Macmillan/McGraw-Hill • Glencoe

W9-AJU-737

Grade
5

Math Triumphs

Assessment Masters

Macmillan/McGraw-Hill
Glencoe

The **McGraw·Hill** Companies

Mc Graw Hill **Macmillan/McGraw-Hill**
Glencoe

Send all inquiries to:
Macmillan/McGraw–Hill•Glencoe/McGraw–Hill
8787 Orion Place
Columbus, OH 43240-4027

ISBN: 978-0-07-888247-0
MHID: 0-07-888247-8

Grade 5 Math Triumphs
Assessment Masters

Printed in the United States of America.

3 4 5 6 7 8 9 10 MAL 18 17 16 15 14 13 12 11 10

Table of Contents

Book 3: Geometry and Measurement

Using the Assessment Masters

Math Triumphs Assessment Masters are an important tool in the evaluation of specific areas of student need, appropriate placement, and determining student success and readiness for transitioning back to on-level curriculum. The assessments in this book provide a comprehensive system that allows for diagnostic, formative, and summative assessment.

Diagnostic and Placement Test

The Diagnostic and Placement Test assesses concepts and skills that are presented in an on-level curriculum. The results can be used to determine whether students require intensive intervention, and, if so, what specific content strands students need.

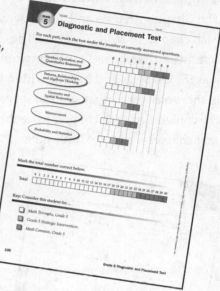

The Diagnostic and Placement Tests for Kindergarten through Grade 2 are oral tests and address the content strands: Number, Operations, and Quantitative Reasoning; Measurement; Probability and Statistics; and Mathematical Processes and Tools. The Kindergarten, Grade 1, and Grade 2 tests each contain 15 questions. The Kindergarten and Grade 1 tests require students to follow simple directions in order to answer each question, while the Grade 2 test is multiple choice.

Grades 3–8 share the same format. Each contains 30 multiple-choice questions and addresses the content strands: Number, Operations, and Quantitative Reasoning; Measurement; Probability and Statistics; and Mathematical Processes and Tools.

See page vii for further explanation and instructions for administering and scoring this test.

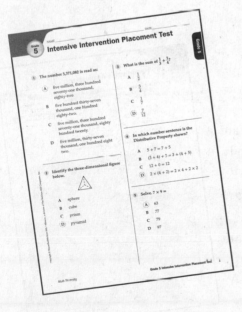

Intensive Intervention Placement Test

The Intensive Intervention Placement Test covers concepts and skills presented strictly in *Math Triumphs*. (It does not cover on-level content.) This test can determine if a student is in need of intensive intervention, as well as identify specific areas in which a student needs intensive intervention. This assessment provides information about the skills and concepts students are struggling with and then indicates in which specific chapter(s) in *Math Triumphs* students should receive instruction.

Book Pretest and Test

The Book Pretests and Tests cover concepts and skills presented in each of the three books in *Math Triumphs.* The Book Pretest can be used to determine student needs and assign specific chapters and lessons. The Book Test can serve as a summative assessment of the contents of each book to determine student success in learning the concepts and skills presented in the book.

Chapter Pretest and Test

The Chapter Pretests and Tests cover concepts and skills presented in each chapter of *Math Triumphs.* The Chapter Pretest is multiple-choice format and can be used to determine specific student needs and assign specific chapters and lessons within that chapter. The Chapter Test is short-answer format and can serve as a summative assessment of the contents of each chapter to determine student success in learning that chapter's concepts and skills.

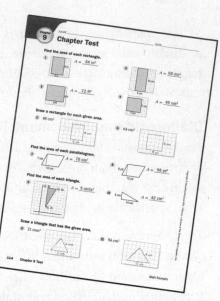

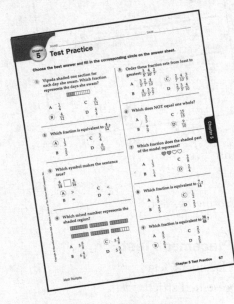

Test Practice

The Test Practice assessment covers concepts and skills presented in each chapter of *Math Triumphs.* It also provides practice for standardized tests by presenting test questions in A, B, C, D standardized-test format. Each chapter's Test Practice can serve as an alternate form of the Chapter Test, providing a summative assessment opportunity.

Performance Assessment

Performance Assessments for each chapter provide an alternate to multiple-choice or fill-in-the-blank assessment. These assessments are multi-step, task-oriented activities that incorporate the concepts and skills learned in the chapter. The activities often involve problem-solving skills and include small projects, games, listening activities, or oral assessments.

In Kindergarten through Grade 3, these performance assessments are led by the teacher. In Grade 4 through Grade 8, these activities can be student self-directed with informal assessment by observation. A scoring rubric is included with each performance assessment.

Answer Key

An Answer Key at the end of this book provides reductions of each student page with answers.

Using the Diagnostic and Placement Test

The **Diagnostic and Placement Test** provides tools to assist teachers in making placement decisions with regard to one of the following on-level, strategic intervention, or intensive intervention resources.

Math Connects

A balanced basal program that provides on-level and strategic intervention instruction.

Math Triumphs

An intensive intervention program for students two or more years behind grade level.

This assessment provides valuable diagnostic information that teachers may also find helpful throughout the school year. The Learning Objectives found before the test provide further information on using these tests as diagnostic tools. These tests are also available in Spanish at macmillanmh.com.

Placement Decisions

In making placement decisions for a student, consider a variety of evidence, such as the student's mathematics grades, classroom observations, teacher recommendations, portfolios of student work, standardized test scores, and placement test scores. Use the results of these placement tests in conjunction with other assessments to determine which mathematics course best fits a student's abilities and needs.

These tests can help determine whether or not students need intervention as well as the level of intervention required. Through strategic intervention, teachers can work with students using on-level content but strategically choose which content strand(s) need further development. Sometimes a student may struggle with a particular strand, but overall the student is able to perform on-level.

Intensive intervention is used with students who are struggling with most or all strands of math content and are unable to work on grade-level. These students will need alternative intervention materials to help meet their needs. These materials, such as the *Math Triumphs* program, offer alternatives that will accelerate achievement in mathematics.

Test Content

These placement tests measure ability, but they are not achievement tests. They cover prerequisite concepts, not every concept found in Macmillan/McGraw-Hill or Glencoe mathematics textbooks or in your state standards.

Mathematics concepts are introduced, developed, and reinforced in consecutive courses. These placement tests measure student mastery of concepts and skills that have been introduced or developed in the student's current mathematics courses and that are further developed in the next course, but that are not developed in the following course.

When to Use the Diagnostic and Placement Test

In most situations, these placement tests are given near the end of the current course in order to help determine student placement for the following year. You can also use these tests in special situations, such as a student transferring into your school mid-year or entering middle school with advanced mathematics ability.

Interpreting Scores

When interpreting scores on the placement tests, consider the student's score on each part, as well as the total score. Scoring Guide Masters before each test can be reproduced and used to record each student's score. A sample of a completed Scoring Guide is shown to the right.

Sample Score and Placement Analysis

On this sample test, this student scored 8 out of 9 questions correct in Number, Operations, and Quantitative Reasoning; 6 in Patterns, Relationships, and Algebraic Thinking; 2 in Geometry and Spatial Reasoning; 3 in Measurement; and 2 in Probability and Statistics. The total number correct was 21 out of 30. **Note:** There is not a direct correlation between the score for each strand and the total test score. Use the total score for class placement decisions and the score by strand when working on particular objectives.

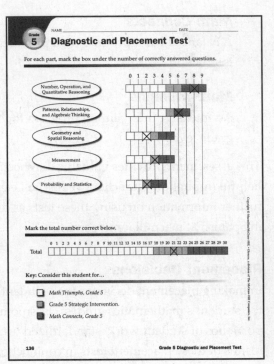

Sample Analysis

This student scored well in the first two parts of the test, but lower in the remaining sections. If these results are similar to other assessments, this student is likely to need intervention materials and may find the grade-level material too challenging without any intervention. The teacher should also note that the student scored particularly low in the Geometry and Spatial Reasoning. This student may require intensive intervention when these skills are taught.

Using Placement Tests for Diagnostic Purposes

These placement tests also provide valuable diagnostic information for classroom teachers. Reproducible learning-objective charts list the learning objective for each test question and can be found before each test. By marking each question the student answered incorrectly, you can see which objectives the student has not mastered.

NAME _____   DATE _____

Intensive Intervention Placement Test

1 The number 5,371,082 is read as:

  A five million, three hundred seventy-one thousand, eighty-two.

  B five hundred thirty-seven thousand, one hundred eighty-two.

  C five million, three hundred seventy-one thousand, eighty hundred twenty.

  D five million, thirty-seven thousand, one hundred eight two.

2 Identify the three-dimensional figure below.

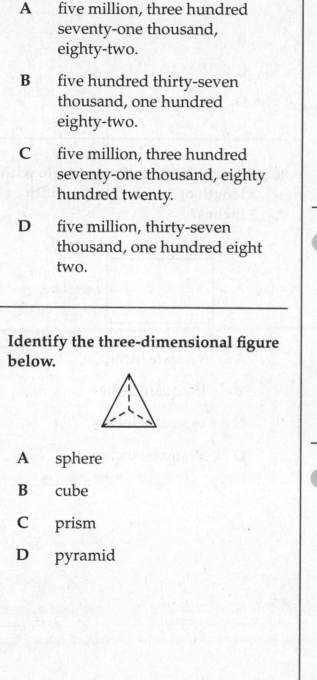

  A sphere

  B cube

  C prism

  D pyramid

3 What is the sum of $\frac{1}{3} + \frac{1}{4}$?

  A $\frac{1}{2}$

  B $\frac{3}{4}$

  C $\frac{1}{7}$

  D $\frac{7}{12}$

4 In which number sentence is the Distributive Property shown?

  A $5 + 7 = 7 + 5$

  B $(3 + 4) + 5 = 3 + (4 + 5)$

  C $12 + 0 = 12$

  D $2 \times (4 + 2) = 2 \times 4 + 2 \times 2$

5 Solve. $7 \times 9 =$

  A 63

  B 77

  C 79

  D 97

6 3 kilograms = _____ grams

    A   30

    B   300

    C   1,000

    D   3,000

7 Place the following decimals in order from least to greatest.

$$1.3, \ 0.31, \ 3.1$$

    A   0.31, 1.3, 3.1

    B   1.3, 3.1, 0.31

    C   3.1, 0.31, 1.3

    D   0.31, 3.1, 1.3

8 Write $\frac{22}{5}$ as a mixed number.

    A $2\frac{2}{5}$

    B $4\frac{2}{5}$

    C $5\frac{5}{22}$

    D $5\frac{4}{5}$

9 Find $35 \div 5$.

    A   5

    B   6

    C   7

    D   8

10 What is the area of a rectangle with a length of 5 inches and a width of 3 inches?

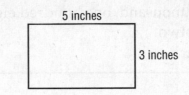

    A   8 square inches

    B   15 square inches

    C   16 square inches

    D   35 square inches

Intensive Intervention
Placement Test, continued

11 Subtract 13.5 − 7.2.

  A   6.3

  B   6.7

  C   7.2

  D   58.5

12 Each side of the cube shown below is 3 centimeters long. What is its surface area?

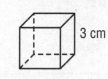

3 cm

  A   9 cm²

  B   36 cm²

  C   54 cm²

  D   64 cm²

13 $4 \times (3 + 1) =$

  A   12

  B   13

  C   16

  D   17

14 What number completes the table below?

Number of Yards	1	2	3	4	5
Number of Feet	3	6	9	12	?

  A   13

  B   15

  C   20

  D   25

15 Which of the fractions below is equivalent to $\frac{2}{3}$?

  A $\frac{2}{4}$

  B $\frac{3}{2}$

  C $\frac{5}{6}$

  D $\frac{6}{9}$

Intensive Intervention
Placement Test, continued

16 7,392 × 0 =

  A   0

  B   1

  C   7,392

  D   73,920

---

17 $\dfrac{11}{12} - \dfrac{10}{12} =$

  A $\dfrac{1}{0}$

  B $\dfrac{1}{12}$

  C $\dfrac{1}{1}$

  D $1\dfrac{9}{12}$

---

18 The radius of the circle below is 1 meter. What is the circle's diameter?

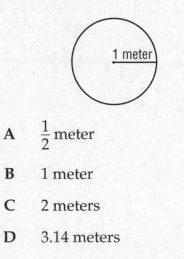

1 meter

  A $\dfrac{1}{2}$ meter

  B   1 meter

  C   2 meters

  D   3.14 meters

19 The triangle below is 5 inches wide and 5 inches high. What is the triangle's area?

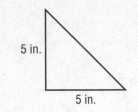

5 in.

5 in.

  A   12.5 in²

  B   25 in²

  C   27 in²

  D   50 in²

---

20 What is the remainder when 15 is divided by 4?

  A   0

  B   2

  C   3

  D   11

21 George measured a box and found it was 2 meters wide, 5 meters long, and 3 meters high. What was the volume of the box?

A 30 m³

B 35 m³

C 60 m³

D 62 m³

22 The base of the parallelogram below is 8 inches long. The height of the parallelogram is 5 inches. What is its area?

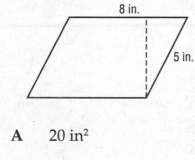

8 in.

5 in.

A 20 in²

B 35 in²

C 40 in²

D 58 in²

23 What is the fraction $\frac{15}{20}$ in simplest form?

A $\frac{5}{20}$

B $\frac{1}{2}$

C $\frac{3}{4}$

D $\frac{4}{5}$

24 $4 \times 6 =$

A 10

B 24

C 46

D 64

25 Write the next three terms in the pattern. 1, 4, 7, 10

A 13, 16, 19

B 14, 18, 22

C 14, 17, 20

D 13, 18, 23

26 Maria divided 78 grapes into 6 equal groups so she could share them with her friends. How many grapes did each of them get?

    A   6

    B   9

    C   11

    D   13

27 In which number sentence is the associative property shown?

    A $12 + 32 = 32 + 12$

    B $(5 + 7) + 32 = 5 + (7 + 32)$

    C $6 \times (2 + 6) = 6 \times 2 + 6 \times 6$

    D $12 + (9 - 3) = (12 - 9) + 3$

28 Which decimal is equivalent to $\frac{1}{4}$?

    A   0.2

    B   0.25

    C   0.33

    D   0.4

29 Identify the figure.

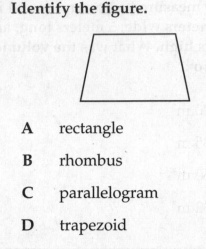

    A   rectangle

    B   rhombus

    C   parallelogram

    D   trapezoid

30 $\frac{2}{5} + \frac{5}{10} =$

    A $\frac{3}{10}$

    B $\frac{6}{20}$

    C $\frac{9}{10}$

    D $\frac{7}{20}$

Grade 5

Intensive Intervention Placement Test
Scoring Guide and Diagnostic Chart

Students missing Exercise . . .	Have trouble with . . .	Should review . . .
1	Reading Numbers in Millions	Chapter 1, Lesson 2
2	Three-Dimensional Figures	Chapter 8, Lesson 4
3	Adding Fractions	Chapter 6, Lesson 3
4	Distributive Property	Chapter 4, Lesson 3
5	Multiplying by 7 and 9	Chapter 2, Lesson 3
6	Metric Mass Conversions	Chapter 10, Lesson 1
7	Ordering Decimals	Chapter 7, Lesson 3
8	Mixed Numbers and Improper Fractions	Chapter 5, Lesson 3
9	Dividing by 5	Chapter 3, Lesson 3
10	Area of Rectangles	Chapter 9, Lesson 2
11	Subtracting Decimals	Chapter 7, Lesson 6
12	Surface Area	Chapter 10, Lesson 3
13	Order of Operations	Chapter 4, Lesson 4
14	Linear Patterns	Chapter 1, Lesson 4
15	Equivalent Fractions	Chapter 5, Lesson 2
16	Multiplying by 0	Chapter 2, Lesson 1
17	Subtracting Fractions	Chapter 6, Lesson 2
18	Circles	Chapter 8, Lesson 3
19	Area of a Triangle	Chapter 9, Lesson 4
20	Dividing by 4	Chapter 3, Lesson 4
21	Volume of Rectangular Solids	Chapter 10, Lesson 5
22	Area of a Parallelogram	Chapter 9, Lesson 3
23	Simplifying Fractions	Chapter 5, Lesson 6
24	Multiplying by 4 and 6	Chapter 2, Lesson 2
25	Number Relationships	Chapter 1, Lesson 3
26	Dividing by 6	Chapter 3, Lesson 5
27	Associative Property	Chapter 4, Lesson 2
28	Equivalent Decimals	Chapter 7, Lesson 2
29	Quadrilaterals	Chapter 8, Lesson 1
30	Adding Fractions	Chapter 6, Lesson 1

Book Pretest

1 What is 3,182 in expanded form?

   A $3,000 + 100 + 80 + 2$ **C** $300 + 1,000 + 80 + 2$

   B $3,000 + 100 + 82$ **D** $3,000 + 100 + 800 + 20$

2 What is 9,450 in expanded form?

   A $9,000 + 45 + 50$ **C** $9,000 + 400 + 5$

   B $900 + 40 + 5$ **D** $9,000 + 400 + 50$

3 What is four million, two hundred eighty-eight thousand, seven hundred three in standard form?

   A 4,288,730   **C** 4,208,873

   B 4,288,703   **D** 428,873

4 What is the next conversion in the pattern?

   A 25 inches in 3 feet   **C** 36 inches in 3 feet

   B 30 inches in 3 feet   **D** 48 inches in 3 feet

Number of Feet	1	2	
Number of Inches	12	24	

5 What is the next conversion in the pattern?

   A 20 in 4 half dozens   **C** 24 in 4 half dozens

   B 22 in 4 half dozens   **D** 28 in 4 half dozens

Number of Half Dozens of Apples	1	2	3	
Number of Apples	6	12	18	

Find each product.

6 $6 \times 10 =$

   A 16   **B** 54   **C** 60   **D** 61

7 $8 \times 12 =$

   A 82   **B** 96   **C** 98   **D** 128

8 $22 \times 0 =$

   A 0   **B** 1   **C** 22   **D** 220

9 $123 \times 5 =$

   A 128   **B** 515   **C** 605   **D** 615

Book 1

Book Pretest, continued

Find each quotient.

10 $66 \div 6 =$

   A 0   **B** 6   **C** 11   **D** 12

11 $60 \div 3 =$

   A 20   **B** 30   **C** 36   **D** 57

12 $72 \div 6 =$

   A 10   **B** 11   **C** 12   **D** 13

13 $100 \div 10 =$

   A 7   **B** 8   **C** 9   **D** 10

Answer the following questions.

14 Which property is shown in the sentence below?

$2 \times (9 + 8) = (2 \times 9) + (2 \times 8)$

   A Associative Property   **C** Order of Operations

   B Commutative Property   **D** Distributive Property

15 Which operation is the inverse of multiplication?

   A division   **B** addition   **C** subtraction   **D** multiplication

Solve.

16 $3 \times (10 + 2) =$

   A 28   **B** 30   **C** 32   **D** 36

17 $(10 - 5) \times 7 + 1 =$

   A 35   **B** 36   **C** 66   **D** 71

18 $7 \times (5 \times 3) =$

   A 7×53 **B** $(7 + 5) \times (7 \times 3)$ **C** $7 \times 5 + 7 \times 3$ **D** $(7 \times 5) \times 3$

19 $124 \times 6 =$

   A $(1 \times 6) + (2 \times 6) + (4 \times 6)$ **C** 6×124

   B 12×46 **D** $(100 \times 6) + (20 \times 4)$

Book 1

Book Pretest
Scoring Guide and Diagnostic Chart

Students missing Exercise . . .	Have trouble with . . .	Should review . . .
1	Whole Numbers Less than 10,000	Chapter 1, Lesson 1
2	Whole Numbers Less than 10,000	Chapter 1, Lesson 1
3	Whole Numbers in the Millions	Chapter 1, Lesson 2
4	Linear Patterns	Chapter 1, Lesson 4
5	Number Relationships	Chapter 1, Lesson 3
6	Multiplying by 10	Chapter 2, Lesson 1
7	Multiplying by 8	Chapter 2, Lesson 3
8	Multiplying by 0	Chapter 2, Lesson 2
9	Multiplying by 5	Chapter 2, Lesson 3
10	Dividing by 6	Chapter 3, Lesson 5
11	Dividing by 3	Chapter 3, Lesson 4
12	Dividing by 6	Chapter 3, Lesson 5
13	Dividing by 10	Chapter 3, Lesson 2
14	Distributive Property	Chapter 4, Lesson 3
15	Model Division	Chapter 3, Lesson 1
16	Properties of Operations	Chapter 4, Lesson 4
17	Properties of Operations	Chapter 4, Lesson 4
18	Associative Property	Chapter 4, Lesson 2
19	Commutative Property	Chapter 4, Lesson 1

Chapter 1

Chapter Pretest

1 Which number completes the statement 1,324 < _____?

    A 1,234   **B** 1,235   **C** 1,324   **D** 1,342

2 Which digit is in the hundreds place in the number 6,895?

    A 5   **B** 6   **C** 8   **D** 9

3 What is the highest place value of a number with three digits?

    A ones   **B** tens   **C** hundreds   **D** thousands

4 What is the standard form of four hundred twenty-seven thousand, one?

    A 427,000   **B** 427,001   **C** 427,010   **D** 427,100

5 What is the word form of 9,021?

    A nine thousand, two hundred ten   **C** nine thousand, two hundred one

    B nine, twenty-one   **D** nine thousand, twenty-one

6 What is the missing number in the table?

4	5	6	7
20	24	?	32

    A 18   **B** 28   **C** 30   **D** 45

7 **TOYS** Jamie is stacking blocks as shown here. If Jamie's first row is the bottom row, how many blocks will he place on the sixth row?

    A 1   **B** 2   **C** 3   **D** 4

8 **RECYCLING** Twyla is collecting plastic bottles. Each day she collects 15 bottles. How many bottles will she collect in 2 weeks?

    A 105   **B** 150   **C** 196   **D** 210

9 **BIRTHDAYS** Aiko had a birthday party. He counted 32 legs among the guests. How many guests did Aiko count?

    A 8   **B** 16   **C** 30   **D** 32

10 Identify the missing number in the pattern.

    4, 8, 12, 16, _____, 24, 28

    A 14   **B** 18   **C** 20   **D** 22

Select the next conversion in each pattern.

11

Number of Yards	1	2	3
Number of Feet	3	6	

    A 1   **B** 7   **C** 9   **D** 10

12

Number of Pounds	1	2	3
Number of Ounces	16	32	

    A 16   **B** 48   **C** 33   **D** 64

Solve.

13 How many sides do 2 rectangles have?

    A 2   **B** 4   **C** 6   **D** 8

14 How many tails do 3 puppies have?

    A 1   **B** 3   **C** 6   **D** 12

15 **AGES** Luke is twice as old as his cousin, Emma. Emma is 6 years old. How old is Luke?

    A 3   **B** 4   **C** 8   **D** 12

16 **SPORTS** The South High track team runs 2 miles during each practice. How many miles will they run in 4 practices?

    A 2   **B** 4   **C** 6   **D** 8

What is the standard form of the number?

17 $3,000 + 700 + 10 + 4$

    A 374   **B** 3,147   **C** 3,714   **D** 37,104

18 $5,000 + 30 + 9$

    A 539   **B** 5,039   **C** 5,309   **D** 53,090

Identify the value of the underlined digit.

19 4,3<u>2</u>0

    A 2   **B** 20   **C** 200   **D** 2,000

20 <u>8</u>,004

    A 8   **B** 80   **C** 800   **D** 8,000

Chapter Pretest
Scoring Guide and Diagnostic Chart

Students missing Exercise . . .	Have trouble with . . .	Should review . . .
1	Whole Numbers Less than 10,000	Chapter 1, Lesson 1
2	Whole Numbers Less than 10,000	Chapter 1, Lesson 1
3	Whole Numbers Less than 10,000	Chapter 1, Lesson 1
4	Read and Write Whole Numbers in the Millions	Chapter 1, Lesson 2
5	Whole Numbers Less than 10,000	Chapter 1, Lesson 1
6	Linear Patterns	Chapter 1, Lesson 4
7	Linear Patterns	Chapter 1, Lesson 4
8	Linear Patterns	Chapter 1, Lesson 4
9	Linear Patterns	Chapter 1, Lesson 4
10	Linear Patterns	Chapter 1, Lesson 4
11	Number Relationships	Chapter 1, Lesson 3
12	Number Relationships	Chapter 1, Lesson 3
13	Linear Patterns	Chapter 1, Lesson 4
14	Linear Patterns	Chapter 1, Lesson 4
15	Linear Patterns	Chapter 1, Lesson 4
16	Linear Patterns	Chapter 1, Lesson 4
17	Whole Numbers Less than 10,000	Chapter 1, Lesson 1
18	Whole Numbers Less than 10,000	Chapter 1, Lesson 1
19	Whole Numbers Less than 10,000	Chapter 1, Lesson 1
20	Whole Numbers Less than 10,000	Chapter 1, Lesson 1

Chapter 1

Chapter Test

Fill in the chart. Identify the value of each underlined digit.

1 9,7̲30 _____

1,000	100	10	1
thousands	hundreds	tens	ones

2 2̲,583 _____

1,000	100	10	1
thousands	hundreds	tens	ones

3 6,1̲03 _____

4 6̲,090 _____

5 1,62̲8 _____

6 42̲9 _____

Write each number in word form.

7 3,256,570

_____

_____

8 2,732,600

_____

_____

9 8,095,277

_____

_____

10 5,803,692

_____

_____

Write each number in standard form.

11 six million, nine hundred fifty-two thousand, six hundred three

_____

12 three million, six hundred thirty-nine thousand, one hundred seventeen _____

13 3,000 + 400 + 20 + 7 _____

14 8,000 + 60 + 4 _____

15 four million, sixty-three thousand, eight hundred _____

16 eight million, three hundred nine thousand, sixty-five _____

Math Triumphs

Chapter 1 · Chapter Test, continued

Write the next three numbers in the pattern.

17 2, 4, 8, _____, _____, _____

18 16, 21, 26, _____, _____, _____

Write the next three conversions in each pattern.

19

Number of Feet	1	2	3	4
Number of Inches	12			

20

Number of Meters	1	2	3	4
Number of Centimeters	100			

Solve.

21 **HIKING** Martin's hiking group hiked 12 miles each day during a one-week vacation in the mountains. How many miles did Martin's group hike? _____

22 **AGES** Alice is half as old as her uncle, Jason. Jason is 34 years old. How old is Alice? _____

Write the rule and the solution for each of the following.

23 How many cookies are in 5 dozen? _____

24 How many legs do 8 spiders have? _____

25 How many sides do 4 triangles have? _____

26 How many fingers do 2 hands have? _____

27 How many shoes are in 7 pairs of shoes? _____

28

Number of Pounds	1	2	3	4
Number of Ounces	16	32		

29

Number of Gallons	1	2	3	4
Number of Quarts	4	8		

NAME _____ DATE _____

Chapter Test
Scoring Guide and Diagnostic Chart

Students missing Exercise . . .	Have trouble with . . .	Should review . . .
1	Whole Numbers Less than 10,000	Chapter 1, Lesson 1
2	Whole Numbers Less than 10,000	Chapter 1, Lesson 1
3	Whole Numbers Less than 10,000	Chapter 1, Lesson 1
4	Whole Numbers Less than 10,000	Chapter 1, Lesson 1
5	Whole Numbers Less than 10,000	Chapter 1, Lesson 1
6	Whole Numbers Less than 10,000	Chapter 1, Lesson 1
7	Read and Write Whole Numbers in the Millions	Chapter 1, Lesson 2
8	Read and Write Whole Numbers in the Millions	Chapter 1, Lesson 2
9	Read and Write Whole Numbers in the Millions	Chapter 1, Lesson 2
10	Read and Write Whole Numbers in the Millions	Chapter 1, Lesson 2
11	Read and Write Whole Numbers in the Millions	Chapter 1, Lesson 2
12	Read and Write Whole Numbers in the Millions	Chapter 1, Lesson 2
13	Whole Numbers Less than 10,000	Chapter 1, Lesson 1
14	Whole Numbers Less than 10,000	Chapter 1, Lesson 1
15	Read and Write Whole Numbers in the Millions	Chapter 1, Lesson 2
16	Read and Write Whole Numbers in the Millions	Chapter 1, Lesson 2
17	Linear Patterns	Chapter 1, Lesson 4
18	Linear Patterns	Chapter 1, Lesson 4
19	Number Relationships	Chapter 1, Lesson 3
20	Number Relationships	Chapter 1, Lesson 3
21	Linear Patterns	Chapter 1, Lesson 4
22	Linear Patterns	Chapter 1, Lesson 4
23	Linear Patterns	Chapter 1, Lesson 4
24	Linear Patterns	Chapter 1, Lesson 4
25	Linear Patterns	Chapter 1, Lesson 4
26	Linear Patterns	Chapter 1, Lesson 4
27	Linear Patterns	Chapter 1, Lesson 4
28	Number Relationships	Chapter 1, Lesson 3
29	Number Relationships	Chapter 1, Lesson 3

Chapter 1 Test Practice

Choose the best answer and fill in the corresponding circle on the answer sheet.

1 Which number shows six hundred eight written in standard form?

A   608   C   680

B   618   D   688

2 $5,000 + 40 + 7 =$

A   547   C   5,407

B   5,047   D   5,447

3 Identify the value of the underlined digit.

4,0<u>9</u>1,532

A   900   C   900,000

B   9,000   D   90,000

4 Which digit is in the thousands place in 1,265,075?

A   1   C   5

B   2   D   7

5 The Cassini spacecraft travels to Saturn at 7<u>7</u>,700 miles per hour. Identify the underlined digit.

A   700   C   70,000

B   7,000   D   700,000

6 Hannah's grandmother is 81 years old. Which shows her grandmother's age written in word form?

A   eighteen   C   eighty

B   eighteen-one   D   eighty-one

Select the next number in the pattern.

7 5, 15, 25, ___

A   26   C   35

B   30   D   40

8 21, 28, 35, ___

A   36   C   42

B   40   D   45

9 Brandon's family is gathered for a family picnic. He has a large family and a few cats. If there is a total of 44 legs at the picnic, which of the following could be an answer for how many humans and how many cats are at the picnic?

    A   8 humans, 6 cats

    B   15 humans, 4 cats

    C   17 humans, 3 cats

    D   18 humans, 2 cats

10 What is the next number in the sequence?

18, 24, 30, 36, 42, 48, 54, ___

    A   60   **C**   64

    B   62   **D**   70

11 What is the rule for this pattern?

15, 22, 29, 36, 43, 50

    A   add 9   **C**   subtract 7

    B   add 7   **D**   subtract 9

12 Find the missing number.

4	8	12	16
16	32	48	?

    A   32   **C**   60

    B   52   **D**   64

ANSWER SHEET

Directions: Fill in the circle of each correct answer.

1 Ⓐ Ⓑ Ⓒ Ⓓ

2 Ⓐ Ⓑ Ⓒ Ⓓ

3 Ⓐ Ⓑ Ⓒ Ⓓ

4 Ⓐ Ⓑ Ⓒ Ⓓ

5 Ⓐ Ⓑ Ⓒ Ⓓ

6 Ⓐ Ⓑ Ⓒ Ⓓ

7 Ⓐ Ⓑ Ⓒ Ⓓ

8 Ⓐ Ⓑ Ⓒ Ⓓ

9 Ⓐ Ⓑ Ⓒ Ⓓ

10 Ⓐ Ⓑ Ⓒ Ⓓ

11 Ⓐ Ⓑ Ⓒ Ⓓ

12 Ⓐ Ⓑ Ⓒ Ⓓ

Test Practice
Scoring Guide and Diagnostic Chart

Students missing Exercise . . .	Have trouble with . . .	Should review . . .
1	Whole Numbers Less than 10,000	Chapter 1, Lesson 1
2	Whole Numbers Less than 10,000	Chapter 1, Lesson 1
3	Place Values of Whole Numbers in the Millions	Chapter 1, Lesson 2
4	Place Values of Whole Numbers in the Millions	Chapter 1, Lesson 2
5	Place Values of Whole Numbers in the Millions	Chapter 1, Lesson 2
6	Linear Patterns	Chapter 1, Lesson 4
7	Linear Patterns	Chapter 1, Lesson 4
8	Linear Patterns	Chapter 1, Lesson 4
9	Number Relationships	Chapter 1, Lesson 3
10	Linear Patterns	Chapter 1, Lesson 4
11	Linear Patterns	Chapter 1, Lesson 4
12	Linear Patterns	Chapter 1, Lesson 4

NAME _____ DATE _____

Performance Assessment

1. Ramon says that the digit 5 in the number 452 stands for 500. Is he correct?

YOUR TASK: Show whether or not Ramon is correct. Use charts, number lines, or any other graphic organizer to help you.

ONE WAY:

- Model 452. Use the correct number of hundreds flats, tens rods, and unit cubes to model 452.

- Use either solid cubes or drawings to complete the model.

- Now count each type of cube. Which type of cubes are shown five times in the model? Are there five hundreds?

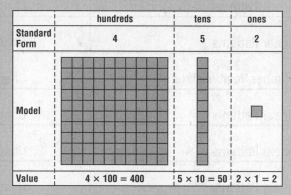

	hundreds	tens	ones
Standard Form	4	5	2
Model			
Value	4 × 100 = 400	5 × 10 = 50	2 × 1 = 2

- Is Ramon correct?

ANOTHER WAY:

- Make a place-value chart and place the digits 4, 5, and 2 in their correct positions. The table should look like this:

100	10	1
hundreds	tens	ones

- Read the value of the 5 on the place-value chart.

- Is it five hundreds? What does the 5 represent?

- Is Ramon correct?

Math Triumphs

Performance Assessment Teacher's Notes

▶ Target Skills

- Extend understanding of place value of whole numbers up to 10,000.
- Solve problems by using models and creating place-value charts.

▶ Task Description

Students will model a three-digit number using their knowledge of place value.

▶ Teacher Notes

This activity is suitable for partner work. Note that many students would benefit if the teacher models the activity before students solve. Ramon is incorrect. The digit 5 stands for 50.

Students can use manipulatives to model place values. Kinesthetic or tactile learners may draw or represent numbers using base-ten blocks or groups of objects.

Scoring Rubric	
Score	**Explanation**
3	Students demonstrate an efficient strategy and a thorough approach that enables them to solve the problem completely. Students will: • correctly use place value to determine that Ramon is incorrect. • evaluate a mathematical proposition. • show their work. • explain their answer in grade-appropriate language.
2	Students demonstrate a strategy that enables them to solve the problem correctly. The strategy is disorganized or less efficient. Students may: • have some difficulty in correctly using place value. • not correctly evaluate the proposition. • find a solution, but have guessed for a few answers.
1	Students demonstrate a confused strategy, which leads to difficulty solving the problem. Most answers are incorrect, but students demonstrate knowledge of at least one concept being assessed. Students may: • demonstrate an understanding of the concept of place value. • correctly evaluate the proposition based on their results. • explain in grade-level language some of the concepts relevant to the problem.

Chapter 2 Chapter Pretest

1 What is the product of 11 and 12?

    A 23   **B** 120   **C** 122   **D** 132

2 Which expression does the array model?

    A $3 + 5$ **C** 15×1

    B 5×3 **D** $5 + 3$

3 **PUZZLES** The grid for a square crossword puzzle has 12 squares along each of its 4 sides. How many smaller squares are in the crossword puzzle?

    A 24   **B** 100   **C** 121   **D** 144

4 What is 9×8?

    A 72   **B** 74   **C** 81   **D** 82

5 **KNITTING** Tara is knitting scarves to sell. Each scarf uses 95 yards of yarn. If she knits 23 scarves, how many yards of yarn will Tara use?

    A 218   **B** 1,955   **C** 2,185   **D** 3,040

6 Which is a multiple of 7?

    A 27   **B** 47   **C** 77   **D** 97

7 What missing factor makes the equation true?

$5 \times$ _____ $= 75$

    A 3   **B** 15   **C** 20   **D** 25

8 **FOOD** On a strip of button candy there are 3 pieces in each row and 12 rows. How many pieces of button candy are on the strip?

    A 15   **B** 30   **C** 36   **D** 39

9 Which fact belongs to the same fact family as $4 \times 3 = 12$?

    A $12 \div 3 = 4$ **B** $4 + 3 = 7$ **C** $6 \times 2 = 12$ **D** $12 \div 1 = 12$

10 **SHOPPING** Marion bought 8 packs of the light bulbs. If there are 4 light bulbs in each pack, how many light bulbs did he buy?

    A 12   **B** 28   **C** 30   **D** 32

11 What is another way to write the product 24×7?

    A $20 + 7 + 7 + 7$ **B** $20 \times 7 + 4 \times 7$ **C** $24 \times 7 + 20 \times 7$ **D** $20 \times 7 + 7$

Chapter 2 Chapter Pretest, continued

Use the Distributive Property of Multiplication to find the product.

12 $18 \times 31 =$

    A 72   **B** 234   **C** 558   **D** 725

13 $27 \times 52 =$

    A 189   **B** 675   **C** 1,304   **D** 1,404

14 $33 \times 34 =$

    A 231   **B** 1,122   **C** 1,452   **D** 3,334

Select the appropriate property.

15 Which property is shown by $120 \times 0 = 0$?

    A Distributive Property of Multiplication   **C** Identity Property of Multiplication

    B Zero Property of Multiplication   **D** Associative Property of Multiplication

16 Which property is shown by $14 \times 82 = 82 \times 14$?

    A Distributive Property   **C** Commutative Property of Multiplication

    B Zero Property of Multiplication   **D** Associative Property of Multiplication

Find each product.

17 $24 \times 1 =$ _____

    A 0   **B** 1   **C** 24   **D** 25

18 $10 \times 62 =$ _____

    A 72   **B** 602   **C** 612   **D** 620

19 $9 \times 11 =$ _____

    A 20   **B** 91   **C** 99   **D** 109

20 **SCHOOL** Each student in a class has 7 textbooks. There are 18 students in the class. How many textbooks do they have altogether?

    A 78   **B** 116   **C** 126   **D** 216

21 **FINANCE** Amelia's grandmother gives her $3 every Saturday. If there are 52 Saturdays this year, how much will her grandmother give her in the year?

    A $55   **B** $152   **C** $153   **D** $156

Chapter
2

Chapter Pretest
Scoring Guide and Diagnostic Chart

Students missing Exercise . . .	Have trouble with . . .	Should review . . .
1	Multiply by 11 and 12	Chapter 2, Lesson 4
2	Modeling Multiplication	Chapter 2, Lesson 6
3	Multiply by 12	Chapter 2, Lesson 4
4	Multiply by 8 and 9	Chapter 2, Lesson 3
5	Multiplying Large Numbers	Chapter 2, Lesson 5
6	Multiply by 7	Chapter 2, Lesson 3
7	Multiply by 5	Chapter 2, Lesson 1
8	Multiply by 12	Chapter 2, Lesson 4
9	Fact Families	Chapter 2, Lesson 6
10	Multiply by 4	Chapter 2, Lesson 2
11	Multiplying by 7	Chapter 2, Lesson 3
12	Multiplying Large Numbers	Chapter 2, Lesson 5
13	Multiplying Large Numbers	Chapter 2, Lesson 5
14	Multiplying Large Numbers	Chapter 2, Lesson 5
15	Modeling Multiplication	Chapter 2, Lesson 1
16	Modeling Multiplication	Chapter 2, Lesson 1
17	Multiply by 1	Chapter 2, Lesson 1
18	Multiply by 10	Chapter 2, Lesson 1
19	Multiply by 9	Chapter 2, Lesson 3
20	Multiply by 7	Chapter 2, Lesson 3
21	Multiply by 3	Chapter 2, Lesson 2

Chapter 2

Chapter Test

Chapter 2

Draw an array to model the expression. Then write and model the commutative fact.

1 6×4 _____

Find each product.

2 6×0 _____

3 2×11 _____

4 5×10 _____

5 0×6 _____

6 5×3 _____

7 12×4 _____

8 3×9 _____

9 5×6 _____

10 9×7 _____

11 7×6 _____

12 12×7 _____

13 2×6 _____

Draw an array to model each expression. Find the product.

14 4×8 _____

15 6×12 _____

Find each product.

16 38×6 _____

17 42×8 _____

18 206×3 _____

19 418×4 _____

20 542×5 _____

21 490×7 _____

Find the missing number that makes the equation true.

22 $7 \times \boxed{} = 63$ _____

23 $8 \times \boxed{} = 32$ _____

Write each product in distributive form.

24 11 × 4 _____

25 22 × 7 _____

26 5 × 43 _____

Solve.

27 **LIBRARY**   Brownsville County Library has 5 shelves in each bookcase. Each shelf holds 24 paperback books. What is the maximum number of paperback books that each bookcase holds?

_____

28 **MOVING**   When Andrea moved to a new house or apartment room, she packed her belongings into 6 boxes. Each box weighed 25 pounds. How many pounds did her boxes weigh in all?

_____

29 **FINANCE**   Mr. Raul wants to buy a big-screen TV that costs about $1,765. He has been saving $150 a month for an entire year. At the end of one year, how much money will he have saved? Is that enough money for the big screen TV? (There are 12 months in a year.)

_____

30 **SCHOOL**   Beth is bringing 10 books home from school in her backpack. Each book weighs 3 pounds. How many pounds of books does she have in her backpack?

_____

Correct the mistakes.

31 Carlos told Julius that he knows a shortcut for multiplying by 100. He said, "You add one zero to the factor." Julius told Carlos that his shortcut was not right. What is the correct shortcut?

_____

Math Triumphs

Chapter 2

Chapter Test
Scoring Guide and Diagnostic Chart

Students missing Exercise . . .	Have trouble with . . .	Should review . . .
1	Modeling Multiplication	Chapter 1, Lesson 6
2	Zero Property of Multiplication	Chapter 2, Lesson 1
3	Multiply by 11	Chapter 2, Lesson 4
4	Multiply by 10	Chapter 2, Lesson 1
5	Zero Property of Multiplication	Chapter 2, Lesson 1
6	Multiply by 3	Chapter 2, Lesson 2
7	Multiply by 4	Chapter 2, Lesson 2
8	Multiply by 9	Chapter 2, Lesson 3
9	Multiply by 6	Chapter 2, Lesson 2
10	Multiply by 7	Chapter 2, Lesson 3
11	Multiply by 6	Chapter 2, Lesson 2
12	Multiply by 7	Chapter 2, Lesson 3
13	Multiply by 6	Chapter 2, Lesson 2
14	Modeling Multiplication	Chapter 1, Lesson 6
15	Modeling Multiplication	Chapter 1, Lesson 6
16	Multiply by 6	Chapter 2, Lesson 2
17	Multiply by 8	Chapter 2, Lesson 3
18	Multiply by 3	Chapter 2, Lesson 2
19	Multiply by 7	Chapter 2, Lesson 3
20	Multiply by 4	Chapter 2, Lesson 2
21	Multiply by 5	Chapter 2, Lesson 1
22	Multiply by 7	Chapter 2, Lesson 3
23	Multiply by 8	Chapter 2, Lesson 3
24	Distributive Property of Multiplication	Chapter 2, Lesson 4
25	Distributive Property of Multiplication	Chapter 2, Lesson 5
26	Distributive Property of Multiplication	Chapter 2, Lesson 5
27	Multiply by 5	Chapter 2, Lesson 1
28	Multiply by 6	Chapter 2, Lesson 2
29	Multiply by 12	Chapter 2, Lesson 4
30	Multiply by 10	Chapter 2, Lesson 1
31	Multiply by 10	Chapter 2, Lesson 1

Test Practice

Choose the best answer and fill in the corresponding circle on the answer sheet.

1 Which number sentence is in the same fact family as $2 \times 6 = 12$?

   A $6 \times 12 = 72$ **C** $6 \div 2 = 3$

   B $12 \div 2 = 6$ **D** $72 \div 6 = 12$

2 What is the product of 1,964 and 1?

   A   0   **C**   1,964

   B   1   **D**   1,965

3 Ernest drinks soda 6 days a month. His friend Oscar drinks soda twice as often in the same month. Which math sentence shows how many sodas Oscar drinks per month?

   A $2 \times 6 = 12$ **C** $2 \times 2 = 4$

   B $6 + 2 = 8$ **D** $6 \times 2 = 10$

4 If the product of 25 and 5 is 125, which of the following is also true?

   A $125 \div 5 = 120$

   B $125 - 25 = 5$

   C $125 \div 25 = 5$

   D $125 \times 5 = 500$

5 An extra-large bag of tortilla chips is on sale for $3. If Larry buys 5 bags, how much does he spend on tortilla chips?

   A $15   **C** $25

   B $18   **D** $30

6 Priscilla's bakery is baking bread. Priscilla makes 12 small loaves in each batch. If she bakes 8 batches, how many loaves of bread does she make?

   A   96 loaves   **C**   124 loaves

   B   114 loaves   **D**   242 loaves

7 Which numbers multiply for a product of 121?

   A   6 and 18   **C**   11 and 11

   B   16 and 11   **D**   13 and 12

8 What is another way to write the product of 18 and 6?

   A $10 \times 8 + 10 \times 6$

   B $10 \times 6 + 8 \times 6$

   C $8 \times 10 + 8 \times 6$

   D $10 + 6 + 8 \times 6$

9 What is the product of 9 and 9?

A   18   C   89

B   81   D   99

10 Which number times 15 equals 0?

A   51   C   0

B   1   D   15

11 Kevin added a zero to the number 32 to make the number 320. This is an example of which of the following?

A   multiplying by 0

B   multiplying by 1

C   dividing by 0

D   multiplying by 10

12 Use partial products to find the product of 59 × 16.

A   596   C   916

B   895   D   944

13 What is the product of 8 and 5?

A   13   C   58

B   40   D   85

ANSWER SHEET

Directions: Fill in the circle of each correct answer.

1 Ⓐ Ⓑ Ⓒ Ⓓ

2 Ⓐ Ⓑ Ⓒ Ⓓ

3 Ⓐ Ⓑ Ⓒ Ⓓ

4 Ⓐ Ⓑ Ⓒ Ⓓ

5 Ⓐ Ⓑ Ⓒ Ⓓ

6 Ⓐ Ⓑ Ⓒ Ⓓ

7 Ⓐ Ⓑ Ⓒ Ⓓ

8 Ⓐ Ⓑ Ⓒ Ⓓ

9 Ⓐ Ⓑ Ⓒ Ⓓ

10 Ⓐ Ⓑ Ⓒ Ⓓ

11 Ⓐ Ⓑ Ⓒ Ⓓ

12 Ⓐ Ⓑ Ⓒ Ⓓ

13 Ⓐ Ⓑ Ⓒ Ⓓ

Test Practice
Scoring Guide and Diagnostic Chart

Students missing Exercise . . .	Have trouble with . . .	Should review . . .
1	Multiplication and Division	Chapter 2, Lesson 6
2	Multiplying by 1	Chapter 2, Lesson 1
3	Multiplying by 2	Chapter 2, Lesson 2
4	Multiplication and Division	Chapter 2, Lesson 6
5	Multiplying by 5	Chapter 2, Lesson 1
6	Multiplying by 8	Chapter 2, Lesson 3
7	Multiplying by 11	Chapter 2, Lesson 4
8	Multiplying by 6	Chapter 2, Lesson 2
9	Multiplying by 9	Chapter 2, Lesson 3
10	Multiplying by 0	Chapter 2, Lesson 1
11	Multiplying by 10	Chapter 2, Lesson 1
12	Multiplying Large Numbers	Chapter 2, Lesson 5
13	Multiplying by 8	Chapter 2, Lesson 3

Chapter 2

Performance Assessment

1. The multiplication table below is missing six of its numbers. Can you find the missing numbers based on the pattern in the table?

Copyright © Macmillan/McGraw-Hill, • Glencoe, a division of The McGraw-Hill Companies, Inc.

Checklist
- ☐ Write your name.
- ☐ Show your work.
- ☐ Explain your reasoning.
- ☐ Write the answer.

YOUR TASK: Write numbers in the empty spaces.

X	10	11	12	13	14
10	100	110		130	140
11		121	132	143	
12	120	132	144		168
13	130		156	169	182
14	140	154		182	196

ONE WAY:

- Locate the empty spaces, such as the space in Column 12 and in Row 10. This space is for the product of 10 and 12.

- Use the fact that 10 × 12 equals 12 × 10. Locate the place in the table that is in Column 10 and Row 12.

- Copy the product from Column 10 and Row 12 into the empty space in Column 12 and Row 10.

- Find another empty space. Then find the matching place in the table and copy the product.

- Continue until all the spaces have been filled.

ANOTHER WAY:

- Locate one of the empty spaces, such as the space in Column 10 and the Row 11.

- Use the fact that the numbers in this column increase by 10s. Write the number that is 10 more than 100 in this space.

- Next find the empty space in Column 11.

- Use the fact that the numbers in this column increase by 11s. Write the number that is 11 more than 132 in this space.

- Find more empty spaces and continue to find the number that belongs in each of them the same way.

Performance Assessment Teacher's Notes

▶ Target Skills

- Develop quick recall of multiplication facts.
- Identify, describe, and extend numeric patterns.

▶ Task Description

Students will use mathematical reasoning to complete a multiplication table.

▶ Teacher Notes

This activity is suitable for partner work. It is preferable to model the activity before students begin to solve.

Students can draw a grid or use manipulatives to represent the multiplication facts in the table. Kinesthetic or tactile learners may use number cubes, counting cubes, or other groups of objects to represent the problems.

Scoring Rubric	
Score	**Explanation**
3	Students demonstrate an efficient strategy and a thorough approach that enables them to solve the problem completely. Students will: • complete the multiplication table correctly. • show their work.
2	Students demonstrate a strategy that enables them to solve the problem correctly. The strategy is disorganized or less efficient. Students may: • have some difficulty determining all of the answers correctly but demonstrate an understanding of general multiplication concepts. • find a solution, but have guessed for a few answers.
1	Students demonstrate a confused strategy, which leads to difficulty solving the problem. Most answers are incorrect, but students demonstrate knowledge of at least one concept being assessed. Students may: • place correct numbers in few of the spaces in the table.

Chapter 3

Chapter Pretest

What division problem does each model represent?

1 A $12 \div 3 = 4$ C $16 \div 4 = 4$

B $15 \div 3 = 5$ D $18 \div 6 = 3$

2 A $25 \div 5 = 5$ C $32 \div 8 = 4$

B $30 \div 6 = 5$ D $36 \div 6 = 6$

3 A $18 \div 2 = 9$ C $21 \div 3 = 7$

B $20 \div 2 = 10$ D $24 \div 2 = 12$

Find each quotient.

4 $56 \div 8 =$ _____

A 4   B 6   C 7   D 8

5 $10 \div 1 =$ _____

A 0   B 1   C 5   D 10

6 $72 \div 6 =$ _____

A 9   B 12   C 13   D 14

7 $11 \div 0 =$ _____

A 0   B 1   C 11   D not possible

8 Find $47 \div 5$. What is the remainder?

A 1   B 2   C 3   D 4

9 Find $14 \div 10$. What is the remainder?

A 0   B 2   C 4   D 5

10 Find $37 \div 3$. What is the remainder?

A 1   B 3   C 4   D 5

Find each quotient. Show the remainder if there is one.

11. $160 \div 4 =$

    A 4   B 14   C 40   D 44

12. $360 \div 6 =$

    A 6   B 16   C 56   D 60

13. $108 \div 9 =$

    A 9   B 11   C 12   D 12 R 5

14. $525 \div 5 =$

    A 105   B 115   C 115 R 3   D 150

15. $724 \div 7 =$

    A 103   B 103 R 3   C 104   D 104 R 1

16. $613 \div 6 =$

    A 101   B 101 R 2   C 102   D 102 R 1

17. **MUSIC** François owns 96 CDs. The cases that he keeps them in hold 6 CDs each. How many cases does he need to hold his CDs?

    A 12   B 14   C 16   D 17

18. **FINANCE** Sally earns $8 for each lawn she mows. Last week she earned $144. How many lawns did she mow?

    A 12   B 16   C 18   D 20

19. **COOKING** Mr. Taylor normally uses 84 eggs when he cooks breakfast for the students at Warm Creek School. Today half the students are away on an overnight field trip, so he will use half as many eggs. How many eggs does he need?

    A 42   B 64   C 82   D 168

Correct the mistakes.

20. Sandy says there is no multiplication fact that is an inverse to $36 \div 1 = 36$. This is incorrect. Which of the number sentences below shows that there is an inverse to $36 \div 1 = 36$?

    A $35 + 1 = 36$ B $36 \times 0 = 0$

    B $36 \times 1 = 36$ D $37 - 1 = 36$

Chapter 3 Chapter Pretest
Scoring Guide and Diagnostic Chart

Students missing Exercise . . .	Have trouble with . . .	Should review . . .
1	Modeling Division	Chapter 3, Lesson 1
2	Modeling Division	Chapter 3, Lesson 1
3	Modeling Division	Chapter 3, Lesson 1
4	Dividing by 8	Chapter 3, Lesson 6
5	Dividing by 1	Chapter 3, Lesson 2
6	Dividing by 6	Chapter 3, Lesson 5
7	Dividing by 0	Chapter 3, Lesson 2
8	Dividing by 5	Chapter 3, Lesson 3
9	Dividing by 10	Chapter 3, Lesson 2
10	Dividing by 3	Chapter 3, Lesson 4
11	Dividing by 4	Chapter 3, Lesson 4
12	Dividing by 6	Chapter 3, Lesson 5
13	Dividing by 9	Chapter 3, Lesson 6
14	Dividing by 5	Chapter 3, Lesson 3
15	Dividing by 7	Chapter 3, Lesson 5
16	Dividing by 6	Chapter 3, Lesson 5
17	Dividing by 6	Chapter 3, Lesson 5
18	Dividing by 8	Chapter 3, Lesson 6
19	Dividing by 2	Chapter 3, Lesson 3
20	Modeling Division	Chapter 3, Lesson 1

Chapter

3

Chapter Test

Write each expression in two different formats.

1 28 ÷ 7 _____   **2** 64 ÷ 8 _____

Write the division problem represented by the model.

3 _____

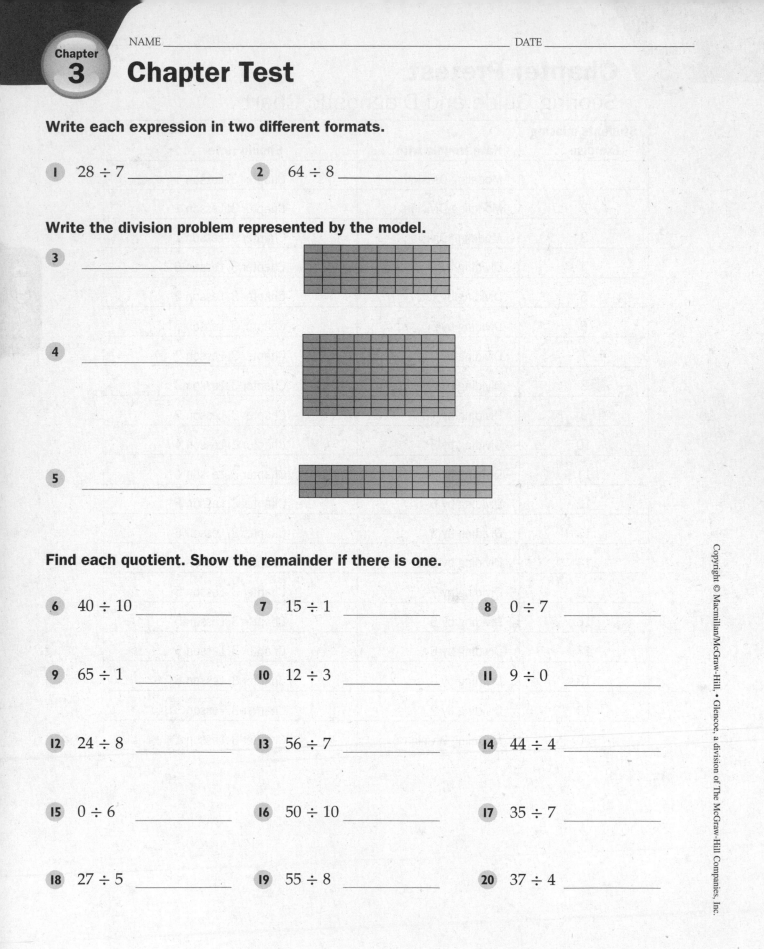

4 _____

5 _____

Find each quotient. Show the remainder if there is one.

6 40 ÷ 10 _____   **7** 15 ÷ 1 _____   **8** 0 ÷ 7 _____

9 65 ÷ 1 _____   **10** 12 ÷ 3 _____   **11** 9 ÷ 0 _____

12 24 ÷ 8 _____   **13** 56 ÷ 7 _____   **14** 44 ÷ 4 _____

15 0 ÷ 6 _____   **16** 50 ÷ 10 _____   **17** 35 ÷ 7 _____

18 27 ÷ 5 _____   **19** 55 ÷ 8 _____   **20** 37 ÷ 4 _____

Find each quotient. Show the remainder if there is one.

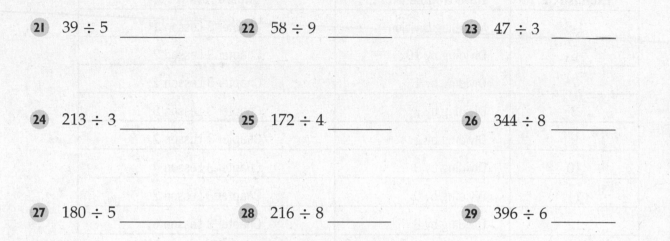

21 39 ÷ 5 _____

22 58 ÷ 9 _____

23 47 ÷ 3 _____

24 213 ÷ 3 _____

25 172 ÷ 4 _____

26 344 ÷ 8 _____

27 180 ÷ 5 _____

28 216 ÷ 8 _____

29 396 ÷ 6 _____

Solve.

30 **SPORTS** Trophies come in boxes of 8. The league ordered 257 trophies, one for each player. How many boxes will the league need? How many trophies will be left over?

_____

31 **BOOKSTORE** The used book store has 324 paperback books that need to be organized into 9 different groups. If each group has the same number of paperback books, how many paperback books will be in each group?

_____

Correct the mistakes.

32 Olivia said that the fact family for 8, 8, 64 has four equations. Is Olivia's statement correct? Explain.

_____

_____

Chapter 3 Chapter Test
Scoring Guide and Diagnostic Chart

Students missing Exercise . . .	Have trouble with . . .	Should review . . .
1-5	Modeling Division	Chapter 3 Lesson 1
6	Dividing by 10	Chapter 3 Lesson 2
7	Dividing by 1	Chapter 3 Lesson 2
8	Dividing by 7	Chapter 3 Lesson 5
9	Dividing by 1	Chapter 3 Lesson 2
10	Dividing by 3	Chapter 3 Lesson 4
11	Dividing by 0	Chapter 3 Lesson 2
12	Dividing by 8	Chapter 3 Lesson 6
13	Dividing by 7	Chapter 3 Lesson 5
14	Dividing by 4	Chapter 3 Lesson 4
15	Dividing by 6	Chapter 3 Lesson 5
16	Dividing by 10	Chapter 3 Lesson 2
17	Dividing by 7	Chapter 3 Lesson 5
18	Dividing by 5	Chapter 3 Lesson 3
19	Dividing by 8	Chapter 3 Lesson 6
20	Dividing by 4	Chapter 3 Lesson 4
21	Dividing by 5	Chapter 3 Lesson 3
22	Dividing by 9	Chapter 3 Lesson 6
23	Dividing by 3	Chapter 3 Lesson 4
24	Dividing by 3	Chapter 3 Lesson 4
25	Dividing by 4	Chapter 3 Lesson 4
26	Dividing by 8	Chapter 3 Lesson 6
27	Dividing by 5	Chapter 3 Lessons 3 and 6
28	Dividing by 8	Chapter 3 Lesson 6
29	Dividing by 6	Chapter 3 Lessons 5 and 6
30	Dividing by 8	Chapter 3 Lesson 2
31	Dividing by 9	Chapter 3 Lesson 6
32	Fact Families	Chapter 3 Lesson 6

Test Practice

Choose the best answer and fill in the corresponding circle on the answer sheet.

1 Which equation can be used to check $10 \times 7 = 70$?

   A $70 \div 5 = 14$

   B $70 \div 10 = 7$

   C $7 \times 7 = 49$

   D $10 \times 10 = 100$

2 Aunt Claudia has 225 music CDs in her collection. If Claudia divides her CDs equally between her 3 nieces, how many CDs will each niece get?

   A 75 CDs   **C** 65 CDs

   B 55 CDs   **D** 45 CDs

3 Sweaters are on sale this week, 2 for $36. How much would 1 sweater cost during this sale?

   A $18   **C** $60

   B $20   **D** $72

4 Which symbol makes this math sentence true?

$$812 \div 4 \;\boxed{}\; 871 \div 3$$

   A >   **C** =

   B <   **D** −

5 Max's scout troop is dividing canned foods equally into 8 boxes for delivery. If the troop has a total of 592 cans of food, how many cans will go in each box?

   A 104 cans of food

   B 86 cans of food

   C 92 cans of food

   D 74 cans of food

6 What division problem does the model below represent?

   A $30 \div 6 = 5$

   B $20 \div 4 = 5$

   C $25 \div 5 = 5$

   D $24 \div 6 = 4$

7 The O'Connor family traveled 621 miles on their summer vacation. If they traveled the same number of miles per day and finished the trip in 9 days, how many miles per day did they travel?

   A 59 miles   **C** 62 miles

   B 69 miles   **D** 68 miles

8 Pablo reads about 30 pages per hour. If he finishes his book in 8 hours, about how many pages are in the book?

A	190 pages	C	320 pages
B	240 pages	D	480 pages

9 What is a different format for the expression $30 \div 5$?

A	$30 + 5$	C	$5 \div 30$
B	30×5	D	$\dfrac{30}{5}$

10 A science teacher wants to divide a box of test tubes into 1 equal group. If there are 107 test tubes, how many will be in the 1 group?

A	106	C	108
B	107	D	0

11 Maria wants to make 84 paper airplanes in 1 week. If she makes the same number of paper airplanes every day for 7 days, how many planes will she have to make each day?

A	7	C	10
B	9	D	12

ANSWER SHEET

Directions: Fill in the circle of each correct answer.

1 Ⓐ Ⓑ Ⓒ Ⓓ
2 Ⓐ Ⓑ Ⓒ Ⓓ
3 Ⓐ Ⓑ Ⓒ Ⓓ
4 Ⓐ Ⓑ Ⓒ Ⓓ
5 Ⓐ Ⓑ Ⓒ Ⓓ
6 Ⓐ Ⓑ Ⓒ Ⓓ
7 Ⓐ Ⓑ Ⓒ Ⓓ
8 Ⓐ Ⓑ Ⓒ Ⓓ
9 Ⓐ Ⓑ Ⓒ Ⓓ
10 Ⓐ Ⓑ Ⓒ Ⓓ
11 Ⓐ Ⓑ Ⓒ Ⓓ

Chapter 3

Test Practice
Scoring Guide and Diagnostic Chart

Students missing Exercise . . .	Have trouble with . . .	Should review . . .
1	Fact Families	Chapter 3, Lesson 6
2	Dividing by 3	Chapter 3, Lesson 4
3	Dividing by 2	Chapter 3, Lesson 3
4	Dividing by 3 and 4	Chapter 3, Lesson 4
5	Dividing by 8	Chapter 3, Lesson 6
6	Modeling Division	Chapter 3, Lesson 1
7	Dividing by 9	Chapter 3, Lesson 6
8	Dividing by 8	Chapter 3, Lesson 6
9	Modeling Division	Chapter 3, Lesson 1
10	Dividing by 1	Chapter 3, Lesson 2
11	Dividing by 7	Chapter 3, Lesson 5

Chapter 3

Chapter 3 Performance Assessment

1. Fred says that he knows what the remainder will be when any whole number is divided by 5 without doing the division. He says that the remainder is always either the same as the last digit of the dividend or equal to the last digit minus 5. Is he correct?

YOUR TASK: Show whether or not Fred is correct.

ONE WAY:

- Write the digits 0 to 9 as in the top row of the table below.
- Write the numbers 0, 10, 20, 30, 40, and 50 in the first column.
- Each space in the table represents each number from 0 to 59. For example, the 10 spaces in the row starting with 30 represent the numbers 30, 31, 32, 33, . . . 39.
- Pick a number between 0 and 59. Find the space in the table that represents that number. Divide by 5 and write the remainder in the space. Complete the table. Some spaces are already filled.
- Check and see if Fred is correct for these numbers. Explain why.

	0	1	2	3	4	5	6	7	8	9
0	0		2					2		
10				3			1			4
20		1				0				4
30					4		1		3	
40	0		2		4			2		
50		1		3		0			3	

Math Triumphs

Chapter 3

Performance Assessment Teacher's Notes

▶ Target Skills

- Develop an understanding of and fluency with division of whole numbers.
- Use patterns, models, and relationships to write and solve simple equations.

▶ Task Description

Students will use mathematical reasoning to find the pattern for remainders when whole numbers are divided by 5.

▶ Teacher Notes

This activity is suitable for partner work. It is preferable to model the activity before students begin to solve.

Students can use manipulatives to model rows of 5. Kinesthetic or tactile learners may represent the digits with number cubes, counting cubes, or groups of objects.

Scoring Rubric	
Score	**Explanation**
3	Students demonstrate an efficient strategy and a thorough approach that enables them to solve the problem completely. Students will: • complete several cells of the table or several number models in rows of 5. • clearly explain in grade level language the pattern of remainders when numbers are divided by 5. • show their work.
2	Students demonstrate a strategy that enables them to solve the problem correctly. The strategy is disorganized or less efficient. Students may: • have some difficulty in correctly calculating all of the remainders. • be unable to clearly explain the pattern of remainders. • find a solution, but have guessed for a few answers.
1	Students demonstrate a confused strategy, which leads to difficulty solving the problem. Most answers are incorrect, but students demonstrate knowledge of at least one concept being assessed. Students may: • correctly calculate most remainders, but be unable to find any pattern. • find an incorrect pattern which still demonstrates some understanding of correct division processes and the remainder concept. • demonstrate the ability to model number operations, but not correctly implement division by 5 or find a pattern for the remainders.

Chapter Pretest

Which number completes each equation?

1 $6 + 9 = $ _____ $+ 6$

   A 3   **B** 6   **C** 9   **D** 15

2 $5 \times 4 = $ _____ $\times 5$

   A 4   **B** 5   **C** 9   **D** 20

3 $(9 \times 3) \times 2 = 9 \times ($ _____ $\times 2)$

   A 2   **B** 3   **C** 6   **D** 9

4 $3 \times 14 = $ _____ $\times 3$

   A 3   **B** 11   **C** 14   **D** 17

5 $19 + 8 = $ _____ $+ 19$

   A 8   **B** 11   **C** 19   **D** 27

6 $(17 + 16) + 4 = 17 + (16 + $ _____ $)$

   A 4   **B** 16   **C** 17   **D** 20

Find the product of each expression.

7 $2 \times 7 \times 5$

   A 14   **B** 35   **C** 60   **D** 70

8 $8 \times (10 + 6)$

   A 96   **B** 128   **C** 140   **D** 148

9 $7 \times (6 + 8)$

   A 98   **B** 100   **C** 196   **D** 336

Solve.

10 $17 - (7 - 4) \times 2 + 3 \times 5$

   A 16   **B** 23   **C** 26   **D** 55

11 $6 + 8 \times 2 - (10 - 7)$

   A 15   **B** 16   **C** 19   **D** 24

12 $9 + (2 + 1) \times 3 + 8 \times 10 \div 2$

   A 49   **B** 57   **C** 58   **D** 76

Identify the properties.

13 Which number sentence is an example of the Distributive Property?

    A $8 \times (3 + 10) = (8 \times 3) + (8 \times 10)$ **C** $8 \times (3 \times 10) = (8 \times 3) \times 10$

    B $8 \times 0 = 0$ **D** $8 \times 3 = 3 \times 8$

14 Which number sentence is an example of the Associative Property?

    A $5 \times 7 + 5 \times 2 = 5 \times 9$ **C** $5 \times (7 \times 2) = (5 \times 7) \times 2$

    B $5 \times 1 = 5$ **D** $5 \times 7 = 7 \times 5$

15 Which number sentence is an example of the Commutative Property?

    A $4 \times 9 + 4 \times 6 = 4 \times 15$ **C** $4 \times (9 \times 6) = (4 \times 9) \times 6$

    B $4 \times 1 = 4$ **D** $4 \times 9 = 9 \times 4$

16 Make the equation true. $26 \times (13 \times 58) =$

    A $26 \times (10 \times 58 + 3 \times 50)$ **C** $26 \times (13 + 58)$

    B $(26 \times 13) \times 58$ **D** $(13 \times 20 + 6) \times 58$

Solve.

17 **FINANCE** To buy school supplies, Randy's mother will give him either $2 each week for 4 weeks or $4 each week for 2 weeks. Which number sentence compares the two choices?

    A $2 \times 4 = 4 \times 2$ **B** $2 \times 4 < 4 \times 2$ **C** $2 \times 4 > 4 \times 2$ **D** $2 \times 2 > 4 \times 2$

18 **SCHOOL** Mrs. Jefferson's class had 18 students. The first month, 2 students moved to a different school. For each of the next 2 months, Mrs. Jefferson's class gained 3 students. Which number sentence shows the change in students in her class?

    A $18 \times (3 - 2) + 2 = 20$ **C** $18 - (2 + 2) \times 3 = 18$

    B $18 - 2 + 2 \times 3 = 22$ **D** $(18 - 2 + 2) \times 3 = 56$

Correct the mistakes.

19 Maria says that the Associative Property allows her to rewrite 15×7 as $10 \times 7 + 5 \times 7$. Did she make a mistake?

    A No, she didn't make any mistake.

    B Yes, she used the wrong order of operations.

    C Yes, she is actually using the Distributive Property.

    D Yes, she is actually using the Commutative Property.

Chapter
4

Chapter Pretest
Scoring Guide and Diagnostic Chart

Students missing Exercise . . .	Have trouble with . . .	Should review . . .
1	Commutative Property	Chapter 4, Lesson 1
2	Commutative Property	Chapter 4, Lesson 1
3	Associative Property	Chapter 4, Lesson 2
4	Commutative Property	Chapter 4, Lesson 1
5	Commutative Property	Chapter 4, Lesson 1
6	Associative Property	Chapter 4, Lesson 2
7	Commutative Property	Chapter 4, Lesson 1
8	Distributive Property	Chapter 4, Lesson 3
9	Distributive Property	Chapter 4, Lesson 3
10	Order of Operations	Chapter 4, Lesson 4
11	Order of Operations	Chapter 4, Lesson 4
12	Order of Operations	Chapter 4, Lesson 4
13	Distributive Property	Chapter 4, Lesson 3
14	Associative Property	Chapter 4, Lesson 2
15	Commutative Property	Chapter 4, Lesson 1
16	Associative Property	Chapter 4, Lesson 2
17	Commutative Property	Chapter 4, Lesson 1
18	Order of Operations	Chapter 4, Lesson 4
19	Distributive Property	Chapter 4, Lesson 3

Chapter 4

Chapter Test

Use the Commutative Properties of Addition and Multiplication to fill in each blank with the correct value. Check your answer.

1. $5 \times 7 = $ _____ $\times 5$

   $35 = $ _____

2. _____ $+ 6 = 6 + 12$

   _____ $= $ _____

3. $8 + 7 = $ _____ $+ $ _____

   _____ $= $ _____

4. $12 \times 4 = $ _____ $\times $ _____

   _____ $= $ _____

5. Give an example of the Commutative Property of Addition. Check your example.

   _____

Use the Associative Property to fill in each blank. Check your answer.

6. $5 \times (5 \times 10)$

   $= ($ _____ $\times 5) \times 10$

   $= $ _____ $\times 10$

   $= $ _____

7. $8 + (13 + 2)$

   $= ($ _____ $+ 2) + 13$

   $= $ _____ $+ 13$

   $= $ _____

8. $3 + (15 + 17)$

   $= ($ _____ $+ $ _____ $) + $ _____

   $= $ _____ $+ $ _____

   $= $ _____

9. $4 \times (6 \times 5)$

   $= ($ _____ $\times $ _____ $) \times $ _____

   $= $ _____ $\times $ _____

   $= $ _____

10. Give an example of the Associative Property of Multiplication. Check your answer.

    _____

Use the Distributive Property of Multiplication to find each product.

11. $7 \times (3 + 4)$

    _____

12. $3 \times (15 - 7)$

    _____

Find the value of each expression.

13. $15 + 3 : 3 \times 7 - (14 - 6)$

    _____

14. $((15 - 5) \div 5) \div 2 + (12 + 8)$

    _____

Math Triumphs

Solve.

15 **JUICE** Lionel wants to make 2 gallons of punch for a party at school. Each gallon requires 2 cans of juice, and each can of juice costs $2.50. How much will the punch cost? _____

16 **PACKAGING** Mrs. Lopez bought 4 packages of hot dogs with 8 hot dogs in each package. Mr. Ruiz bought 5 packages of hamburgers with 6 hamburgers in each package. Who bought more food?

_____

_____

17 **MOVIES** Anna watched two 50-minute history videos last week and three 40-minute science videos this week. How many minutes did she spend watching videos during both weeks? _____

18 **BASEBALL** The baseball team stored their baseballs in boxes. Five boxes had 3 baseballs in each box, and two boxes had 4 baseballs in each box. For one game they used 11 baseballs. What is the total number of baseballs left?

_____

Correct the mistakes.

19 **LIGHTBULBS** Rita went to the hardware store and purchased 6 boxes of the lightbulbs labeled "box A." Her friend Ava went to the discount store and purchased 4 boxes of the lightbulbs labeled "box B." Rita told Ava that she bought more lightbulbs because she bought more boxes. What mistake did Rita make?

_____

_____

20 **BAKERY** At the Bake Shop, the baker had 7 dozen rolls in a case. Two customers purchased 2 dozen rolls each, and 3 dozen more went to another customer. The baker then brought out 4 more dozen rolls but dropped 1 dozen on the floor, so they had to be thrown away. The baker exclaimed, "Now we only have 5 dozen rolls to sell." Was the baker correct? Explain.

_____

_____

Math Triumphs

Chapter 4

Chapter Test
Scoring Guide and Diagnostic Chart

Students missing Exercise . . .	Have trouble with . . .	Should review . . .
1	Commutative Property	Chapter 4, Lesson 1
2	Commutative Property	Chapter 4, Lesson 1
3	Commutative Property	Chapter 4, Lesson 1
4	Commutative Property	Chapter 4, Lesson 1
5	Commutative Property	Chapter 4, Lesson 1
6	Associative Property	Chapter 4, Lesson 2
7	Associative Property	Chapter 4, Lesson 2
8	Associative Property	Chapter 4, Lesson 2
9	Associative Property	Chapter 4, Lesson 2
10	Associative Property	Chapter 4, Lesson 2
11	Distributive Property	Chapter 4, Lesson 3
12	Distributive Property	Chapter 4, Lesson 3
13	Order of Operations	Chapter 4, Lesson 4
14	Order of Operations	Chapter 4, Lesson 4
15	Order of Operations	Chapter 4, Lesson 4
16	Associative Property	Chapter 4, Lesson 2
17	Order of Operations	Chapter 4, Lesson 4
18	Order of Operations	Chapter 4, Lesson 4
19	Commutative Property	Chapter 4, Lesson 1
20	Order of Operations	Chapter 4, Lesson 4

Math Triumphs

Choose the best answer and fill in the corresponding circle on the answer sheet.

1 If $5 \times 8 \times 6 = 240$, then what is $6 \times 5 \times 8$?

A   160   C   480

B   240   D   520

2 $94 \times (203 \times 26) =$

A $(84 \times 230) \times 26$

B $(94 \times 230) \times 62$

C $(94 \times 203) \times 26$

D $(49 \times 203) \times 26$

3 Mr. Palo wants to put up a fence. If he knows the dimensions of two sides, which expression shows how much fencing he needs?

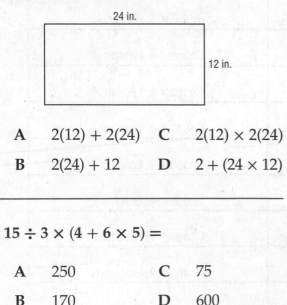

24 in.

12 in.

A $2(12) + 2(24)$ C $2(12) \times 2(24)$

B $2(24) + 12$ D $2 + (24 \times 12)$

4 $15 \div 3 \times (4 + 6 \times 5) =$

A   250   C   75

B   170   D   600

5 Which property is shown in the sentence below?

$(12 \times 4) + (12 \times 5) = 12 \times (4 + 5)$

A   Associative Property of Addition

B   Distributive Property of Multiplication over Addition

C   Commutative Property of Addition

D   Identity Property of Multiplication

6 Which property is shown in the sentence below?

$(152 \times 577) \times 183 = 152 \times (577 \times 183)$

A   Associative Property of Multiplication

B   Distributive Property of Multiplication over Addition

C   Commutative Property of Multiplication

D   Identity Property of Multiplication

Math Triumphs

7 Which property is shown in the sentence below?

$$22 \times 3 = 3 \times 22$$

A   Associative Property of Multiplication

B   Distributive Property of Multiplication over Addition

C   Commutative Property of Multiplication

D   Identity Property of Multiplication

8 Carlos buys 8 model cars on sale. Which expression has a value equal to the cost of 8 model cars?

Item	Cost
model car	$9
puzzle	$6
board game	$12

A $(3 \times 9) + (5 \times 9)$

B $(3 \times 12) + (5 \times 12)$

C $(3 \times 6) + (5 \times 6)$

D $(3 \times 9) + (6 \times 9)$

9 Which expression is equal to 26×9?

A $(2 \times 9) + (6 \times 9)$

B $(20 \times 9) + (6 \times 9)$

C $(26 \times 26) + (9 \times 9)$

D $(9 \times 60) + (9 \times 2)$

10 What is the first step in solving $5 \times (4 - 3) \div 2$?

A   Multiply 5 times 4

B   Subtract 3 from 4

C   Divide 3 by 2

D   Multiply 5 times 2

11 Which of the following is true if $(10 \times 12) \times 3 = 360$?

A $(10 \times 12) + (10 \times 3) = 360$

B $3 \times 360 = 10 \times 12$

C $10 \times (12 \times 3) = 360$

D $(10 + 12) \times 3 = 360$

ANSWER SHEET

Directions: Fill in the circle of each correct answer.

1   Ⓐ Ⓑ Ⓒ Ⓓ
2   Ⓐ Ⓑ Ⓒ Ⓓ
3   Ⓐ Ⓑ Ⓒ Ⓓ
4   Ⓐ Ⓑ Ⓒ Ⓓ
5   Ⓐ Ⓑ Ⓒ Ⓓ
6   Ⓐ Ⓑ Ⓒ Ⓓ
7   Ⓐ Ⓑ Ⓒ Ⓓ
8   Ⓐ Ⓑ Ⓒ Ⓓ
9   Ⓐ Ⓑ Ⓒ Ⓓ
10   Ⓐ Ⓑ Ⓒ Ⓓ
11   Ⓐ Ⓑ Ⓒ Ⓓ

Test Practice
Scoring Guide and Diagnostic Chart

Students missing Exercise . . .	Have trouble with . . .	Should review . . .
1	Associative Property	Chapter 4, Lesson 2
2	Associative Property	Chapter 4, Lesson 2
3	Distributive Property	Chapter 4, Lesson 3
4	Order of Operations	Chapter 4, Lesson 4
5	Distributive Property	Chapter 4, Lesson 3
6	Associative Property	Chapter 4, Lesson 2
7	Commutative Property	Chapter 4, Lesson 1
8	Distributive Property	Chapter 4, Lesson 3
9	Distributive Property	Chapter 4, Lesson 3
10	Order of Operations	Chapter 4, Lesson 4
11	Associative Property	Chapter 4, Lesson 2

Math Triumphs

Chapter 4 Performance Assessment

1. Use the Distributive Property and the fact that 796 is equal to 800 − 4 to solve 796 × 3.

YOUR TASK: Use the Distributive Property to write a number sentence equal to 796 × 3. Then solve the problem.

ONE WAY:

- Write the problem 796 × 3.
- Replace 796 with 800 − 4.
- Use the Distributive Property and multiply by 3.

  _____ × 3 = ___ − ___ × 3 = ___

- Subtract the products to find the answer.

  ___ − ___ = ___

ANOTHER WAY:

Make a place-value chart with three columns: hundreds, tens, and ones. Use yellow and red counters to represent numbers. Yellow counters are added; red counters are subtracted.

- Use yellow counters to represent the hundreds place, tens place, and ones place in 796.

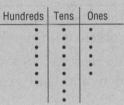

- Show 796 a different way. Place one more yellow counter in the hundreds place to total 8, and four red counters in the ones place. The counters now represent 796. (800 yellow counters − 4 red counters = 796)

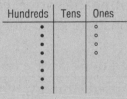

- Repeat the new model of 796 three times to show multiplying by 3.
- Total all the counters to find the solution for 796 × 3. First count all the yellow hundreds counters, then subtract the red ones counters.

Chapter 4 Performance Assessment Teacher's Notes

 Target Skills

- Use patterns, models, and relationships to write and solve simple equations.
- Understand and use properties of operations.
- Extend understanding of place value of numbers to millions.
- Develop an understanding of and fluency with multiplication of whole numbers.

 Task Description

Students will use the Distributive Property to solve a problem involving the multiplication of large numbers.

▶ **Teacher Notes**

This activity is suitable for partner work. It is preferable to model the activity before students begin to solve.

Students can draw symbols or use manipulatives to represent the hundreds, tens, and ones in the problem. Kinesthetic or tactile learners may use number cubes, counting cubes, or other groups of objects to represent the problem.

Scoring Rubric	
Score	**Explanation**
3	Students demonstrate an efficient strategy and a thorough approach that enables them to solve the problem completely. Students will: • write an expression equivalent to 796 × 3. • correctly solve the problem and get the product 2,388. • show their work.
2	Students demonstrate a strategy that enables them to solve the problem correctly. The strategy is disorganized or less efficient. Students may: • have some difficulty writing the correct expression or completing the multiplication but demonstrate an understanding of the Distributive Property. • find a solution, but have guessed for a few answers.
1	Students demonstrate a confused strategy, which leads to difficulty solving the problem. Most answers are incorrect, but students demonstrate knowledge of at least one concept being assessed. Students may: • write an expression equivalent to 796 × 3, but not understand its meaning or how to use it to solve the problem. • correctly solve the original problem 796 × 3, but not make any use of the Distributive Property.

Book Test

Identify the place of each underlined digit. Fill in the chart to help you.

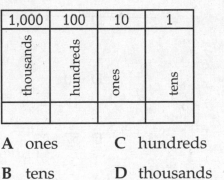

1 9,01<u>2</u>

1,000	100	10	1
thousands	hundreds	ones	tens

A ones   **C** hundreds

B tens   **D** thousands

2 <u>7</u>,413

1,000	100	10	1
thousands	hundreds	ones	tens

A ones   **C** hundreds

B tens   **D** thousands

Answer the following questions.

3 What is 5,412,091 in word form?

A five million, four hundred twelve thousand, nine hundred ten

B fifty-four million, twelve thousand, ninety-one

C five million, four hundred twelve thousand, ninety-one

D five million, forty-one thousand, two hundred ninety-one

4 What are the next two numbers in the pattern below?

A 1,100; 1,200   **C** 2,000; 4,000

B 2,000; 3,000   **D** 3,000; 4,000

Number of Liters	1	2	3	4
Number of Milliliters	1,000	2,000		

5 How many cookies are in 3 dozen?

A 30   **B** 32   **C** 36   **D** 38

Find each product.

6 $8 \times 9 =$

A 72   **B** 78   **C** 89   **D** 98

7 $11 \times 12 =$

A 110   **B** 120   **C** 130   **D** 132

8 $13 \times 0 =$

A 13   **B** 1,300   **C** 0   **D** 130

9 $145 \times 2 =$

A 147   **B** 245   **C** 290   **D** 1,452

Book 1

Book Test, continued

Find each quotient.

10 $145 \div 29 =$

   A 0   **B** 3   **C** 5   **D** 10

11 $72 \div 9 =$

   A 7   **B** 8   **C** 9   **D** 10

12 $60 \div 3 =$

   A 20   **B** 30   **C** 36   **D** 57

13 $72 \div 6 =$

   A 10   **B** 11   **C** 12   **D** 13

Answer the following questions below.

14 Which operation is the inverse of division?

   A division   **B** addition   **C** subtraction   **D** multiplication

15 $3 \times (4 - 1) =$

   A 8   **C** 11

   B 9   **D** 15

16 $(15 - 15) \times 6 + 3 =$

   A 0   **C** 78

   B 3   **D** 93

17 Which property is shown in the sentence below?

$3 + (17 + 1) = (3 + 17) + 1$

   A Associative Property   **C** Order of Operations

   B Commutative Property   **D** Distributive Property

18 $12 \times (5 + 9) =$

   A $(10 \times 5) + (2 \times 9)$ **C** $5 \times 12 + 5 \times 9$

   B $12 \times 5 \times 9$ **D** $12 \times 5 + 12 \times 9$

19 $139 \times 47 =$

   A $139 + 47$ **C** 47×139

   B $(100 + 39) \times (40 - 7)$ **D** $(139 \times 1) + (47 \times 0)$

Book 1

Book Test
Scoring Guide and Diagnostic Chart

Students missing Exercise . . .	Have trouble with . . .	Should review . . .
1	Whole Numbers Less than 10,000	Chapter 1, Lesson 1
2	Whole Numbers Less than 10,000	Chapter 1, Lesson 1
3	Read and Write Whole Numbers in the Millions	Chapter 1, Lesson 2
4	Linear Patterns	Chapter 1, Lesson 4
5	Number Relationships	Chapter 1, Lesson 3
6	Multiplying by 8 and 9	Chapter 2, Lesson 3
7	Multiplying by 11 and 12	Chapter 2, Lesson 4
8	Multiplying by 0	Chapter 2, Lesson 1
9	Multiplying Large Numbers	Chapter 2, Lesson 5
10	Dividing by 5	Chapter 3, Lesson 3
11	Dividing by 9	Chapter 3, Lesson 6
12	Dividing by 3	Chapter 3, Lesson 4
13	Dividing by 6	Chapter 3, Lesson 5
14	Modeling Division	Chapter 3, Lesson 1
15	Order of Operations	Chapter 4, Lesson 4
16	Order of Operations	Chapter 4, Lesson 4
17	Associative Property	Chapter 4, Lesson 2
18	Distributive Property	Chapter 4, Lesson 3
19	Commutative Property	Chapter 4, Lesson 1

Book 1 Test

Book 2

Book Pretest

Solve.

1 $\frac{3}{7} - \frac{1}{14} =$

A $\frac{3}{14}$　　　　B $\frac{5}{14}$　　　　C $\frac{7}{14}$　　　　D $\frac{5}{7}$

2 $\frac{4}{5} - \frac{2}{3} =$

A $\frac{1}{15}$　　　　B $\frac{2}{15}$　　　　C $\frac{1}{3}$　　　　D $\frac{4}{15}$

3 $\frac{5}{11} + \frac{3}{11} =$

A $\frac{2}{11}$　　　　B $\frac{4}{11}$　　　　C $\frac{6}{11}$　　　　D $\frac{8}{11}$

4 $\frac{5}{8} - \frac{3}{8} =$

A 2　　　　B $\frac{8}{8}$　　　　C 1　　　　D $\frac{1}{4}$

5 Add. Write the sum in simplest form.

$\frac{3}{8} + \frac{5}{12} =$

A $\frac{3}{4}$　　　　B $\frac{19}{24}$　　　　C $\frac{5}{6}$　　　　D $\frac{7}{8}$

6 $0.67 - 0.4 =$

A 0.27　　　　B 0.37　　　　C 0.63　　　　D 1.07

7 $5.94 + 3.82 =$

A 8.66　　　　B 8.76　　　　C 9.76　　　　D 9.86

Order the following numbers from least to greatest.

8 $\frac{2}{5}, \frac{1}{2}, \frac{3}{7}$

A $\frac{2}{5}, \frac{1}{2}, \frac{3}{7}$　　　　B $\frac{1}{2}, \frac{3}{7}, \frac{2}{5}$　　　　C $\frac{2}{5}, \frac{3}{7}, \frac{1}{2}$　　　　D $\frac{3}{7}, \frac{1}{2}, \frac{2}{5}$

9 $\frac{3}{4}, \frac{4}{5}, \frac{2}{3}, \frac{1}{2}$

A $\frac{4}{5}, \frac{3}{4}, \frac{2}{3}, \frac{1}{2}$　　　　C $\frac{1}{2}, \frac{3}{4}, \frac{4}{5}, \frac{2}{3}$

B $\frac{1}{2}, \frac{2}{3}, \frac{3}{4}, \frac{4}{5}$　　　　D $\frac{2}{3}, \frac{1}{2}, \frac{3}{4}, \frac{4}{5}$

10 0.25, 0.05, 0.52

A 0.52, 0.05, 0.25　　　　B 0.05, 0.52, 0.25　　　　C 0.25, 0.05, 0.52　　　　D 0.05, 0.25, 0.52

Book Pretest, continued

Answer the following questions.

11 Which fraction does the shaded part of the model represent?

A $\frac{9}{14}$ **B** $\frac{8}{14}$ **C** $\frac{7}{14}$ **D** $\frac{5}{14}$

12 Which number in the fraction $\frac{13}{24}$ represents the number of equal parts into which an object is divided?

A 1 **B** 2 **C** 13 **D** 24

13 The least common multiple of the denominators of two or more fractions is referred to as the _____.

A least common multiple **C** greatest common factor

B least common denominator **D** equivalent fraction

14 Write $4\frac{1}{6}$ as an improper fraction.

A $\frac{25}{6}$ **B** $\frac{24}{6}$ **C** $\frac{11}{6}$ **D** $\frac{10}{6}$

15 Which fraction is equal to 1?

A $\frac{26}{27}$ **B** $\frac{27}{27}$ **C** $\frac{28}{27}$ **D** $\frac{27}{1}$

16 Write $\frac{19}{7}$ as a mixed number.

A $2\frac{4}{7}$ **B** $2\frac{5}{7}$ **C** $5\frac{2}{7}$ **D** $7\frac{2}{5}$

17 Select the equivalent decimal and mixed number for six and four tenths.

A $6.04; 6\frac{4}{100}$ **B** $6.04; 6\frac{1}{25}$ **C** $6.4; 6\frac{2}{50}$ **D** $6.4; 6\frac{4}{10}$

18 **PAINTING** Javon, Nissa, Lulu, and Marcus each painted an unfinished wooden toy. Javon used $\frac{2}{3}$ of his paint, Nissa used $\frac{1}{4}$ of her paint, Lulu used $\frac{1}{6}$ of her paint, and Marcus used $\frac{1}{2}$ of his paint. Who used the greatest amount of paint?

A Javon **B** Nissa **C** Lulu **D** Marcus

19 **LANDSCAPING** Samantha needs mulch for her gardens. She usually needs $\frac{1}{2}$ bag for the front gardens and $\frac{2}{3}$ bag for the back gardens. How many total bags of mulch does she need?

A $\frac{3}{5}$ **B** $\frac{4}{5}$ **C** $\frac{5}{6}$ **D** $1\frac{1}{6}$

Book Pretest
Scoring Guide and Diagnostic Chart

Students missing Exercise . . .	Have trouble with . . .	Should review . . .
1	Subtract Fractions with Unlike Denominators	Chapter 6, Lesson 4
2	Subtract Fractions with Unlike Denominators	Chapter 6, Lesson 4
3	Add Fractions with Like Denominators	Chapter 6, Lesson 2
4	Subtract Fractions with Like Denominators	Chapter 6, Lesson 2
5	Add Fractions with Unlike Denominators	Chapter 6, Lesson 3
6	Subtract Decimals	Chapter 7, Lesson 5
7	Add Decimals	Chapter 7, Lesson 4
8	Compare and Order Fractions	Chapter 5, Lesson 5
9	Compare and Order Decimals	Chapter 7, Lesson 3
10	Compare and Order Decimals	Chapter 7, Lesson 3
11	Parts of a Whole	Chapter 5, Lesson 1
12	Parts of a Whole	Chapter 5, Lesson 1
13	Least Common Denominator	Chapter 5, Lesson 4
14	Mixed Numbers and Improper Fractions	Chapter 5, Lesson 3
15	Fraction equivalent to 1	Chapter 5, Lesson 6
16	Mixed Numbers and Improper Fractions	Chapter 5, Lesson 3
17	Equivalent Decimals	Chapter 7, Lesson 2
18	Compare and Order Fractions	Chapter 5, Lesson 5
19	Add Fractions with Like Denominators	Chapter 6, Lesson 1

Chapter Pretest

Gr.5

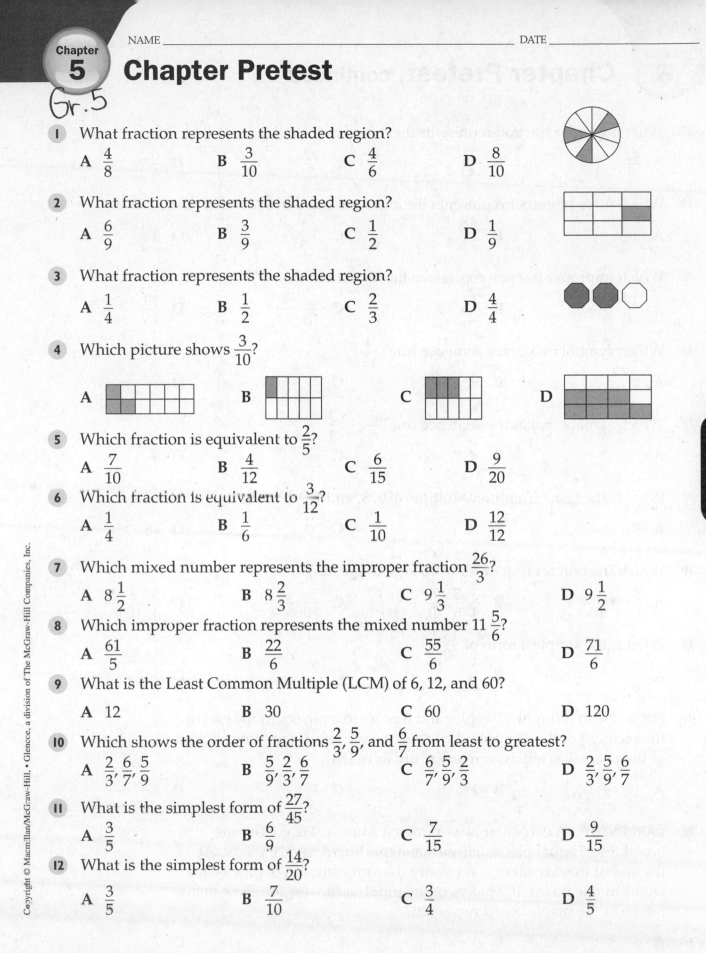

1 What fraction represents the shaded region?

A $\frac{4}{8}$ B $\frac{3}{10}$ C $\frac{4}{6}$ D $\frac{8}{10}$

2 What fraction represents the shaded region?

A $\frac{6}{9}$ B $\frac{3}{9}$ C $\frac{1}{2}$ D $\frac{1}{9}$

3 What fraction represents the shaded region?

A $\frac{1}{4}$ B $\frac{1}{2}$ C $\frac{2}{3}$ D $\frac{4}{4}$

4 Which picture shows $\frac{3}{10}$?

A   B   C   D

5 Which fraction is equivalent to $\frac{2}{5}$?

A $\frac{7}{10}$ B $\frac{4}{12}$ C $\frac{6}{15}$ D $\frac{9}{20}$

6 Which fraction is equivalent to $\frac{3}{12}$?

A $\frac{1}{4}$ B $\frac{1}{6}$ C $\frac{1}{10}$ D $\frac{12}{12}$

7 Which mixed number represents the improper fraction $\frac{26}{3}$?

A $8\frac{1}{2}$ B $8\frac{2}{3}$ C $9\frac{1}{3}$ D $9\frac{1}{2}$

8 Which improper fraction represents the mixed number $11\frac{5}{6}$?

A $\frac{61}{5}$ B $\frac{22}{6}$ C $\frac{55}{6}$ D $\frac{71}{6}$

9 What is the Least Common Multiple (LCM) of 6, 12, and 60?

A 12   B 30   C 60   D 120

10 Which shows the order of fractions $\frac{2}{3}$, $\frac{5}{9}$, and $\frac{6}{7}$ from least to greatest?

A $\frac{2}{3}, \frac{6}{7}, \frac{5}{9}$ B $\frac{5}{9}, \frac{2}{3}, \frac{6}{7}$ C $\frac{6}{7}, \frac{5}{9}, \frac{2}{3}$ D $\frac{2}{3}, \frac{5}{9}, \frac{6}{7}$

11 What is the simplest form of $\frac{27}{45}$?

A $\frac{3}{5}$ B $\frac{6}{9}$ C $\frac{7}{15}$ D $\frac{9}{15}$

12 What is the simplest form of $\frac{14}{20}$?

A $\frac{3}{5}$ B $\frac{7}{10}$ C $\frac{3}{4}$ D $\frac{4}{5}$

Chapter 5

13 What improper fraction represents the mixed number $4\frac{2}{5}$?

     A $\frac{42}{5}$ **B** $\frac{22}{4}$ **C** $\frac{22}{5}$ **D** $\frac{6}{4}$

14 Which mixed number represents the improper fraction $\frac{8}{3}$?

     A $2\frac{1}{2}$ **B** $2\frac{2}{3}$ **C** $3\frac{1}{3}$ **D** $3\frac{1}{2}$

15 Which improper fraction represents the mixed number $3\frac{1}{4}$?

     A $\frac{13}{4}$ **B** $\frac{42}{4}$ **C** $\frac{3}{16}$ **D** $\frac{13}{16}$

16 Which symbol makes the sentence true? $\frac{4}{12} \bigcirc \frac{3}{9}$

     A >   **B** <   **C** =   **D** +

17 Which symbol makes the sentence true? $\frac{5}{6} \bigcirc \frac{3}{4}$

     A >   **B** <   **C** =   **D** +

18 What is the Least Common Multiple of 6, 8, and 16?

     A 8   **B** 12   **C** 32   **D** 48

19 Which fraction set is in order from least to greatest?

     A $\frac{5}{6}, \frac{3}{4}, \frac{9}{10}$ **B** $\frac{3}{4}, \frac{5}{6}, \frac{9}{10}$ **C** $\frac{9}{10}, \frac{5}{6}, \frac{3}{4}$ **D** $\frac{3}{4}, \frac{9}{10}, \frac{5}{6}$

20 What is the simplest form of $\frac{15}{30}$?

     A $\frac{3}{6}$ **B** $\frac{2}{5}$ **C** $\frac{2}{3}$ **D** $\frac{1}{2}$

21 **FOOD** Sean brought 12 apples and 8 pears to a picnic. At the end of the picnic, 3 of the 12 apples he brought were left. If the same fraction of the pears was left, how many pears were left?

     A 1   **B** 2   **C** 3   **D** 4

22 **CARPENTRY** A carpenter is working on a house. He cuts a pine board into 5 equal pieces. He cuts a maple board into 10 pieces. At the end of the day there was exactly the same amount of pine board left as maple board. If 3 pieces of the pine board were left, how many pieces of the maple board remained?

     A 6   **B** 3   **C** 5   **D** 7

Chapter 5

Chapter Pretest
Scoring Guide and Diagnostic Chart

Students missing Exercise . . .	Have trouble with . . .	Should review . . .
1	Parts of a Whole	Chapter 5, Lesson 1
2	Parts of a Whole	Chapter 5, Lesson 1
3	Parts of a Set	Chapter 5, Lesson 1
4	Parts of a Whole	Chapter 5, Lesson 1
5	Equivalent Fractions	Chapter 5, Lesson 2
6	Equivalent Fractions	Chapter 5, Lesson 2
7	Mixed Numbers and Improper Fractions	Chapter 5, Lesson 3
8	Mixed Numbers and Improper Fractions	Chapter 5, Lesson 3
9	Least Common Denominators	Chapter 5, Lesson 4
10	Compare and Order Fractions	Chapter 5, Lesson 5
11	Simplify Fractions	Chapter 5, Lesson 6
12	Simplify Fractions	Chapter 5, Lesson 6
13	Mixed Numbers and Improper Fractions	Chapter 5, Lesson 3
14	Mixed Numbers and Improper Fractions	Chapter 5, Lesson 3
15	Mixed Numbers and Improper Fractions	Chapter 5, Lesson 3
16	Compare and Order Fractions	Chapter 5, Lesson 5
17	Compare and Order Fractions	Chapter 5, Lesson 5
18	Least Common Denominators	Chapter 5, Lesson 4
19	Compare and Order Fractions	Chapter 5, Lesson 5
20	Simplify Fractions	Chapter 5, Lesson 6
21	Equivalent Fractions	Chapter 5, Lesson 2
22	Equivalent Fractions	Chapter 5, Lesson 2

Math Triumphs

Chapter Test

Gr.5

Write a fraction to represent each shaded region or part of a set.

1 [grid image] _____

2 [hearts image] _____

Draw a picture to model each fraction. Use equal parts of a whole.

3 $\frac{3}{8}$

4 $\frac{1}{6}$

Name two equivalent fractions.

5 $\frac{1}{5}$ _____

6 $\frac{3}{4}$ _____

Write each mixed number as an improper fraction.

7 $5\frac{2}{7}$ ▭/▭

8 $8\frac{1}{4}$ ▭/▭

Write each improper fraction as a mixed number.

9 $\frac{14}{3}$ ▭ ▭/▭

10 $\frac{25}{7}$ ▭ ▭/▭

Use <, =, or > to compare the fractions. Rename the fractions using a common denominator.

11 $\frac{1}{2} \bigcirc \frac{2}{3}$ _____

12 $\frac{4}{5} \bigcirc \frac{3}{4}$ _____

Find the Least Common Multiple (LCM) of each set of numbers.

13 6, 4, and 9 _____

14 5, 3, and 6 _____

Order the fraction sets from least to greatest.

15 $\dfrac{5}{8}, \dfrac{2}{3}, \dfrac{3}{6}$ _____

16 $\dfrac{2}{5}, \dfrac{3}{4}, \dfrac{6}{10}$ _____

17 Write $\dfrac{24}{36}$ in simplest form.

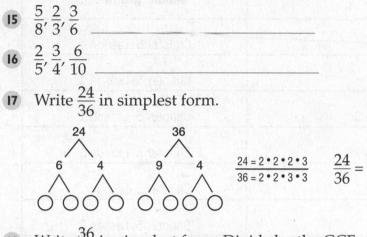

$\dfrac{24 = 2 \cdot 2 \cdot 2 \cdot 3}{36 = 2 \cdot 2 \cdot 3 \cdot 3}$ $\dfrac{24}{36} = $ _____

18 Write $\dfrac{36}{54}$ in simplest form. Divide by the GCF.

_____

Solve.

19 **PACKAGING** There are 2 boxes of mini-muffins at a party. One box has 24 muffins, while the other box has 36 muffins. At the end of the party, the same fraction of each box is remaining. If 12 muffins of the 24-piece box are left, then how many muffins of the 36-piece box are left?

_____

20 In March, $\dfrac{1}{3}$ of students went outside at recess. In May, $\dfrac{2}{4}$ of students went outside at recess. In which month did more students go outside at recess?

_____

21 **HOBBIES** Ira had 2 pieces of rope that were the same size. He used $\dfrac{4}{5}$ of the first piece and $\dfrac{5}{8}$ of the second piece for a project he made. Which piece of rope did he use more of? _____

Correct the mistakes.

22 Rasha brought 63 bottles of water to sell at the football game. After the game he had 7 bottles remaining. He told his father that only $\dfrac{3}{4}$ of the bottles were sold. What mistake did Rasha make?

_____

Chapter Test
Scoring Guide and Diagnostic Chart

Students missing Exercise . . .	Have trouble with . . .	Should review . . .
1	Parts of a Whole	Chapter 5, Lesson 1
2	Parts of a Set	Chapter 5, Lesson 1
3	Parts of a Whole and a Set	Chapter 5, Lesson 1
4	Parts of a Whole and a Set	Chapter 5, Lesson 1
5	Equivalent Fractions	Chapter 5, Lesson 2
6	Equivalent Fractions	Chapter 5, Lesson 2
7	Mixed Numbers and Improper Fractions	Chapter 5, Lesson 3
8	Mixed Numbers and Improper Fractions	Chapter 5, Lesson 3
9	Mixed Numbers and Improper Fractions	Chapter 5, Lesson 3
10	Mixed Numbers and Improper Fractions	Chapter 5, Lesson 3
11	Compare and Order Fractions	Chapter 5, Lesson 5
12	Compare and Order Fractions	Chapter 5, Lesson 5
13	Least Common Denominators	Chapter 5, Lesson 4
14	Least Common Denominators	Chapter 5, Lesson 4
15	Compare and Order Fractions	Chapter 5, Lesson 5
16	Compare and Order Fractions	Chapter 5, Lesson 5
17	Simplify Fractions	Chapter 5, Lesson 6
18	Simplify Fractions	Chapter 5, Lesson 6
19	Equivalent Fractions	Chapter 5, Lesson 2
20	Compare and Order Fractions	Chapter 5, Lesson 5
21	Compare and Order Fractions	Chapter 5, Lesson 5
22	Simplify Fractions	Chapter 5, Lesson 6

Chapter 5 **Test Practice**

Gr.5

Choose the best answer and fill in the corresponding circle on the answer sheet.

1 Vipada shaded one section for each day she swam. Which fraction represents the days she swam?

A $\frac{1}{4}$

C $\frac{8}{12}$

B $\frac{4}{12}$

D $\frac{4}{4}$

2 Which fraction is equivalent to $\frac{4}{12}$?

A $\frac{1}{3}$

C $\frac{3}{4}$

B $\frac{2}{5}$

D $\frac{6}{10}$

3 Which symbol makes the sentence true?

$$\frac{6}{18} \,\square\, \frac{4}{16}$$

A >

C <

B =

D +

4 Which mixed number represents the shaded region?

A $5\frac{8}{8}$

C $5\frac{1}{8}$

B $6\frac{4}{8}$

D $5\frac{3}{4}$

5 Order these fraction sets from least to greatest: $\frac{3}{5}, \frac{4}{10}, \frac{2}{7}$.

A $\frac{3}{5}, \frac{2}{7}, \frac{4}{10}$

C $\frac{2}{7}, \frac{4}{10}, \frac{3}{5}$

B $\frac{4}{10}, \frac{3}{5}, \frac{2}{7}$

D $\frac{2}{7}, \frac{3}{5}, \frac{4}{10}$

6 Which does NOT equal one whole?

A $\frac{3}{3}$

C $\frac{15}{15}$

B $\frac{9}{9}$

D $\frac{9}{10}$

7 Which fraction does the shaded part of the model represent?

A $\frac{1}{3}$

C $\frac{2}{8}$

B $\frac{1}{4}$

D $\frac{2}{4}$

8 Which fraction is equivalent to $\frac{7}{14}$?

A $\frac{4}{5}$

C $\frac{1}{2}$

B $\frac{2}{5}$

D $\frac{2}{3}$

9 Which fraction is equivalent to $\frac{36}{48}$?

A $\frac{4}{5}$

C $\frac{2}{3}$

B $\frac{3}{4}$

D $\frac{3}{5}$

Chapter 5

Choose the best answer and fill in the corresponding circle on the sheet at right.

10 Which fraction represents the shaded region?

A $\dfrac{8}{12}$ C $\dfrac{10}{12}$

B $\dfrac{7}{11}$ D $\dfrac{2}{4}$

11 What is three-tenths written as a fraction?

A $\dfrac{3}{10}$ C $\dfrac{10}{30}$

B $\dfrac{1}{3}$ D $\dfrac{1}{30}$

12 Which model represents $\dfrac{4}{8}$?

A   C

B   D

13 Which symbol makes the sentence true?

$\dfrac{1}{5}$ ☐ $\dfrac{1}{15}$

A =   C +

B >   D <

ANSWER SHEET

Directions: Fill in the circle of each correct answer.

1 Ⓐ Ⓑ Ⓒ Ⓓ
2 Ⓐ Ⓑ Ⓒ Ⓓ
3 Ⓐ Ⓑ Ⓒ Ⓓ
4 Ⓐ Ⓑ Ⓒ Ⓓ
5 Ⓐ Ⓑ Ⓒ Ⓓ
6 Ⓐ Ⓑ Ⓒ Ⓓ
7 Ⓐ Ⓑ Ⓒ Ⓓ
8 Ⓐ Ⓑ Ⓒ Ⓓ
9 Ⓐ Ⓑ Ⓒ Ⓓ
10 Ⓐ Ⓑ Ⓒ Ⓓ
11 Ⓐ Ⓑ Ⓒ Ⓓ
12 Ⓐ Ⓑ Ⓒ Ⓓ
13 Ⓐ Ⓑ Ⓒ Ⓓ

Chapter 5 Test Practice

Scoring Guide and Diagnostic Chart

Students missing Exercise . . .	Have trouble with . . .	Should review . . .
1	Parts of a Whole	Chapter 5, Lesson 1
2	Equivalent Fractions	Chapter 5, Lesson 2
3	Compare and Order Fractions	Chapter 5, Lesson 5
4	Mixed Numbers and Improper Fractions	Chapter 5, Lesson 3
5	Compare and Order Fractions	Chapter 5, Lesson 5
6	Parts of a Whole	Chapter 5, Lesson 1
7	Equivalent Forms of One	Chapter 5, Lesson 2
8	Simplify Fractions	Chapter 5, Lesson 6
9	Simplify Fractions	Chapter 5, Lesson 6
10	Parts of a Whole	Chapter 5, Lesson 1
11	Parts of a Whole and Parts of a Set	Chapter 5, Lesson 1
12	Parts of a Set	Chapter 5, Lesson 1
13	Compare and Order Fractions	Chapter 5, Lesson 5

Chapter 5

Chapter 5

Performance Assessment

1. What is the Least Common Denominator (LCD) for the fractions $\frac{5}{12}$ and $\frac{7}{20}$? Which fraction is larger?

Checklist
☐ Write your name.
☐ Show your work.
☐ Explain your reasoning.
☐ Write the answer.

YOUR TASK: Compare the fractions $\frac{5}{12}$ and $\frac{7}{20}$ by finding the Least Common Denominator and writing the fractions as equivalent fractions. Show your work and explain your answer.

ONE WAY:

- To find the Least Common Denominator, first write the denominators 12 and 20 as products of smaller numbers. For instance, $12 = 3 \times 4$, and $20 = 5 \times 4$.

- The Least Common Denominator is the product of each of the smaller numbers used once: $3 \times 4 \times 5 = ?$

- Multiply the numerator of each fraction by the number in $3 \times 4 \times 5$ that is only in the denominator of the other fraction:

$$\frac{5 \times 5}{60} \qquad \frac{7 \times 3}{60}$$

- Select the fraction with the larger numerator.

ANOTHER WAY:

To find the LCD, make a table of the multiples of 12 and 20. The table is started here. Find the LCM of 12 and 20.

	Multiples of 12	Multiples of 20
1	$12 \times 1 = 12$	$20 \times 1 = 20$
2	$12 \times 2 = 24$	$20 \times 2 = 40$
3	$12 \times 3 = 36$	$20 \times 3 = 60$
4	$12 \times 4 = 48$	$20 \times 4 = 80$
5	$12 \times 5 = 60$	$20 \times 5 = 100$

The LCD is 20.

Rename each fraction as an equivalent fraction with a denominator of 60.

Compare the numerators of the equivalent fractions.

The fraction with the larger numerator is equivalent to the larger fraction.

Chapter 5

Performance Assessment Teacher's Notes

▶ Target Skills

- Develop an understanding of fractions.
- Use patterns, models, and relationships to write and solve simple equations.

▶ Task Description

Students will use mathematical reasoning to find the Least Common Denominator and compare two fractions.

▶ Teacher Notes

This activity is suitable for partner work. It is preferable to model the activity before students begin to solve.

Students can use manipulatives to model the two fractions. Kinesthetic or tactile learners may draw or represent fractions with number cubes, counting cubes, or groups of objects. Visual learners may draw simple diagrams to represent the problem.

Scoring Rubric	
Score	**Explanation**
3	Students demonstrate an efficient strategy and a thorough approach that enables them to solve the problem completely. Students will: • correctly find the Least Common Denominator. • find the equivalent fractions to compare the fractions. • explain their answer in grade-appropriate language.
2	Students demonstrate a strategy that enables them to solve the problem correctly. The strategy is disorganized or less efficient. Students may: • have difficulty in finding the Least Common Denominator. • not find the equivalent fractions or properly compare the two fractions. • find a solution, but have guessed for a few answers.
1	Students demonstrate a confused strategy, which leads to difficulty solving the problem. Most answers are incorrect, but students demonstrate knowledge of at least one concept being assessed. Students may: • demonstrate an understanding of the Least Common Denominator. • correctly find equivalent fractions or compare the fractions which they compare. • explain in grade-level language some of the concepts relevant to the problem.

Math Triumphs

Chapter Pretest

Gr.5

1 In simplest form, what is the sum represented in the drawing?

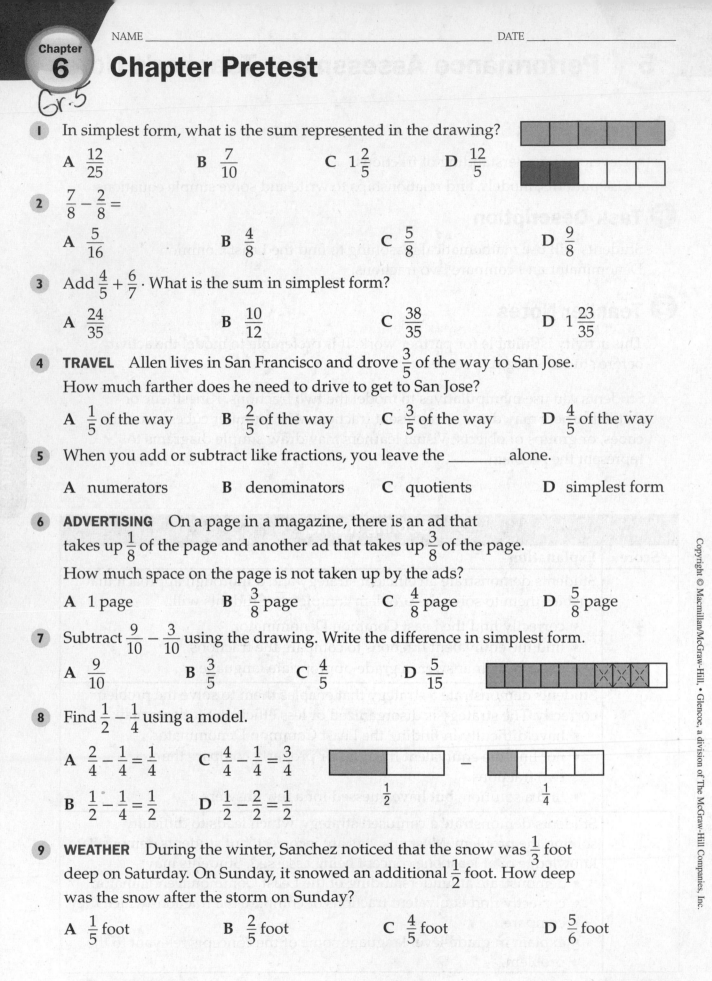

   A $\frac{12}{25}$ **B** $\frac{7}{10}$ **C** $1\frac{2}{5}$ **D** $\frac{12}{5}$

2 $\frac{7}{8} - \frac{2}{8} =$

   A $\frac{5}{16}$ **B** $\frac{4}{8}$ **C** $\frac{5}{8}$ **D** $\frac{9}{8}$

3 Add $\frac{4}{5} + \frac{6}{7}$. What is the sum in simplest form?

   A $\frac{24}{35}$ **B** $\frac{10}{12}$ **C** $\frac{38}{35}$ **D** $1\frac{23}{35}$

4 **TRAVEL** Allen lives in San Francisco and drove $\frac{3}{5}$ of the way to San Jose. How much farther does he need to drive to get to San Jose?

   A $\frac{1}{5}$ of the way   **B** $\frac{2}{5}$ of the way   **C** $\frac{3}{5}$ of the way   **D** $\frac{4}{5}$ of the way

5 When you add or subtract like fractions, you leave the _____ alone.

   A numerators   **B** denominators   **C** quotients   **D** simplest form

6 **ADVERTISING** On a page in a magazine, there is an ad that takes up $\frac{1}{8}$ of the page and another ad that takes up $\frac{3}{8}$ of the page. How much space on the page is not taken up by the ads?

   A 1 page   **B** $\frac{3}{8}$ page   **C** $\frac{4}{8}$ page   **D** $\frac{5}{8}$ page

7 Subtract $\frac{9}{10} - \frac{3}{10}$ using the drawing. Write the difference in simplest form.

   A $\frac{9}{10}$ **B** $\frac{3}{5}$ **C** $\frac{4}{5}$ **D** $\frac{5}{15}$

8 Find $\frac{1}{2} - \frac{1}{4}$ using a model.

   A $\frac{2}{4} - \frac{1}{4} = \frac{1}{4}$ **C** $\frac{4}{4} - \frac{1}{4} = \frac{3}{4}$

   B $\frac{1}{2} - \frac{1}{4} = \frac{1}{2}$ **D** $\frac{1}{2} - \frac{2}{2} = \frac{1}{2}$

$\frac{1}{2}$ $\frac{1}{4}$

9 **WEATHER** During the winter, Sanchez noticed that the snow was $\frac{1}{3}$ foot deep on Saturday. On Sunday, it snowed an additional $\frac{1}{2}$ foot. How deep was the snow after the storm on Sunday?

   A $\frac{1}{5}$ foot   **B** $\frac{2}{5}$ foot   **C** $\frac{4}{5}$ foot   **D** $\frac{5}{6}$ foot

10 **HARVESTING**   Michele picked 35 apples at the apple farm. She separated the apples into the 3 baskets: one had 16 green apples, one had 12 red apples, and one had 7 yellow apples. What fraction of the apples is either green or red?

A $\frac{1}{5}$ B $\frac{4}{7}$ C $\frac{3}{4}$ D $\frac{4}{5}$

Add. What is the sum in simplest form?

11 $\frac{2}{3} + \frac{1}{5} =$

A $\frac{3}{8}$ B $\frac{13}{15}$ C $\frac{10}{15}$ D $\frac{3}{5}$

12 $\frac{2}{6} + \frac{1}{3} =$

A $\frac{1}{3}$ B $\frac{2}{18}$ C $\frac{2}{3}$ D $\frac{5}{6}$

Subtract. What is the difference in simplest form?

13 $\frac{5}{8} - \frac{1}{2} =$

A $\frac{7}{8}$ B $\frac{6}{8}$ C $\frac{1}{8}$ D $\frac{4}{8}$

14 $\frac{7}{10} - \frac{1}{4} =$

A $\frac{6}{10}$ B $\frac{6}{6}$ C $\frac{4}{20}$ D $\frac{9}{20}$

15 $\frac{4}{5} - \frac{2}{3} =$

A $\frac{1}{15}$ B $\frac{2}{15}$ C $\frac{1}{3}$ D $\frac{3}{8}$

16 **COOKING**   Hector is baking a cake. The recipe calls for $\frac{1}{2}$ cup of flour. However, Hector's teacher tells him to put in $\frac{1}{4}$ cup less flour than the recipe calls for. How much flour should Hector put in the cake?

A $\frac{2}{4}$ cup   B $\frac{2}{3}$ cup   C $\frac{3}{4}$ cup   D $\frac{1}{4}$ cup

17 **EXERCISE**   Wanda jogs $\frac{3}{4}$ mile with her brother every morning. In the afternoon she jogs $\frac{1}{8}$ of a mile with her friends. How far does she jog in all?

A $\frac{5}{8}$ mile   B $\frac{6}{8}$ mile   C $\frac{7}{8}$ mile   D 1 mile

Chapter 6

Chapter 6 Chapter Pretest
Scoring Guide and Diagnostic Chart

Students missing Exercise . . .	Have trouble with . . .	Should review . . .
1	Adding Fractions with Like Denominators	Chapter 6, Lesson 1
2	Subtracting Fractions with Like Denominators	Chapter 6, Lesson 2
3	Adding Fractions with Unlike Denominators	Chapter 6, Lesson 3
4	Subtracting Fractions with Like Denominators	Chapter 6, Lesson 2
5	Fractions with Like Denominators	Chapter 6, Lesson 2
6	Adding Fractions with Like Denominators	Chapter 6, Lesson 1
7	Subtracting Fractions with Like Denominators	Chapter 6, Lesson 2
8	Subtracting Fractions with Unlike Denominators	Chapter 6, Lesson 4
9	Adding Fractions with Unlike Denominators	Chapter 6, Lesson 3
10	Adding Fractions with Unlike Denominators	Chapter 6, Lesson 3
11	Adding Fractions with Unlike Denominators	Chapter 6, Lesson 3
12	Adding Fractions with Unlike Denominators	Chapter 6, Lesson 3
13	Subtracting Fractions with Unlike Denominators	Chapter 6, Lesson 4
14	Subtracting Fractions with Unlike Denominators	Chapter 6, Lesson 4
15	Subtracting Fractions with Unlike Denominators	Chapter 6, Lesson 4
16	Subtracting Fractions with Unlike Denominators	Chapter 6, Lesson 4
17	Adding Fractions with Unlike Denominators	Chapter 6, Lesson 3

Chapter
6

Chapter Test

Gr.5

Add. Write each sum in simplest form.

1   $\dfrac{4}{8} + \dfrac{2}{8}$ _____

3   $\dfrac{3}{4} + \dfrac{1}{3}$ _____

2   $\dfrac{3}{9} + \dfrac{3}{9}$ _____

4   $\dfrac{2}{7} + \dfrac{4}{14}$ _____

Subtract. Write each difference in simplest form.

5   $\dfrac{7}{8} - \dfrac{5}{8}$ _____

7   $\dfrac{6}{12} - \dfrac{2}{6}$ _____

6   $\dfrac{5}{10} - \dfrac{2}{10}$ _____

8   $\dfrac{8}{20} - \dfrac{1}{5}$ _____

Add or subtract. Write each answer in simplest form.

9   $\dfrac{9}{10} - \dfrac{3}{10}$ _____

11   $\dfrac{1}{4} + \dfrac{2}{4}$ _____

10   $\dfrac{2}{5} + \dfrac{1}{10}$ _____

12   $\dfrac{5}{8} - \dfrac{1}{2}$ _____

Solve.

13   **DESSERT**   Grace's mother has a cookie recipe that calls for $\dfrac{1}{3}$ cup sugar, and her grandma has a cookie recipe that calls for $\dfrac{1}{2}$ cup sugar. How much sugar is needed altogether for both recipes?

_____

14   **TRAVEL**   Harry is driving to the store from his house. He stops along the way at Luis's house, which is $\dfrac{1}{2}$ mile from his house. How much farther does Harry have to drive to get to the store?

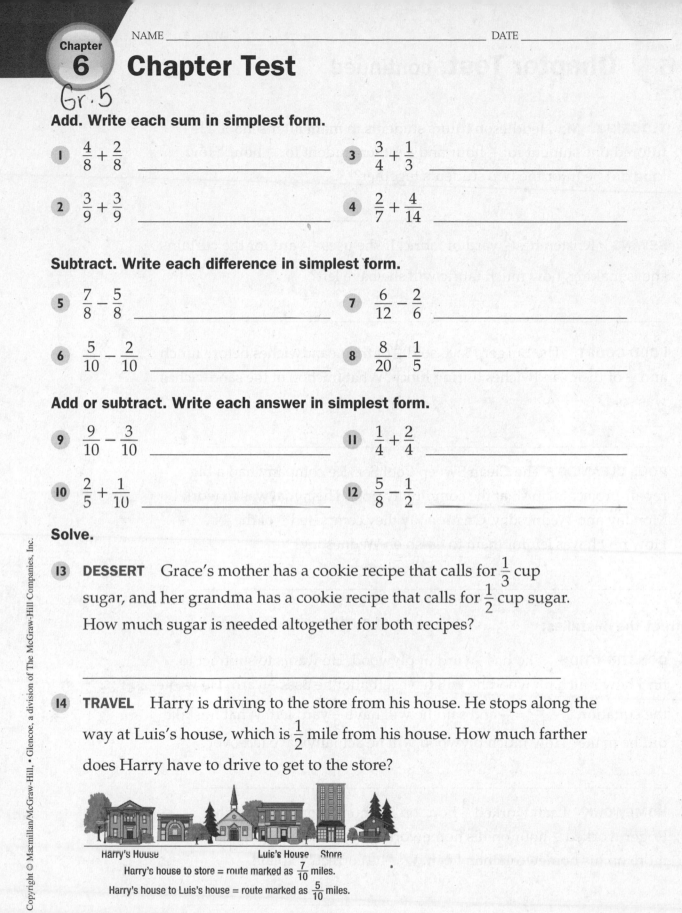

Harry's House   Luis's House   Store

Harry's house to store = route marked as $\dfrac{7}{10}$ miles.

Harry's house to Luis's house = route marked as $\dfrac{5}{10}$ miles.

_____

Chapter 6

15 **TUTORING** Mr. Heddleson tutors students in math after school. He tutored one student for $\frac{5}{8}$ hour and another student for $\frac{1}{4}$ hour. How long did he tutor the two students together?

_____

16 **SEWING** Kristen has $\frac{4}{5}$ yard of fabric. If she uses $\frac{1}{2}$ yard for the curtains she is making, how much fabric will she have left?

_____

17 **FOOD COURT** The Burger Place sold $\frac{2}{5}$ of their sandwiches before lunch and $\frac{4}{8}$ of their sandwiches during lunch. What fraction of the sandwiches was sold?

_____

18 **POOL CLEANING** The Clean Sweep Pool Service company had a big repair project to finish at the community pool. Their goal was to work Monday and Wednesday. On Monday they completed $\frac{1}{3}$ of the job. How much was left for them to finish on Wednesday?

_____

Correct the mistakes.

19 **CONSTRUCTION** Elio has $\frac{6}{9}$ yard of plywood. He wants to subtract to find how much plywood he will have left after he uses $\frac{1}{3}$ yard. He wrote the equation $\frac{6}{9} - \frac{6}{18} = \frac{6}{9}$ and said he will have $\frac{6}{9}$ yard left. What mistake did he make? How much plywood will he actually have left over?

_____

20 **HOMEWORK** Leah worked $\frac{3}{4}$ hour on her homework. Her brother Roger worked $\frac{2}{3}$ hour on his homework. Roger said he spent $\frac{1}{12}$ hour more on his homework than Leah. Was he correct? Explain.

_____

Chapter 6

Chapter Test
Scoring Guide and Diagnostic Chart

Students missing Exercise . . .	Have trouble with . . .	Should review . . .
1	Add Fractions with Like Denominators	Chapter 6, Lesson 1
2	Add Fractions with Like Denominators	Chapter 6, Lesson 1
3	Add Fractions with UnLike Denominators	Chapter 6, Lesson 3
4	Add Fractions with Unlike Denominators	Chapter 6, Lesson 3
5	Subtract Fractions with Like Denominators	Chapter 6, Lesson 2
6	Subtract Fractions with Like Denominators	Chapter 6, Lesson 2
7	Subtract Fractions with Unlike Denominators	Chapter 6, Lesson 4
8	Subtract Fractions with Unlike Denominators	Chapter 6, Lesson 4
9	Subtract Fractions with Like Denominators	Chapter 6, Lesson 2
10	Add Fractions with Unlike Denominators	Chapter 6, Lesson 3
11	Add Fractions with Like Denominators	Chapter 6, Lesson 1
12	Subtract Fractions with Unlike Denominators	Chapter 6, Lesson 4
13	Add Fractions with Unlike Denominators	Chapter 6, Lesson 3
14	Subtract Fractions with Unlike Denominators	Chapter 6, Lesson 4
15	Add Fractions with Unlike Denominators	Chapter 6, Lesson 3
16	Subtract Fractions with Unlike Denominators	Chapter 6, Lesson 4
17	Add Fractions with Unlike Denominators	Chapter 6, Lesson 3
18	Add Fractions with Unlike Denominators	Chapter 6, Lesson 3
19	Subtract Fractions with Unlike Denominators	Chapter 6, Lesson 4
20	Subtract Fractions with Unlike Denominators	Chapter 6, Lesson 4

6r.5

Choose the best answer and fill in the corresponding circle on the answer sheet.

1 Logan used $\frac{2}{8}$ gallon of paint for one wall and $\frac{4}{8}$ gallon of paint for another wall. How much paint did he use for both walls?

A $\frac{6}{16}$ gallon   C $\frac{1}{2}$ gallon

B $\frac{3}{4}$ gallon   D $\frac{2}{8}$ gallon

2 Which fraction has a value equal to

$$\frac{5}{10} - \frac{3}{10}?$$

A $\frac{2}{0}$ C $\frac{2}{20}$

B $\frac{8}{10}$ D $\frac{1}{5}$

3 Elijah, Brooke, and Klaus went on a trip together. The three friends took turns driving. The table shows how much time each person drove. How much more did Brooke drive than Elijah?

Name	Drive Time
Brooke	$\frac{7}{14}$
Klaus	$\frac{4}{14}$
Elijah	$\frac{3}{14}$

A $\frac{4}{14}$ or $\frac{2}{7}$ C $\frac{5}{14}$

B $\frac{1}{14}$ D $\frac{7}{14}$ or $\frac{1}{2}$

4 Add $\frac{2}{3} + \frac{1}{4}$. What is the sum in simplest form?

A $\frac{3}{7}$ C $\frac{11}{12}$

B $\frac{5}{6}$ D $\frac{3}{12}$

5 Gita has a $\frac{3}{4}$ foot long roll of bread dough. She uses a piece $\frac{1}{4}$ foot long. How long is the remaining roll of dough?

A $\frac{4}{4}$ or 1 foot   C $\frac{2}{4}$ or $\frac{1}{2}$ foot

B $\frac{3}{4}$ foot   D $\frac{1}{4}$ foot

6 Which symbol makes the sentence below true?

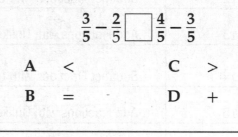

$$\frac{3}{5} - \frac{2}{5} \;\square\; \frac{4}{5} - \frac{3}{5}$$

A   <   C   >

B   =   D   +

7 Add. Write the sum in simplest form.

$$\frac{10}{24} + \frac{4}{24}$$

A $\frac{6}{32}$ C $\frac{6}{16}$

B $\frac{3}{4}$ D $\frac{7}{12}$

Math Triumphs

8 Employees at Brentwood Farms harvest part of their fields in September and October. What part of the fields did Brentwood Farms harvest in those 2 months?

Months	Harvested
September	$\frac{1}{4}$
October	$\frac{3}{8}$

A $\frac{5}{8}$ C $\frac{4}{8}$ or $\frac{1}{2}$

B $\frac{6}{8}$ or $\frac{3}{4}$ D $\frac{5}{16}$

9 Which symbol makes this sentence true?

$$\frac{5}{6} \square \frac{20}{24}$$

A $=$ C $<$

B $>$ D $+$

10 Hector rides the bus $\frac{2}{3}$ mile to school each morning. The bus picks up Gina after Hector has ridden $\frac{1}{2}$ mile. How far does Gina ride to school?

A $\frac{1}{2}$ mile C $\frac{1}{4}$ mile

B $\frac{1}{3}$ mile D $\frac{1}{6}$ mile

11 What is $\frac{24}{48}$ in simplest form?

A $\frac{3}{4}$ C $\frac{1}{2}$

B $\frac{1}{3}$ D $\frac{3}{8}$

12 In Ms. Roger's class, $\frac{1}{3}$ of the students are studying history and $\frac{1}{3}$ of the students are studying music. What fraction of the students is studying either history or music?

A $\frac{1}{6}$ C $\frac{1}{2}$

B $\frac{1}{3}$ D $\frac{2}{3}$

ANSWER SHEET

Directions: Fill in the circle of each correct answer.

1 Ⓐ Ⓑ Ⓒ Ⓓ
2 Ⓐ Ⓑ Ⓒ Ⓓ
3 Ⓐ Ⓑ Ⓒ Ⓓ
4 Ⓐ Ⓑ Ⓒ Ⓓ
5 Ⓐ Ⓑ Ⓒ Ⓓ
6 Ⓐ Ⓑ Ⓒ Ⓓ
7 Ⓐ Ⓑ Ⓒ Ⓓ
8 Ⓐ Ⓑ Ⓒ Ⓓ
9 Ⓐ Ⓑ Ⓒ Ⓓ
10 Ⓐ Ⓑ Ⓒ Ⓓ
11 Ⓐ Ⓑ Ⓒ Ⓓ
12 Ⓐ Ⓑ Ⓒ Ⓓ

Chapter 6

Test Practice
Scoring Guide and Diagnostic Chart

Students missing Exercise . . .	Have trouble with . . .	Should review . . .
1	Add Fractions with Like Denominators	Chapter 6, Lesson 1
2	Subtract Fractions with Like Denominators	Chapter 6, Lesson 2
3	Subtract Fractions with Like Denominators	Chapter 6, Lesson 2
4	Add Fractions with Unlike Denominators	Chapter 6, Lesson 3
5	Subtract Fractions with Like Denominators	Chapter 6, Lesson 2
6	Subtract Fractions with Like Denominators	Chapter 6, Lesson 2
7	Add Fractions with Like Denominators	Chapter 6, Lesson 1
8	Add Fractions with Unlike Denominators	Chapter 6, Lesson 3
9	Simplifying Fractions	Chapter 6, Lesson 3 and 4
10	Subtract Fractions with Unlike Denominators	Chapter 6, Lesson 4
11	Add Fractions with Like Denominators	Chapter 6, Lesson 1
12	Simplifying Fractions	Chapter 6, Lesson 3 and 4

NAME _____ DATE _____

Performance Assessment

YOUR TASK: Find $\frac{1}{2} + \frac{3}{8}$.

ONE WAY:

- Use the rectangle below. Divide it into eight equal pieces.
- Color $\frac{1}{2}$ of the rectangle yellow.
- Color 3 of the other pieces of the rectangle red.

The colored portion of the entire rectangle is $\frac{1}{2} + \frac{3}{8}$.

- Count the number of colored pieces. What is $\frac{1}{2} + \frac{3}{8}$?

ANOTHER WAY:

- Use 8 counters. Set $\frac{1}{2}$ of the counters in a pile.
- Make a separate pile using 3 of the remaining counters.

  The two piles will look like the figure below:

- What fraction represents both piles of counters? (Hint: Out of the eight counters, how many are in the two piles combined?)
- This fraction represents $\frac{1}{2} + \frac{3}{8}$. What is $\frac{1}{2} + \frac{3}{8}$?

Chapter 6

Performance Assessment Teacher's Notes

 ## Target Skills

- Perform calculations and solve problems involving addition and subtraction of fractions.
- Use patterns, models, and relationships to write simple equations.

 ## Task Description

Students will use mathematical reasoning to perform calculations with fractions.

Teacher Notes

This activity is suitable for partner work. Kinesthetic or tactile learners may use other manipulatives to represent the fractions, such as fraction tiles and fraction strips. Its is preferable to model the activity before students begin to solve.

This chapter focuses on making diagrams and solving simpler problems. Model this frequently and encourage students to use this strategy repeatedly as they work through the problems in the chapter.

Scoring Rubric	
Score	**Explanation**
3	Students demonstrate an efficient strategy and a thorough approach that enables them to solve the problem completely. Students will: • complete the diagram and/or manipulative activity correctly. • find the correct solution. • show their work and explain their reasoning.
2	Students demonstrate a strategy that enables them to solve the problem correctly. The strategy is disorganized or less efficient. Students may: • have some difficulty determining the answer correctly, but demonstrate an understanding of general numerical concepts. • find a solution, but guessed for the answer.
1	Students demonstrate a confused strategy, which leads to difficulty solving the problem. The answer is incorrect, but students demonstrate knowledge of at least one concept being assessed. Students may: • correctly complete the diagram and/or manipulative activity, but are unable to write the answer in symbolic form correctly. • be unable to explain their reasoning.

Chapter Pretest

Gr-5

1 What is the equivalent decimal of the grid?

    A 0.86   **C** 0.75

    B 0.33   **D** 0.34

2 What fraction is equivalent to 0.4?

    A $\frac{4}{10}$ **C** $\frac{2}{7}$

    B $\frac{1}{4}$ **D** $\frac{6}{10}$

3 What is the equivalent decimal for seventy and two hundredths?

    A 0.72   **B** 70.2   **C** 70.02   **D** 72.00

4 Which decimal is represented on the number line?

    0 0.5 1 1.5 2 2.5 3 3.5 4 4.5 5

    A 2.2   **B** 2.8   **C** 3.4   **D** 5.5

5 **GAMES** Lorenzo spent two dollars and a quarter at the arcade. What is the amount he spent written in decimal form?

    A $2.14   **B** $2.24   **C** $2.25   **D** $2.41

6 Compare the decimals below. Which symbol makes the statement true?

    5.07 ◯ 5.7

    A +   **B** =   **C** >   **D** <

7 Add. $13.5 + 8 =$ _____

    A 13.58   **B** 14.3   **C** 21.5   **D** 93.5

8 Subtract. $40.17 - 18.2 =$ _____

    A 21.97   **B** 38.17   **C** 38.35   **D** 41.75

9 Add. $1.21 + 2.46 =$ _____

    A 1.25   **B** 3.57   **C** 3.67   **D** 14.56

10 Subtract. $8.54 - 3.13 =$ _____

    A 5.41   **B** 5.67   **C** 8.23   **D** 11.67

Chapter 7

11 Which set of numbers is in order from least to greatest?

    A 1.4, 1.05, 1.45   **B** 1.05, 1.4, 1.45   **C** 1.4, 1.45, 1.05   **D** 1.45, 1.05, 1.4

12 Which decimal represents 7 tenths plus 5 hundredths?

    A 0.57   **B** 0.705   **C** 0.75   **D** 57.0

13 Which decimal represents seven thousandths?

    A 0.007   **B** 0.070   **C** 0.07   **D** 0.700

14 Which decimal is equivalent to 6.2?

    A 06.002   **B** 6.02   **C** 6.20   **D** 60.2

15 Add. 12.62 + 5.7 = _____

    A 17.32   **B** 17.69   **C** 18.32   **D** 18.69

16 Subtract. 34.89 − 25.27 = _____

    A 9.62   **B** 10.16   **C** 19.62   **D** 32.37

17 Subtract. 5.06 − 4.66 = _____

    A 0.4   **B** 0.61   **C** 1.49   **D** 1.61

18 Add. 13.72 + 3.6 = _____

    A 16.12   **B** 16.32   **C** 17.12   **D** 17.32

19 Estimate the sum of 1.75 and 2.32.

    A 2   **B** 3   **C** 4   **D** 5

20 **SCHOOL** Ellen's average grade in music class was 93.2 points. Her teacher added 4.5 bonus points to her grade. To the nearest whole number, what is Ellen's grade now?

    A 96   **B** 97   **C** 98   **D** 99

21 **MEASUREMENT** Frank measured his pencil to be 5.3 inches long one month ago. Yesterday, he measured it again and found it was 1.9 inches long. To the nearest inch, how much shorter was his pencil yesterday than it was one month ago?

    A 1 inch   **B** 2 inches   **C** 3 inches   **D** 4 inches

22 **TRAVEL** Sam spent thirty-five hundredths of an hour on the bus when he went to visit his grandmother. How is thirty-five hundredths written as a decimal?

    A $3\frac{1}{2}$ **B** $\frac{35}{10}$ **C** $\frac{3}{5}$ **D** $\frac{7}{20}$

Chapter 7

Chapter Pretest
Scoring Guide and Diagnostic Chart

Students missing Exercise . . .	Have trouble with . . .	Should review . . .
1	Introduction to Decimals	Chapter 7, Lesson 1
2	Introduction to Decimals	Chapter 7, Lesson 1
3	Introduction to Decimals	Chapter 7, Lesson 1
4	Comparing and Ordering Decimals	Chapter 7, Lesson 3
5	Introduction to Decimals	Chapter 7, Lesson 1
6	Comparing and Ordering Decimals	Chapter 7, Lesson 3
7	Adding Decimals	Chapter 7, Lesson 4
8	Subtracting Decimals	Chapter 7, Lesson 5
9	Adding Decimals	Chapter 7, Lesson 4
10	Subtracting Decimals	Chapter 7, Lesson 5
11	Comparing Decimals	Chapter 7, Lesson 3
12	Introduction to Decimals	Chapter 7, Lesson 1
13	Introduction to Decimals	Chapter 7, Lesson 1
14	Equivalent Decimals	Chapter 7, Lesson 2
15	Adding Decimals	Chapter 7, Lesson 4
16	Subtracting Decimals	Chapter 7, Lesson 5
17	Subtracting Decimals	Chapter 7, Lesson 5
18	Adding Decimals	Chapter 7, Lesson 4
19	Estimating Decimal Sums	Chapter 7, Lesson 6
20	Estimating Decimal Sums	Chapter 7, Lesson 6
21	Estimating Decimal Differences	Chapter 7, Lesson 6
22	Introduction to Decimals	Chapter 7, Lesson 1

Chapter 7

Chapter 7 — Chapter Test

Gr.5

Write the equivalent decimal and fraction in simplest form.

1 _____

2 twenty-six and thirty-four hundredths

_____

3 Order the numbers 7.61, 6.17, and 1.67 from least to greatest.

_____

4 Find the sum of 15.34 + 8.25.

_____

5 Find the difference between 0.83 and 0.42.

_____

Compare each pair of decimals using place value.
Write <, =, or > in each circle to make a true statement.

6 0.18 ◯ 0.24

7 82.3 ◯ 82.09

8 9.21 ◯ 9.29

9 0.65 ◯ 0.57

Order the numbers from least to greatest.

10 0.6, 0.8, 0.40, 0.5, _____, _____, _____, _____

11 0.45, 0.43, 0.75, 0.25, _____, _____, _____, _____

Add.

12 16.38 + 29.85 = _____

13 82.01 + 13.59 = _____

Subtract.

14 48.36 − 19.08 = _____

15 27.14 − 5.24 = _____

Math Triumphs

Add or subtract.

16   1.45
      + 2.23

17   7.62
      − 2.17

18   3.7 − 2.4 = _____

19   23.61
       + 6.46

Estimate to the nearest tenth.

20   3.5
      + 1.27

21   41.52
      − 16.49

Solve.

22 **SEWING**   Maria worked with her mom to sew blankets and pillows for a craft fair. Maria sewed $\frac{2}{8}$ of the blankets and $\frac{10}{16}$ of the pillows. Write the amounts Maria sewed as decimals.

_____

23 **YARD SALE**   Susan made potted plants to sell at her school's yard sale. She paid $1.21 for the materials for each potted plant, and she sold the potted plants for $3.88. Estimate to the nearest dollar how much she earned on each plant she sold. _____

24 **SUPPLIES**   DaJon tracks the monthly cost of his cleaning supplies. How much less was the cost of cleaning supplies in April than in March?

_____

Month	Cost of Supplies
March	$ 98.59
April	$ 45.23

Correct the mistakes.

25 Roger has a job painting. He earned $50.35 for painting one room and $65.40 for painting a second room. He told his friends, "I made about $700 for painting two rooms."

What mistake did Roger make? About how much did he make for painting the two rooms?

_____

_____

Chapter 7

Chapter 7

Chapter Test
Scoring Guide and Diagnostic Chart

Students missing Exercise . . .	Have trouble with . . .	Should review . . .
1	Introduction to Decimals	Chapter 7, Lesson 1
2	Introduction to Decimals	Chapter 7, Lesson 1
3	Comparing and Ordering Decimals	Chapter 7, Lesson 3
4	Adding Decimals	Chapter 7, Lesson 4
5	Subtracting Decimals	Chapter 7, Lesson 5
6	Comparing and Ordering Decimals	Chapter 7, Lesson 3
7	Comparing and Ordering Decimals	Chapter 7, Lesson 3
8	Comparing and Ordering Decimals	Chapter 7, Lesson 3
9	Comparing and Ordering Decimals	Chapter 7, Lesson 3
10	Comparing and Ordering Decimals	Chapter 7, Lesson 3
11	Comparing and Ordering Decimals	Chapter 7, Lesson 3
12	Adding Decimals	Chapter 7, Lesson 4
13	Adding Decimals	Chapter 7, Lesson 4
14	Subtracting Decimals	Chapter 7, Lesson 5
15	Subtracting Decimals	Chapter 7, Lesson 5
16	Adding Decimals	Chapter 7, Lesson 4
17	Subtracting Decimals	Chapter 7, Lesson 5
18	Subtracting Decimals	Chapter 7, Lesson 5
19	Adding Decimals	Chapter 7, Lesson 4
20	Estimating Decimal Sums	Chapter 7, Lesson 6
21	Estimating Decimal Differences	Chapter 7, Lesson 6
22	Introduction to Decimals	Chapter 7, Lesson 1
23	Estimating Decimal Differences	Chapter 7, Lesson 6
24	Subtracting Decimals	Chapter 7, Lesson 5
25	Estimating Decimal Sums	Chapter 7, Lesson 6

NAME _____

DATE _____

Choose the best answer and fill in the corresponding circle on the answer sheet.

1 Regina has 2.25 dollars in her pocket. Which point on the number line represents this amount of money?

```
        A       B              C       D
◄───┼───●───┼───●───┼───┼───●───┼───●──►
    0  0.25 0.5 0.75  1  1.25 1.5 1.75  2  2.25
```

A   A   C   C

B   B   D   D

---

2 Round 56.37 to the nearest tenth.

A   56

B   56.3

C   56.4

D   57

---

3 Louisa drove her family 38.59 miles to an amusement park. On the way home, she drove another 23.81 miles before she needed to stop for gas. How many miles did she drive before she stopped for gas?

A   52.30 miles

B   61.40 miles

C   62.4 miles

D   63.30 miles

4 Harold finished his science test in 43.17 minutes. He finished his math test in 34.61 minutes. How much faster did Harold finish his math test than his science test?

A   8.56 minutes

B   8.82 minutes

C   10.18 minutes

D   10.42 minutes

---

5 Add. 57.46 + 7.2 =

A   58.18

B   64.66

C   129.46

D   581.8

---

6 Mrs. Creed's class raised $12.39 for a school fundraiser. Mr. Brown's class raised $7.62. What is the difference in the amounts the two classes raised?

A $4.77

B $11.63

C $63.82

D $96.39

Chapter 7

7 Order these decimals from least to greatest.

0.75, 0.36, 0.6, 0.25

   A   0.6, 0.25, 0.36, 0.75

   B   0.6, 0.25, 0.75, 0.36

   C   0.25, 0.36, 0.6, 0.75

   D   0.25, 0.6, 0.36, 0.75

8 Yolanda has a coin jar containing $4.75 in quarters, $1.10 in dimes, $0.85 in nickels, and $0.21 in pennies. If she rounds each amount to the nearest dollar, what is the best estimate for the total amount of money she has in the jar?

   A $5   **C** $7

   B $6   **D** $8

9 Roderick is setting up a model train track. He puts together three pieces of track that are 0.7 feet, 1.3 feet, and 2.1 feet long. What is the best estimate to the nearest foot of the length of the combined track?

   A   4 feet   **C**   7 feet

   B   5 feet   **D**   10 feet

10 Tran has four of the five pieces of a pie. What decimal represents the amount of pie Tran has?

   A   0.4   **C**   0.8

   B   0.5   **D**   4.5

11 Estimate to the nearest tenth. What is 1.62 + 3.89?

   A   5.5   **C**   20.1

   B   5.6   **D**   40.6

12 Which symbol makes the sentence below true?

$1.45 - 0.75 \, \square \, 3.91 - 3.21$

   A   <   **C**   >

   B   =   **D**   +

ANSWER SHEET

Directions: Fill in the circle of each correct answer.

1 Ⓐ Ⓑ Ⓒ Ⓓ

2 Ⓐ Ⓑ Ⓒ Ⓓ

3 Ⓐ Ⓑ Ⓒ Ⓓ

4 Ⓐ Ⓑ Ⓒ Ⓓ

5 Ⓐ Ⓑ Ⓒ Ⓓ

6 Ⓐ Ⓑ Ⓒ Ⓓ

7 Ⓐ Ⓑ Ⓒ Ⓓ

8 Ⓐ Ⓑ Ⓒ Ⓓ

9 Ⓐ Ⓑ Ⓒ Ⓓ

10 Ⓐ Ⓑ Ⓒ Ⓓ

11 Ⓐ Ⓑ Ⓒ Ⓓ

12 Ⓐ Ⓑ Ⓒ Ⓓ

Chapter 7

Test Practice
Scoring Guide and Diagnostic Chart

Students missing Exercise . . .	Have trouble with . . .	Should review . . .
1	Comparing and Ordering Decimals	Chapter 7, Lesson 3
2	Comparing and Ordering Decimals	Chapter 7, Lesson 3
3	Adding Decimals	Chapter 7, Lesson 4
4	Subtracting Decimals	Chapter 7, Lesson 5
5	Adding Decimals	Chapter 7, Lesson 4
6	Subtracting Decimals	Chapter 7, Lesson 5
7	Comparing and Ordering Decimals	Chapter 7, Lesson 3
8	Adding Decimals	Chapter 7, Lesson 4
9	Adding Decimals	Chapter 7, Lesson 4
10	Introduction to Decimals	Chapter 7, Lesson 1
11	Estimating Decimal Sums	Chapter 7, Lesson 6
12	Subtracting Decimals	Chapter 7, Lesson 5

Chapter 7

Math Triumphs

NAME _____ DATE _____

Performance Assessment

1. When Lydia goes to school, she goes 1.3 miles down one street, 0.75 mile down the next street, and 2.15 miles down the third street. Estimate to the nearest mile how far Lydia goes in all.

Checklist
- ☐ Write your name.
- ☐ Show your work.
- ☐ Eplain your reasoning.
- ☐ Write the answer.

YOUR TASK: Estimate the sum of 1.3 + 0.75 + 2.15 to find the distance in miles that Lydia goes to school. Show your work and explain your answer.

ONE WAY:

1. Line up the decimal points of the three numbers.

   1 . 3

   _____ . _____ _____

   _____ . _____ _____

2. Then add down the columns to get an exact answer.

3. Finally, round the answer to the nearest whole number.

ANOTHER WAY:

1. Round each number to the nearest whole number first.

   1.3 rounded to the nearest whole number = _____

   0.75 rounded to the nearest whole number = _____

   2.15 rounded to the nearest whole number = _____

2. Now add the three whole numbers:

   _____ + _____ + _____ = _____

Lydia's Home

School

Chapter 7

Performance Assessment Teacher's Notes

▶ Target Skills

- Develop an understanding of and fluency with addition and subtraction of decimals.
- Use patterns, models, and relationships to write and solve simple equations.
- Extend understanding of place value of numbers up to thousands and thousandths in various contexts.

▶ Task Description

Students will use mathematical reasoning to estimate the sum of decimal numbers.

▶ Teacher Notes

This activity is suitable for partner work.

Students can use manipulatives to model rows of 5. Kinesthetic or tactile learners may represent the decimals with number cubes, counting cubes, or groups of objects. Visual learners may draw simple diagrams to represent the problem.

Scoring Rubric	
Score	**Explanation**
3	Students demonstrate an efficient strategy and a thorough approach that enables them to solve the problem completely. Students will: • round decimal numbers to the correct whole number. • correctly add to find the sum of three numbers. • show their work. • explain their answer in grade-appropriate language.
2	Students demonstrate a strategy that enables them to solve the problem correctly. The strategy is disorganized or less efficient. Students may: • have some difficulty in correctly rounding decimal numbers. • not correctly compute the sum of the three numbers. • find a solution, but have guessed for a few answers.
1	Students demonstrate a confused strategy, which leads to difficulty solving the problem. Most answers are incorrect, but students demonstrate knowledge of at least one concept being assessed. Students may: • correctly round some decimals to the nearest whole number. • compute the correct sum for whole numbers, but not demonstrate an understanding of decimals. • explain in grade-level language concepts relevant to the problem.

Book 2

Gr.5

Book Test

Solve.

1 $\frac{2}{3} - \frac{1}{5} =$

A $\frac{7}{15}$ B $\frac{1}{15}$ C $\frac{1}{8}$ D $\frac{13}{15}$

2 $\frac{6}{13} + \frac{1}{2} =$

A $\frac{11}{13}$ B $\frac{23}{26}$ C $\frac{25}{26}$ D $1\frac{1}{13}$

3 $\frac{9}{11} - \frac{3}{11} =$

A $\frac{2}{8}$ B $\frac{12}{11}$ C $\frac{6}{11}$ D 1

4 $\frac{1}{6} + \frac{2}{5} =$

A $\frac{1}{10}$ B $\frac{17}{30}$ C $\frac{12}{30}$ D $\frac{2}{3}$

5 $\frac{2}{3} - \frac{6}{15} =$

A $\frac{1}{5}$ B $\frac{4}{15}$ C $\frac{2}{5}$ D $\frac{1}{2}$

6 $\frac{2}{7} + \frac{4}{7} - \frac{3}{7} =$

A $\frac{2}{7}$ B $\frac{3}{7}$ C $\frac{4}{7}$ D $\frac{9}{7}$

7 $\frac{2}{7} + \frac{4}{7} =$

A $\frac{7}{6}$ B $\frac{6}{7}$ C $\frac{6}{14}$ D $\frac{8}{49}$

Order the following numbers from least to greatest.

8 $\frac{3}{5}, \frac{1}{3}, 0.65, 0.24$

A $\frac{3}{5}, \frac{1}{3}, 0.65, 0.24$ B $0.24, \frac{1}{3}, 0.65, \frac{3}{5}$ C $\frac{1}{3}, 0.24, 0.65, \frac{3}{5}$ D $0.24, \frac{1}{3}, \frac{3}{5}, 0.65$

9 $0.9, 0.65, \frac{2}{3}, 1\frac{1}{8}$

A $0.65, \frac{2}{3}, 0.9, 1\frac{1}{8}$ B $\frac{2}{3}, 0.65, 0.9, 1\frac{1}{8}$ C $1\frac{1}{8}, \frac{2}{3}, 0.65, 0.9$ D $0.9, 1\frac{1}{8}, 0.65, \frac{2}{3}$

Answer the following question.

10 Which fraction does the shaded part of the model represent?

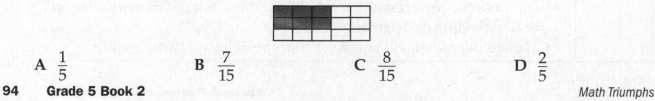

A $\frac{1}{5}$ B $\frac{7}{15}$ C $\frac{8}{15}$ D $\frac{2}{5}$

Math Triumphs

Book
2 **Book Test**

Gr. 5

Answer the following questions.

11 What are the equivalent fractions for $\frac{4}{5}$ and $\frac{7}{8}$?

A $\frac{16}{40}, \frac{32}{40}$ B $\frac{9}{10}, \frac{14}{20}$ C $\frac{7}{15}, \frac{8}{9}$ D $\frac{12}{15}, \frac{14}{16}$

12 Write $\frac{12}{5}$ as a mixed number.

A $2\frac{2}{5}$ B $5\frac{2}{5}$ C $7\frac{2}{5}$ D $2\frac{3}{5}$

13 Write $4\frac{3}{7}$ as an improper fraction.

A $\frac{29}{28}$ B $\frac{30}{28}$ C $\frac{31}{7}$ D $\frac{32}{28}$

14 What is the least common multiple (LCM) of 5, 7, and 10?

A 350   B 35   C 70   D 50

15 What decimal is equivalent to the fraction $\frac{3}{5}$?

A 0.3   B 0.5   C 0.6   D 0.8

16 Select the equivalent decimal and mixed number which the model represents.

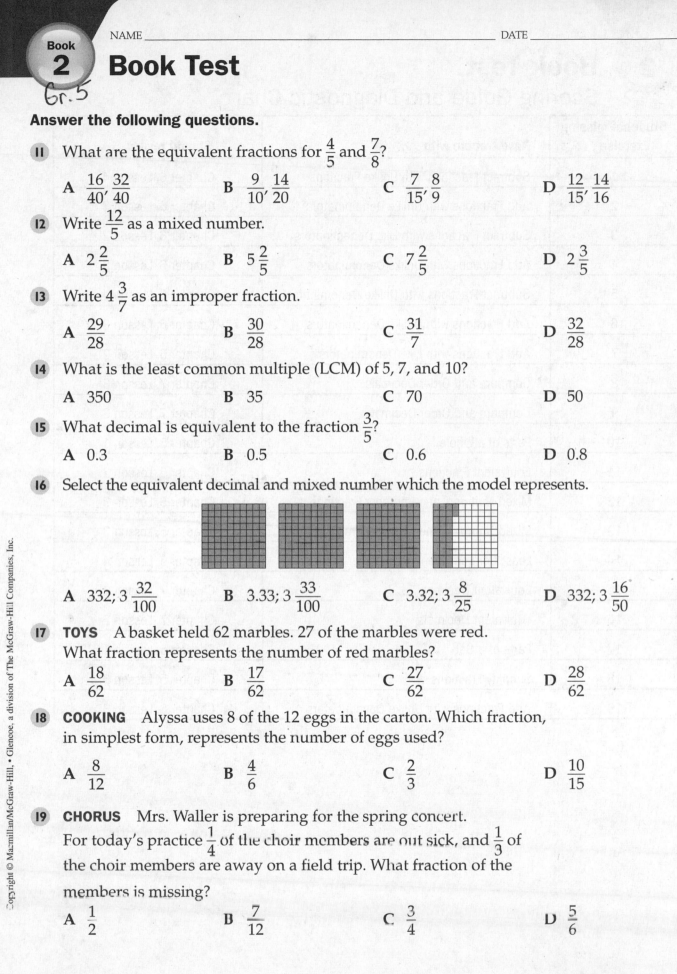

A $332; 3\frac{32}{100}$ B $3.33; 3\frac{33}{100}$ C $3.32; 3\frac{8}{25}$ D $332; 3\frac{16}{50}$

17 **TOYS** A basket held 62 marbles. 27 of the marbles were red. What fraction represents the number of red marbles?

A $\frac{18}{62}$ B $\frac{17}{62}$ C $\frac{27}{62}$ D $\frac{28}{62}$

18 **COOKING** Alyssa uses 8 of the 12 eggs in the carton. Which fraction, in simplest form, represents the number of eggs used?

A $\frac{8}{12}$ B $\frac{4}{6}$ C $\frac{2}{3}$ D $\frac{10}{15}$

19 **CHORUS** Mrs. Waller is preparing for the spring concert. For today's practice $\frac{1}{4}$ of the choir members are out sick, and $\frac{1}{3}$ of the choir members are away on a field trip. What fraction of the members is missing?

A $\frac{1}{2}$ B $\frac{7}{12}$ C $\frac{3}{4}$ D $\frac{5}{6}$

Math Triumphs

Book 2
Test

Book Test
Scoring Guide and Diagnostic Chart

Students missing Exercise . . .	Have trouble with . . .	Should review . . .
1	Subtract Fractions with Unlike Fractions	Chapter 6, Lesson 4
2	Add Fractions with Unlike Denominators	Chapter 6, Lesson 3
3	Subtract Fractions with Like Denominators	Chapter 6, Lesson 2
4	Add Fractions with Unlike Denominators	Chapter 6, Lesson 3
5	Subtract Fractions with Unlike Denominators	Chapter 6, Lesson 4
6	Add Fractions with Unlike Denominators	Chapter 6, Lesson 3
7	Add Fractions with Like Denominators	Chapter 6, Lesson 2
8	Compare and Order Decimals	Chapter 7, Lesson 3
9	Compare and Order Decimals	Chapter 7, Lesson 3
10	Parts of a Whole	Chapter 5, Lesson 1
11	Equivalent Fractions	Chapter 5, Lesson 2
12	Mixed Numbers and Improper Fractions	Chapter 5, Lesson 3
13	Mixed Numbers and Improper Fractions	Chapter 5, Lesson 3
14	Least Common Denominator	Chapter 5, Lesson 4
15	Equivalent Decimals	Chapter 7, Lesson 2
16	Equivalent Decimals	Chapter 7, Lesson 2
17	Parts of a Set	Chapter 5, Lesson 1
18	Simplify Fractions	Chapter 5, Lesson 5
19	Add Fractions with Unlike Denominators	Chapter 6, Lesson 3

Book
3

G 5

Book Pretest

Convert.

① 3 gallons = _____ quarts

    A 4   B 12   C 24   D 30

② 7L = _____ mL

    A 0.07   B 0.7   C 700   D 7,000

③ 2.5 kilograms = _____ grams

    A 200.5 grams   B 250 grams   C 2,000 grams   D 2,500 grams

Find the surface area of the following figures.

④ A 13 square units   C 100 square units

    B 56 square units   D 30 square units

    7

    2   4

⑤ A 4 ft²   B 8 ft²   C 16 ft²   D 24 ft²

    2 ft
    2 ft
    2 ft

Identify the figure.

⑥ A square   C parallelogram

    B rectangle   D trapezoid

⑦ A sphere   C pyramid

    B cone   D prism

⑧ A square   C parallelogram

    B rectangle   D trapezoid

⑨ A triangle with two sides that are 4 centimeters long, and one side
that is 4.5 centimeters long.

    A equilateral   B scalene   C right   D isosceles

Answer the following questions.

10 Which three-dimensional figure is shaped like a ball?

   A cube   **B** sphere   **C** prism   **D** pyramid

11 What is the best estimate for the weight of one apple?

   A 1 ounce   **B** 6 ounces   **C** 10 pounds   **D** $\frac{1}{2}$ ton

Find the area.

12 **A** 8 in.   **B** 8 sq in.   **C** 15 in.   **D** 15 sq in.

13 **A** 152 m   **C** 76 m

    B 152 sq m   **D** 76 sq m

    $h = 19$ m
    $b = 8$ m

14 A rectangle with length 3 inches and width 2 inches.

   A 5 in²   **B** 6 in²   **C** 10 in²   **D** 12 in²

Answer the following questions.

15 What is the volume of the solid figure?

   A 13 cubic units   **C** 60 cubic units

   B 32 cubic units   **D** 17 cubic units

   5
   6   2

16 Which of the following measures the number of cubic units a solid
    figure contains?

   A perimeter   **B** surface area   **C** volume   **D** diameter

17 A grape weighs about 1 ounce. About how much do 100 grapes weigh?

   A 1 pound   **B** 6 pounds   **C** 16 pounds   **D** 25 pounds

18 **FARMING** A potato farmer wants to put netting over his potato crop.
    The potato patch is 20 feet in length and 45 feet wide. What is the area
    of the potato crop that he will have to net?

   A 65 ft   **B** 130 sq ft   **C** 900 sq ft   **D** 900 ft

19 **SPORTS** The radius of a certain flying disk is 7 centimeters.
    What is the disk's diameter?

   A 7 cm   **B** 9 cm   **C** 14 cm   **D** 21.9 cm

Math Triumphs

Book Test
Scoring Guide and Diagnostic Chart

Students missing Exercise . . .	Have trouble with . . .	Should review . . .
1	Customary Capacity	Chapter 10, Lesson 2
2	Metric Capacity	Chapter 10, Lesson 1
3	Metric Mass	Chapter 10, Lesson 1
4	Surface Area of Rectangular Solids	Chapter 10, Lesson 3
5	Surface Area of Rectangular Solids	Chapter 10, Lesson 3
6	Quadrilaterals	Chapter 8, Lesson 1
7	Three-Dimensional Shapes	Chapter 8, Lesson 4
8	Quadrilaterals	Chapter 8, Lesson 1
9	Triangles	Chapter 8, Lesson 2
10	Three-Dimensional Shapes	Chapter 8, Lesson 4
11	Customary Weight	Chapter 10, Lesson 2
12	Area of a Parallelogram	Chapter 9, Lesson 3
13	Area of a Triangle	Chapter 9, Lesson 4
14	Area of a Rectangle	Chapter 9, Lesson 2
15	Volume of Rectangular Solids	Chapter 10, Lesson 5
16	Concept of Volume	Chapter 10, Lesson 4
17	Customary Weight	Chapter 10, Lesson 2
18	Area of a Rectangle	Chapter 9, Lesson 2
19	Circles	Chapter 8, Lesson 3

Chapter Pretest

Gr.5

Choose the correct name of each figure.

1   A   square   C   parallelogram

    B   rhombus   D   rectangle

2   A   scalene triangle   C   equilateral triangle

    B   right triangle   D   obtuse triangle

    5 inches   5 inches
    5 inches

3   A   parallelogram   C   rectangle

    B   rhombus   D   trapezoid

4   A   isosceles triangle   C   equilateral triangle

    B   right triangle   D   obtuse triangle

5   A   rhombus   C   rectangle

    B   parallelogram   D   trapezoid

6   A   rhombus   C   square

    B   parallelogram   D   trapezoid

7   A   rhombus   C   square

    B   parallelogram   D   trapezoid

Answer the following questions.

8   The diameter of a circle is 4 feet. What is the circle's radius?

    A   1 foot   B   2 feet   C   4 feet   D   8 feet

9   A box is 12 inches long, 5 inches wide, and 3 inches high. What is the
    box's shape?

    A   pyramid   B   cube   C   prism   D   cone

10 Mrs. Jacobs draws a line from one corner of a square to the opposite
    corner. What are the two new figures?

    A   rectangles   C   equilateral triangles

    B   trapezoids   D   right triangles

Choose the correct name of each three-dimensional figure.

11 A triangular prism   C cube

    B sphere   D triangular pyramid

12 A cube   C rectangular pyramid

    B sphere   D triangular prism

13 A cube   C prism

    B cone   D sphere

14 A cube   C prism

    B cone   D sphere

15 A cube   C prism

    B cone   D sphere

16 Choose the correct diameter measure of the circle.

$$r = 5$$
$$d = ?$$

    A 2.5   B 5   C 7.5   D 10

Solve.

17 **GAMES** Jess's sister said she was thinking of a three-dimensional figure with four faces. What figure could she be thinking about?

    A cube   B pyramid   C sphere   D prism

18 **SPORTS** Alice's pen pal from Ghana asked Alice what shape a bowling ball is. Which name can she use to describe a bowling ball?

    A prism   B cube   C sphere   D cylinder

Chapter Pretest
Scoring Guide and Diagnostic Chart

Students missing Exercise . . .	Have trouble with . . .	Should review . . .
1	Quadrilaterals	Chapter 8, Lesson 1
2	Triangles	Chapter 8, Lesson 2
3	Quadrilaterals	Chapter 8, Lesson 1
4	Triangles	Chapter 8, Lesson 2
5	Quadrilaterals	Chapter 8, Lesson 1
6	Quadrilaterals	Chapter 8, Lesson 1
7	Quadrilaterals	Chapter 8, Lesson 1
8	Circles	Chapter 8, Lesson 3
9	Three-Dimensional Figures	Chapter 8, Lesson 4
10	Triangles	Chapter 8, Lesson 2
11	Three-Dimensional Figures	Chapter 8, Lesson 4
12	Three-Dimensional Figures	Chapter 8, Lesson 4
13	Three-Dimensional Figures	Chapter 8, Lesson 4
14	Three-Dimensional Figures	Chapter 8, Lesson 4
15	Three-Dimensional Figures	Chapter 8, Lesson 4
16	Circles	Chapter 8, Lesson 3
17	Three-Dimensional Figures	Chapter 8, Lesson 4
18	Three-Dimensional Figures	Chapter 8, Lesson 4

Chapter 8 Chapter Test

Gr.5

Identify each figure.

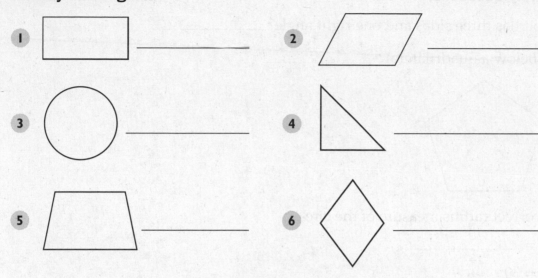

1. [rectangle] _____

2. [parallelogram] _____

3. [circle] _____

4. [triangle] _____

5. [trapezoid] _____

6. [rhombus] _____

Identify each three-dimensional figure.

7. A solid figure that is shaped like a soup can. _____

8. A solid figure with six square faces. _____

9. A solid figure that has a diameter. _____

Identify each three-dimensional figure.

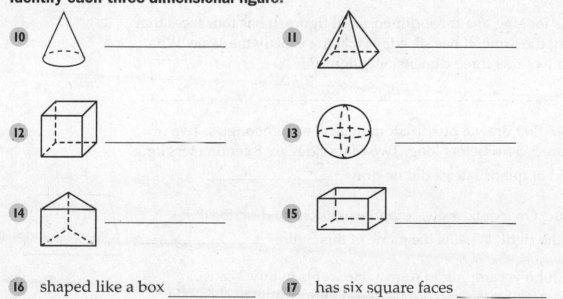

10. [cone] _____

11. [pyramid] _____

12. [cube] _____

13. [sphere] _____

14. [triangular prism] _____

15. [rectangular prism] _____

16. shaped like a box _____

17. has six square faces _____

Chapter 8

Answer the following questions.

18 What polygon has three sides and one right angle? _____

19 Is the figure below a quadrilateral? _____

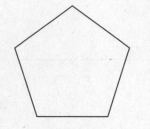

20 What is the correct radius measure of the circle?

$r =$ _____

$d = 30$

21 What is the correct radius measure of the circle?

$r =$ _____

$d = 8$

Fill in the missing number.

22 Diameter of a circle = 4 inches

Radius of a circle = _____ inches

$d = 4$ inches

23 Michael is looking at a three-dimensional figure. It has four faces that are exactly the same. It has six edges that are exactly the same. What is the name of this three-dimensional figure?

_____

24 **DRAWING** Bob drew a quadrilateral with four right angles. Two of its sides are 5 centimeters long. Two of its sides are 8 centimeters long. What kind of quadrilateral did he draw? _____

25 **CONTESTS** On a quiz show, Naomi was asked to describe the figure at the right. What is the name of this figure? _____

26 **TRAVEL** John is camping in Kenya. He wants to buy 2 cans of soup to cook for dinner, but he doesn't know how to speak the local language. Instead, John decides to draw a picture of a can of soup. What shape should John draw?

_____

Chapter 8

Chapter Test
Scoring Guide and Diagnostic Chart

Students missing Exercise . . .	Have trouble with . . .	Should review . . .
1	Quadrilaterals	Chapter 8, Lesson 1
2	Quadrilaterals	Chapter 8, Lesson 1
3	Circles	Chapter 8, Lesson 3
4	Triangles	Chapter 8, Lesson 2
5	Quadrilaterals	Chapter 8, Lesson 1
6	Quadrilaterals	Chapter 8, Lesson 1
7	Three-Dimensional Figures	Chapter 8, Lesson 4
8	Three-Dimensional Figures	Chapter 8, Lesson 4
9	Three-Dimensional Figures	Chapter 8, Lesson 4
10	Three-Dimensional Figures	Chapter 8, Lesson 4
11	Three-Dimensional Figures	Chapter 8, Lesson 4
12	Three-Dimensional Figures	Chapter 8, Lesson 4
13	Three-Dimensional Figures	Chapter 8, Lesson 4
14	Three-Dimensional Figures	Chapter 8, Lesson 4
15	Three-Dimensional Figures	Chapter 8, Lesson 4
16	Three-Dimensional Figures	Chapter 8, Lesson 4
17	Three-Dimensional Figures	Chapter 8, Lesson 4
18	Triangles	Chapter 8, Lesson 2
19	Quadrilaterals	Chapter 8, Lesson 1
20	Circles	Chapter 8, Lesson 3
21	Circles	Chapter 8, Lesson 3
22	Circles	Chapter 8, Lesson 3
23	Three-Dimensional Figures	Chapter 8, Lesson 4
24	Quadrilaterals	Chapter 8, Lesson 1
25	Quadrilaterals	Chapter 8, Lesson 1
26	Three-Dimensional Figures	Chapter 8, Lesson 4

Chapter 8

Test Practice

Gr 5

Choose the best answer and fill in the corresponding circle on the answer sheet.

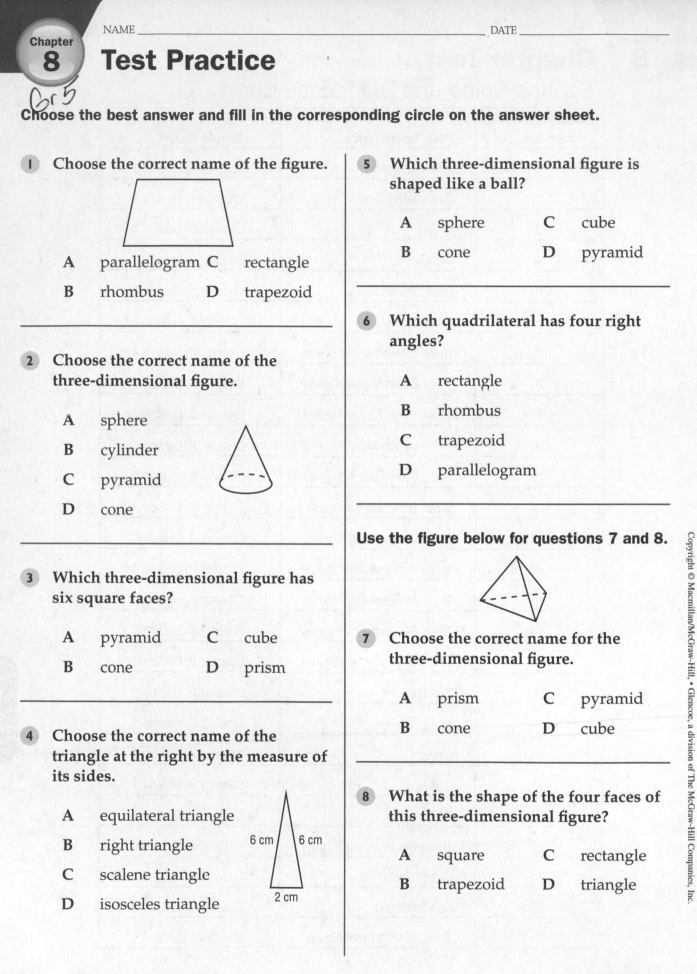

1 Choose the correct name of the figure.

 A parallelogram   C   rectangle

 B rhombus   D   trapezoid

2 Choose the correct name of the three-dimensional figure.

 A sphere

 B cylinder

 C pyramid

 D cone

3 Which three-dimensional figure has six square faces?

 A pyramid   C   cube

 B cone   D   prism

4 Choose the correct name of the triangle at the right by the measure of its sides.

 A equilateral triangle

 B right triangle   6 cm   6 cm

 C scalene triangle

 D isosceles triangle   2 cm

5 Which three-dimensional figure is shaped like a ball?

 A sphere   C   cube

 B cone   D   pyramid

6 Which quadrilateral has four right angles?

 A rectangle

 B rhombus

 C trapezoid

 D parallelogram

Use the figure below for questions 7 and 8.

7 Choose the correct name for the three-dimensional figure.

 A prism   C   pyramid

 B cone   D   cube

8 What is the shape of the four faces of this three-dimensional figure?

 A square   C   rectangle

 B trapezoid D   triangle

9 Choose the correct diameter.

$r = 6$ centimeters
$d = ?$

A   3 centimeters

B   6 centimeters

C   9 centimeters

D   12 centimeters

10 What figure has all sides the same length?

A   rectangle

B   trapezoid

C   isosceles triangle

D   rhombus

11 Choose the correct name for the triangle at the right.

A   equilateral triangle

B   scalene triangle

C   obtuse triangle

D   right triangle

ANSWER SHEET

Directions: Fill in the circle of each correct answer.

1   Ⓐ Ⓑ Ⓒ Ⓓ

2   Ⓐ Ⓑ Ⓒ Ⓓ

3   Ⓐ Ⓑ Ⓒ Ⓓ

4   Ⓐ Ⓑ Ⓒ Ⓓ

5   Ⓐ Ⓑ Ⓒ Ⓓ

6   Ⓐ Ⓑ Ⓒ Ⓓ

7   Ⓐ Ⓑ Ⓒ Ⓓ

8   Ⓐ Ⓑ Ⓒ Ⓓ

9   Ⓐ Ⓑ Ⓒ Ⓓ

10 Ⓐ Ⓑ Ⓒ Ⓓ

11 Ⓐ Ⓑ Ⓒ Ⓓ

Chapter 8

Test Practice

Scoring Guide and Diagnostic Chart

Students missing Exercise . . .	Have trouble with . . .	Should review . . .
1	Quadrilaterals	Chapter 8, Lesson 1
2	Three-Dimensional Figures	Chapter 8, Lesson 4
3	Three-Dimensional Figures	Chapter 8, Lesson 4
4	Triangles	Chapter 8, Lesson 2
5	Three-Dimensional Figures	Chapter 8, Lesson 4
6	Quadrilaterals	Chapter 8, Lesson 1
7	Three-Dimensional Figures	Chapter 8, Lesson 4
8	Three-Dimensional Figures	Chapter 8, Lesson 4
9	Circles	Chapter 8, Lesson 3
10	Quadrilaterals	Chapter 8, Lesson 1
11	Triangles	Chapter 8, Lesson 2

Chapter 8 Performance Assessment

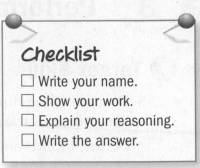

1. Count the faces of the three-dimensional figure below. This three-dimensional figure has four edges that are 100 meters long and four edges that are 200 meters long. It also has four right angles. Identify the three-dimensional figure. Make a list showing and describing each face.

Checklist
- ☐ Write your name.
- ☐ Show your work.
- ☐ Explain your reasoning.
- ☐ Write the answer.

YOUR TASK: Identify the figure and each of its faces.

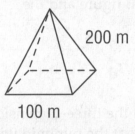

200 m

100 m

- Identify the shapes of the faces of the three-dimensional figure.
- Make a list with one row for each face of the three-dimensional figure.
- Identify the faces by how many sides they have.
- In the middle column, identify the faces by whether their sides have equal lengths and by the angles between the sides.

Your list could look like this:

Sides of the Three-Dimensional Figure

Face	Equal Sides or Angles?	Number of Sides
1 Square	Yes	4
2		
3		
4		
5		

- Identify this figure by the base opposite its point. Place the name for this figure on the first line.
- Think about three-dimensional figures that come to a point. Place the name for this three-dimensional figure on the second line.

_____   _____
name of base   *name of three-dimensional figure*

Chapter 8

Performance Assessment Teacher's Notes

▶ Target Skills

- Describe three-dimensional figures and analyze their properties, including volume and surface area.
- Connect solids and volume to capacity, weight, and mass.

▶ Task Description

Students will identify a three-dimensional figure and the two-dimensional figure of each of its faces.

▶ Teacher Notes

This activity is suitable for partner work.

Students can use manipulatives to model the three-dimensional figure. Kinesthetic or tactile learners may represent the pyramid with concrete physical objects. Visual learners may draw simple diagrams to represent the problem.

Scoring Rubric	
Score	**Explanation**
3	Students demonstrate an efficient strategy and a thorough approach that enables them to solve the problem completely. Students will: • correctly identify the square pyramid. • list the square base and four isosceles triangle sides that are faces of the pyramid. • explain their answer in grade-appropriate language.
2	Students demonstrate a strategy that enables them to solve the problem correctly. The strategy is disorganized or less efficient. Students may: • identify either the three-dimensional figure or its faces. • incorrectly relate the three-dimensional figure to the five faces that make its surface. • find a solution, but have guessed for a few answers.
I	Students demonstrate a confused strategy, which leads to difficulty solving the problem. Most answers are incorrect, but students demonstrate knowledge of at least one concept being assessed. Students may: • demonstrate an understanding of three-dimensional or plane geometry. • correctly identify some geometric figures that were based on the problem. • explain in grade-level language some of the concepts relevant to the problem.

Chapter 9

Gr.5

Chapter Pretest

1 What is the area of this figure?

A 5 cm²   B 13 cm²   C 26 cm²   D 36 cm²

2 What is the area of this figure?

A 24 in²   C 72 in²

B 48 in²   D 144 in²

3 What is the area of the shaded figure?

A 9 square units   C 19 square units

B 18 square units   D 81 square units

4 What is the area of this figure?

A 16 m²   B 32 m²   C 63 m²   D 252 m²

5 What is the area of this figure?

A 17 yd²   B 33 yd²   C 34 yd²   D 66 yd²

6 The area of the figure below covers _____ square units.

A $14\frac{1}{2}$ C $15\frac{1}{2}$

B 15   D 20

7 What is the area of a rectangle with length 11 yards and width 8 yards?

A 19 yd²   B 38 yd²   C 88 yd²   D 98 yd²

8 What is the area of a parallelogram with a base of 10 inches and a height of 9 inches?

A 19 in²   B 38 in²   C 90 in²   D 99 in²

9 What is the area of a triangle with a base 6 meters long and a height 7 meters long?

A 13 m²   B 21 m²   C 26 m²   D 42 m²

10 What is the area of the rectangle at the right?

A 13 cm²   C 30 cm²

B 26 cm²   D 33 cm²

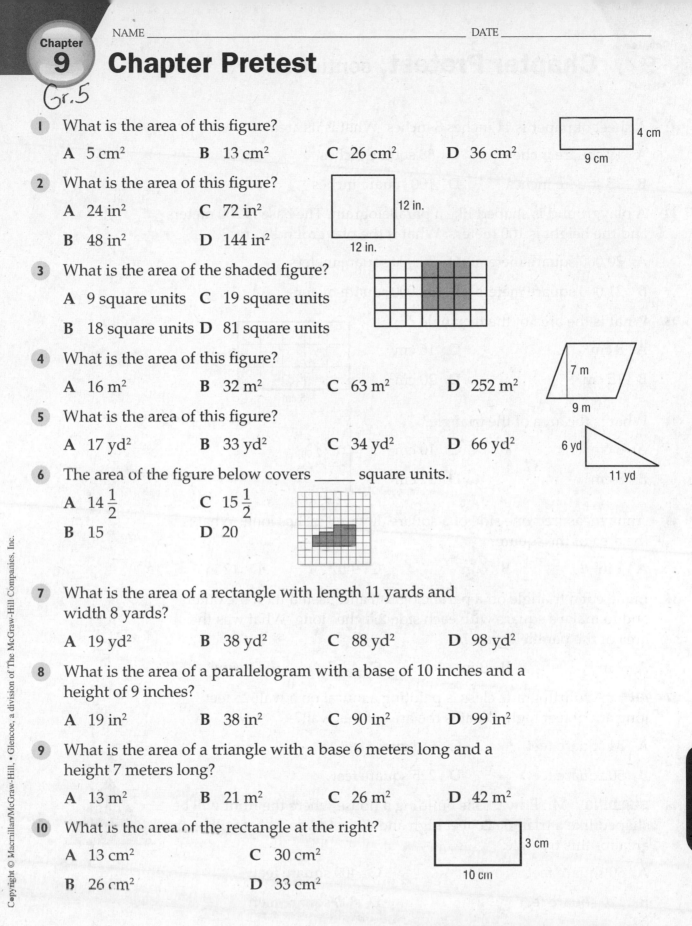

Chapter 9

Math Triumphs

11 A sheet of paper is 11 inches 8 inches. What is its area?

    A 19 square inches   **C** 88 square inches

    B 38 square inches   **D** 100 square inches

12 A playground is shaped like a parallelogram. The base is 200 meters and the height is 100 meters. What is the playground's area?

    A 20,000 square meters   **C** 30,000 square meters

    B 21,000 square meters   **D** 32,000 square meters

13 What is the area of the rectangle ?

    A 8 cm^2 **C** 16 cm^2

    B 15 cm^2 **D** 20 cm^2

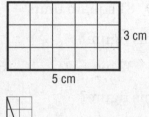

3 cm

5 cm

14 What is the area of the triangle?

    A 6 cm^2 **C** 10 cm^2

    B 8 cm^2 **D** 12 cm^2

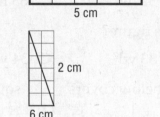

2 cm

6 cm

15 Anna measured one side of a square. It was 3 inches long. What is the area of the square?

    A 3 in^2 **B** 6 in^2 **C** 9 in^2 **D** 12 in^2

16 Liang cut a triangle off a parallelogram and pasted it on the other end to make a square with each side 2 inches long. What was the area of the parallelogram?

    A 2 in^2 **B** 3 in^2 **C** 4 in^2 **D** 6 in^2

17 **ART** A fourth grade class is painting a mural on a wall 25 feet long and 9 feet high. What is the area of this wall?

    A 34 square feet   **C** 68 square feet

    B 50 square feet   **D** 225 square feet

18 **BUILDING** Mr. Edwards is building a house where the front will be shaped like a triangle 20 feet high and 40 feet wide. What will be the area for this triangle?

    A 60 square feet   **C** 400 square feet

    B 120 square feet   **D** 800 square feet

Chapter Pretest
Scoring Guide and Diagnostic Chart

Students missing Exercise . . .	Have trouble with . . .	Should review . . .
1	Area of a Rectangle	Chapter 9, Lesson 2
2	Area of a Rectangle	Chapter 9, Lesson 2
3	Understanding Area	Chapter 9, Lesson 1
4	Area of a Parallelogram	Chapter 9, Lesson 3
5	Area of a Triangle	Chapter 9, Lesson 4
6	Understanding Area	Chapter 9, Lesson 1
7	Area of a Rectangle	Chapter 9, Lesson 2
8	Area of a Parallelogram	Chapter 9, Lesson 3
9	Area of a Triangle	Chapter 9, Lesson 4
10	Area of a Rectangle	Chapter 9, Lesson 2
11	Area of a Rectangle	Chapter 9, Lesson 2
12	Area of a Parallelogram	Chapter 9, Lesson 3
13	Area of a Rectangle	Chapter 9, Lesson 2
14	Area of a Triangle	Chapter 9, Lesson 4
15	Area of a Rectangle	Chapter 9, Lesson 2
16	Area of a Parallelogram	Chapter 9, Lesson 3
17	Area of a Rectangle	Chapter 9, Lesson 2
18	Area of a Triangle	Chapter 9, Lesson 4

Chapter Test

Gr. 5

Find the area of each rectangle.

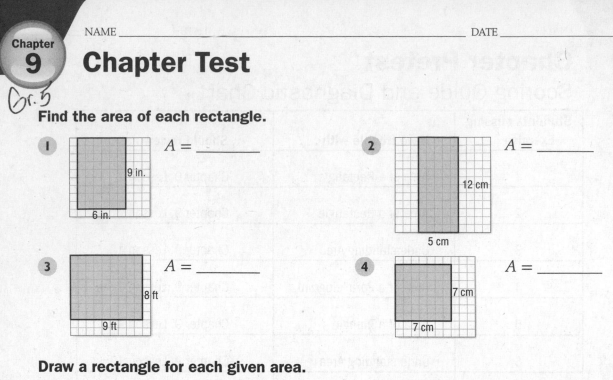

1 9 in. 6 in. $A =$ _____

2 12 cm 5 cm $A =$ _____

3 8 ft 9 ft $A =$ _____

4 7 cm 7 cm $A =$ _____

Draw a rectangle for each given area.

5 48 cm^2

6 64 cm^2

Find the area of each parallelogram.

7 7 cm 10 cm $A =$ _____

8 8 yd 12 yd $A =$ _____

Find the area of each triangle.

9

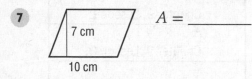

(2, 8) (5, 8) (2, 2) $A =$ _____

10 6 cm 14 cm $A =$ _____

Draw a triangle that has the given area.

11 21 mm^2

12 54 cm^2

Copyright © Macmillan/McGraw-Hill, • Glencoe, a division of The McGraw-Hill Companies, Inc.

Math Triumphs

Find the area of each figure.

13 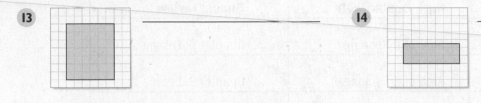 _____

14 _____

Draw a figure that has the given area.

15 27 square units

Solve.

16 **TENT** The front of the Brewster's tent is the shape of a triangle with a base of 16 feet and a height of 9 feet. What is the area of this triangle? _____

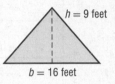

$h = 9$ feet
$b = 16$ feet

17 **PHOTOGRAPHY** Makawee ordered an 18 inch by 24 inch photograph to hang on her wall. What is the area of the photograph? _____

18 **TRAVEL** Regina is taking a cruise. The floor of the cabin where she will be staying is a rectangle 10 feet long and 8 feet wide. What is the area of the floor in Regina's cabin in square feet? _____

Correct the mistakes.

19 Locke measured his bedroom for carpeting. The floor is in the shape of a rectangle and has a length of 15 feet and a width of 12 feet. Locke said the area was 54 square feet. Tell what mistake he made.

_____

_____

20 Show how you would answer Locke's problem.

_____

_____

Chapter 9

Chapter 9

Chapter Test
Scoring Guide and Diagnostic Chart

Students missing Exercise . . .	Have trouble with . . .	Should review . . .
1	Area of a Rectangle	Chapter 9, Lesson 2
2	Area of a Rectangle	Chapter 9, Lesson 2
3	Area of a Rectangle	Chapter 9, Lesson 2
4	Area of a Rectangle	Chapter 9, Lesson 2
5	Area of a Rectangle	Chapter 9, Lesson 2
6	Area of a Rectangle	Chapter 9, Lesson 2
7	Area of a Parallelogram	Chapter 9, Lesson 3
8	Area of a Parallelogram	Chapter 9, Lesson 3
9	Area of a Triangle	Chapter 9, Lesson 4
10	Area of a Triangle	Chapter 9, Lesson 4
11	Area of a Triangle	Chapter 9, Lesson 4
12	Area of a Triangle	Chapter 9, Lesson 4
13	Area of a Rectangle	Chapter 9, Lesson 2
14	Area of a Rectangle	Chapter 9, Lesson 2
15	Concept of Area	Chapter 9, Lesson 1
16	Area of a Triangle	Chapter 9, Lesson 4
17	Area of a Rectangle	Chapter 9, Lesson 2
18	Area of a Rectangle	Chapter 9, Lesson 2
19	Area of a Rectangle	Chapter 9, Lesson 2
20	Area of a Rectangle	Chapter 9, Lesson 2

Math Triumphs

Gr.5

Choose the best answer and fill in the corresponding circle on the sheet at right.

1 What is the area of a rectangle with a length of 22 m and a width of 8 m?

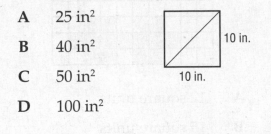

8 m
22 m

A   30 m²   C   160 m²
B   60 m²   D   176 m²

2 One wall of Mr. Dagmar's office measures 53 feet by 14 feet. What is the area of this wall?

A   67 ft²   C   268 ft²
B   134 ft²   D   742 ft²

3 Find the area of each figure. Which sentence is true?

Figure A   Figure B
6 cm   6 cm
8 cm   8 cm

A   Area A > Area B
B   Area B > Area A
C   Area A < Area B
D   Area A = Area B

4 Tai has a parallelogram-shaped notepad. It has a base length of 8 inches and a height of 9 inches. What is the area of the notepad?

A   18 in²   C   64 in²
B   36 in²   D   72 in²

5 What is the area of each triangle in the figure?

A   25 in²
B   40 in²
C   50 in²
D   100 in²

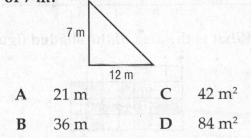

10 in.
10 in.

6 What is the area of a right triangle with a base of 12 m and a height of 7 m?

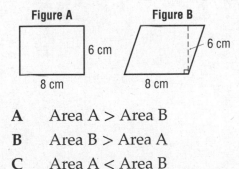

7 m
12 m

A   21 m   C   42 m²
B   36 m   D   84 m²

7 What is the area of the rectangle?

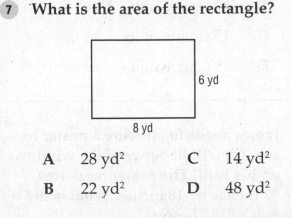

6 yd
8 yd

A   28 yd²   C   14 yd²
B   22 yd²   D   48 yd²

8 What is the area of a square with sides 7 inches long?

A   28 in²   C   54 in²
B   49 in²   D   70 in²

Chapter 9

9 What is the area of the shaded figure?

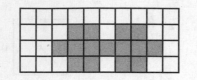

A   12 square units

B   15 square units

C   17 square units

D   20 square units

10 What is the area of the shaded figure?

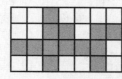

A   12 square units

B   13 square units

C   15 square units

D   18 square units

11 James needs to measure a poster to see if it will fit between the windows on his wall. The poster measures 32 inches by 18 inches. What is the area of the poster?

A   576 in²

B   100 in²

C   256 in²

D   50 in²

ANSWER SHEET
Directions: Fill in the circle of each correct answer.

1 Ⓐ Ⓑ Ⓒ Ⓓ

2 Ⓐ Ⓑ Ⓒ Ⓓ

3 Ⓐ Ⓑ Ⓒ Ⓓ

4 Ⓐ Ⓑ Ⓒ Ⓓ

5 Ⓐ Ⓑ Ⓒ Ⓓ

6 Ⓐ Ⓑ Ⓒ Ⓓ

7 Ⓐ Ⓑ Ⓒ Ⓓ

8 Ⓐ Ⓑ Ⓒ Ⓓ

9 Ⓐ Ⓑ Ⓒ Ⓓ

10 Ⓐ Ⓑ Ⓒ Ⓓ

11 Ⓐ Ⓑ Ⓒ Ⓓ

Chapter 9

Test Practice
Scoring Guide and Diagnostic Chart

Students missing Exercise . . .	Have trouble with . . .	Should review . . .
1	Area of a Rectangle	Chapter 9, Lesson 2
2	Area of a Rectangle	Chapter 9, Lesson 2
3	Area of a Parallelogram	Chapter 9, Lesson 3
4	Area of a Parallelogram	Chapter 9, Lesson 3
5	Area of a Triangle	Chapter 9, Lesson 4
6	Area of a Triangle	Chapter 9, Lesson 4
7	Area of a Rectangle	Chapter 9, Lesson 2
8	Area of a Rectangle	Chapter 9, Lesson 2
9	Concept of Area	Chapter 9, Lesson 1
10	Concept of Area	Chapter 9, Lesson 1
11	Area of a Rectangle	Chapter 9, Lesson 2

Chapter 9

NAME _____ DATE _____

Performance Assessment

YOUR TASK: Find the area of a triangle with a base of 8 units and a height of 8 units.

ONE WAY:

Draw a square that measures 8 units by 8 units. Make a diagonal line across one side of the square. Now use **one** of the triangles and find its area.

a. Count the number of whole square units.
   There are _____ whole square units inside the triangle.

b. Now count the $\frac{1}{2}$ square units. There are _____ $\frac{1}{2}$ square units.
   _____ $\frac{1}{2}$ square units = _____ whole square units.

c. Add the answers for parts a and b. The area of the triangle is

   _____.

Performance Assessment Teacher's Notes

▶ Target Skills

- Determine the area by covering solid figures with squares.
- Measure the area of rectangular shapes by using appropriate units, such as square centimeter (cm^2).
- Use the formula for area of a triangle.

▶ Task Description

Students will use mathematical reasoning to find the area of a triangle.

▶ Teacher Notes

This activity is suitable for partner work. Kinesthetic or tactile learners may need other alternatives, such as centimeter tiles. Students can use the tiles to estimate and compare the area of the triangle and the rectangle.

Scoring Rubric	
Score	**Explanation**
3	Students demonstrate an efficient strategy and a thorough approach that enables them to solve the problem completely. Students will: • provide the correct answer for the problem. • show their work. • meet all the requirements of the problem.
2	Students demonstrate a strategy that enables them to solve the problem correctly. The strategy is disorganized or less efficient. Students may: • have some difficulty determining how to approach the problem. • find the correct solutions, but are unable to provide symbolic representation or have difficulty building the models.
1	Students demonstrate a confused strategy, which leads to difficulty solving the problem. Most answers are incorrect, but students demonstrate knowledge of at least one concept being assessed. Students may: • correctly solve part of the problem. • provide a partial answer. • be unable to provide an explanation of their answer.

Gr.5

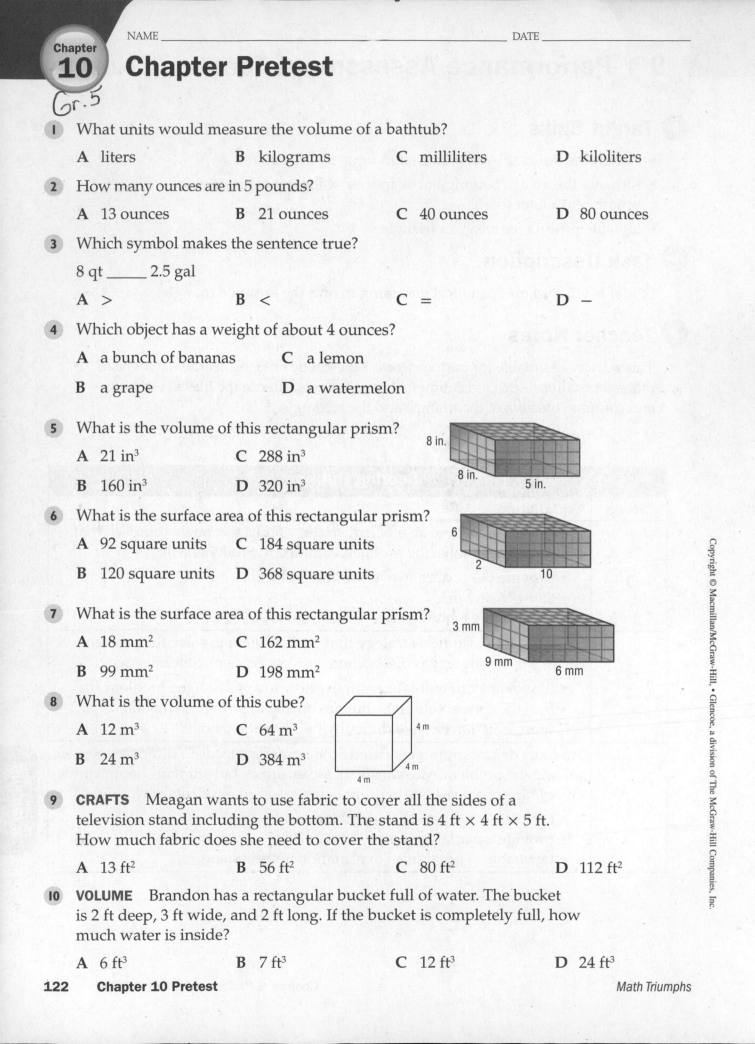

1   What units would measure the volume of a bathtub?

   A liters   **B** kilograms   **C** milliliters   **D** kiloliters

2   How many ounces are in 5 pounds?

   A 13 ounces   **B** 21 ounces   **C** 40 ounces   **D** 80 ounces

3   Which symbol makes the sentence true?

   8 qt _____ 2.5 gal

   A >   **B** <   **C** =   **D** −

4   Which object has a weight of about 4 ounces?

   A a bunch of bananas   **C** a lemon

   B a grape   **D** a watermelon

5   What is the volume of this rectangular prism?

   A 21 in³   **C** 288 in³

   B 160 in³   **D** 320 in³

   8 in.   8 in.   5 in.

6   What is the surface area of this rectangular prism?

   A 92 square units   **C** 184 square units

   B 120 square units   **D** 368 square units

   6   2   10

7   What is the surface area of this rectangular prism?

   A 18 mm²   **C** 162 mm²

   B 99 mm²   **D** 198 mm²

   3 mm   9 mm   6 mm

8   What is the volume of this cube?

   A 12 m³   **C** 64 m³

   B 24 m³   **D** 384 m³

   4 m   4 m   4 m

9   **CRAFTS**   Meagan wants to use fabric to cover all the sides of a
   television stand including the bottom. The stand is 4 ft × 4 ft × 5 ft.
   How much fabric does she need to cover the stand?

   A 13 ft²   **B** 56 ft²   **C** 80 ft²   **D** 112 ft²

10 **VOLUME**   Brandon has a rectangular bucket full of water. The bucket
   is 2 ft deep, 3 ft wide, and 2 ft long. If the bucket is completely full, how
   much water is inside?

   A 6 ft³   **B** 7 ft³   **C** 12 ft³   **D** 24 ft³

11 Which item has a mass of about 4 kilograms?

   A a watermelon   **B** a cow   **C** a carrot   **D** an ear of corn

12 5,302 milliliters = _____ liters

   A 10.604   **B** 5.302   **C** 2.651   **D** 0.5302

13 A prism is 3 meters high, 2 meters long, and 1 meter wide. What is its surface area?

   A 6 m²   **B** 11 m²   **C** 22 m²   **D** 24 m²

14 48 ounces = _____ pounds

   A 2   **B** 3   **C** 4   **D** 6

15 What is the volume of the prism?

   A 60 cubic units   **C** 184 cubic units

   B 160 cubic units   **D** 200 cubic units

16 **COOKING** A recipe calls for 3 kilograms of flour. How many grams of flour are needed to make the recipe?

   A 300 grams   **B** 600 grams   **C** 3,000 grams   **D** 30,000 grams

17 **PAINTING** Jane is painting her brother's toy box. The toy box is 8 inches high, 10 inches wide, and 16 inches long. How many square inches will she paint?

   A 368 in²   **B** 480 in²   **C** 736 in²   **D** 960 in²

18 **SCIENCE** An scientist wants to fill a 5,000 milliliter container with water. How many 1-liter bottles of water will it take to fill the 5,000 milliliter container?

   A 5   **B** 50   **C** 100   **D** 500

19 **TRAVEL** Isaac needs a trunk that holds at least 300 cubic meters of luggage. Which trunk dimensions should he choose?

   A 5 meters high, 3 meters wide, and 10 meters long

   B 6 meters high, 7 meters wide, and 8 meters long

   C 4 meters high, 8 meters wide, and 9 meters long

   D 6 meters high, 5 meters wide, and 7 meters long

Chapter Pretest
Scoring Guide and Diagnostic Chart

Students missing Exercise . . .	Have trouble with . . .	Should review . . .
1	Metric Capacity	Chapter 10, Lesson 1
2	Customary Weight	Chapter 10, Lesson 2
3	Customary Capacity	Chapter 10, Lesson 2
4	Customary Weight	Chapter 10, Lesson 2
5	Volume of Rectangular Solids	Chapter 10, Lesson 5
6	Surface Area of Rectangular Solids	Chapter 10, Lesson 3
7	Surface Area of Rectangular Solids	Chapter 10, Lesson 3
8	Volume of Rectangular Solids	Chapter 10, Lesson 5
9	Surface Area of Rectangular Solids	Chapter 10, Lesson 3
10	Volume of Rectangular Solids	Chapter 10, Lesson 5
11	Metric Mass	Chapter 10, Lesson 1
12	Metric Capacity	Chapter 10, Lesson 1
13	Surface Area of Rectangular Solids	Chapter 10, Lesson 3
14	Customary Weight	Chapter 10, Lesson 2
15	Volume of Rectangular Solids	Chapter 10, Lesson 5
16	Metric Mass	Chapter 10, Lesson 1
17	Surface Area of Rectangular Solids	Chapter 10, Lesson 3
18	Metric Capacity	Chapter 10, Lesson 1
19	Volume of Rectangular Solids	Chapter 10, Lesson 5

Gr.5

Chapter Test

Convert using a table.

1   64 oz. = _____ lb

Pounds	1	2	3	4	5
Ounces	16				

2   24 pt = _____ qt

Pints	2	4								
Quarts	1	2								

3   500 g = _____ kg

4   1.6 L = _____ mL

Convert.

5   6 T = _____ lb

6   15 gal = _____ fl oz

7   6 lb = _____ oz

8   64 pt = _____ gal

9   **PLASTER**   Twan needs 30 cups of plaster for his model of a castle. How many pints of plaster does Twan need? _____

10   Find the volume of the rectangular prism.

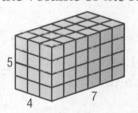

5
4   7

11   Find the volume of a rectangular prism with a width of 3, depth of 4 and height of 4 units. _____

12   Find the volume of a rectangular prism with a width of 2, depth of 5 and height of 6 units. _____

A rectangular prism is 5 inches long, 4 inches wide, and 2 inches high.

13   What is its volume? _____

14   What is its surface area? _____

Find the volume of each rectangular prism.

15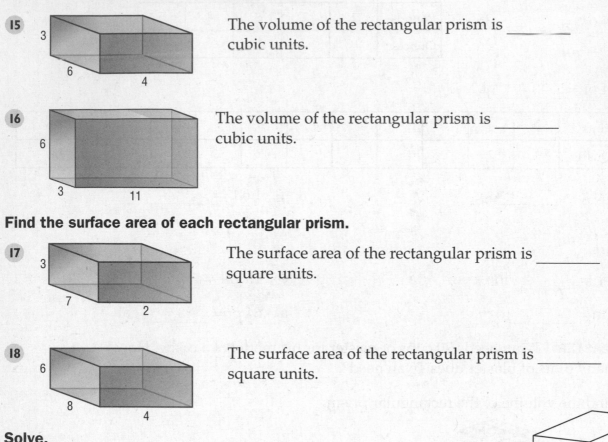
3
6
4

The volume of the rectangular prism is _____ cubic units.

16
6
3
11

The volume of the rectangular prism is _____ cubic units.

Find the surface area of each rectangular prism.

17
3
7
2

The surface area of the rectangular prism is _____ square units.

18
6
8
4

The surface area of the rectangular prism is _____ square units.

Solve.

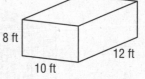
8 ft
10 ft
12 ft

19 The front of the Brewsters' tent is the shape of a rectangle 12 feet wide and 8 feet high. The tent is 10 feet long. What is the volume of the tent? _____

20 **STORAGE**   A storage building has dimensions of 9 feet × 15 feet × 20 feet. What is the surface area of the storage building? _____

Correct the mistakes.

21 Louisa is wrapping a present for her brother. The present measures 5 inches by 5 inches by 8 inches. She calculates its surface area to find out how much wrapping paper she needs. Her calculations are shown. What mistake did Louisa make?

Present has six surfaces
25+25+40+40 = 130
5×5+5×5+5×8+5×8 = Surface area

_____

_____

Chapter 10

Chapter Test
Scoring Guide and Diagnostic Chart

Students missing Exercise . . .	Have trouble with . . .	Should review . . .
1	Customary Weight	Chapter 10, Lesson 2
2	Customary Capacity	Chapter 10, Lesson 2
3	Metric Mass	Chapter 10, Lesson 1
4	Metric Capacity	Chapter 10, Lesson 1
5	Customary Capacity	Chapter 10, Lesson 2
6	Customary Capacity	Chapter 10, Lesson 2
7	Customary Weight	Chapter 10, Lesson 2
8	Customary Capacity	Chapter 10, Lesson 2
9	Customary Capacity	Chapter 10, Lesson 2
10	Concept of Volume	Chapter 10, Lesson 4
11	Volume of Rectangular Solids	Chapter 10, Lesson 5
12	Volume of Rectangular Solids	Chapter 10, Lesson 5
13	Volume of Rectangular Solids	Chapter 10, Lesson 5
14	Surface Area of Rectangular Solids	Chapter 10, Lesson 3
15	Volume of Rectangular Solids	Chapter 10, Lesson 5
16	Volume of Rectangular Solids	Chapter 10, Lesson 5
17	Surface Area of Rectangular Solids	Chapter 10, Lesson 3
18	Surface Area of Rectangular Solids	Chapter 10, Lesson 3
19	Volume of Rectangular Solids	Chapter 10, Lesson 5
20	Surface Area of Rectangular Solids	Chapter 10, Lesson 3
21	Surface Area of Rectangular Solids	Chapter 10, Lesson 3

Chapter 10

Math Triumphs

Choose the best answer and fill in the corresponding circle on the sheet at right.

1 About how much is the mass of 1 watermelon?

    A 2 grams

    B 2 milligrams

    C 4 kilograms

    D 20 kilograms

2 How many cups can a 6-quart pot hold?

    A 12

    B 24

    C 36

    D 48

3 About how much is the weight of a button?

    A 1 ounce

    B 5 kilograms

    C 2 pounds

    D 1 ton

4 How many milliliters can a 1-liter bottle hold?

    A 10

    B 100

    C 1,000

    D 10,000

Use the figure below for questions 5 and 6.

5 What is the surface area of the prism?

    A 24 square units

    B 48 square units

    C 36 square units

    D 72 square units

6 What is the volume of the prism?

    A 18 cubic units

    B 24 cubic units

    C 36 cubic units

    D 48 cubic units

Use the figure below for questions 7 and 8.

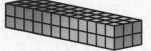

7 What is the surface area of the prism?

    A 100 units^2 **C** 132 units^2

    B 124 units^2 **D** 144 units^2

8 What is the volume of the prism?

    A 24 units^3 **C** 56 units^3

    B 48 units^3 **D** 72 units^3

Use the cube below to answer questions 9 and 10.

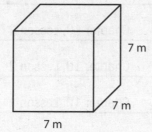

7 m
7 m
7 m

9 **What is the surface area of the cube?**

A   21 m²

B   196 m²

C   294 m²

D   343 m²

10 **What is the volume of the cube?**

A   294 m³

B   300 m³

C   343 m³

D   350 m³

11 **Which units would be used to measure the volume of a swimming pool?**

A   kiloliters

B   liters

C   mililiters

D   kilograms

12 **What is the volume of a cube with 4 cm sides?**

A   16 cm³

B   64 cm³

C   24 cm³

D   96 cm³

ANSWER SHEET

Directions: Fill in the circle of each correct answer.

1   Ⓐ Ⓑ Ⓒ Ⓓ

2   Ⓐ Ⓑ Ⓒ Ⓓ

3   Ⓐ Ⓑ Ⓒ Ⓓ

4   Ⓐ Ⓑ Ⓒ Ⓓ

5   Ⓐ Ⓑ Ⓒ Ⓓ

6   Ⓐ Ⓑ Ⓒ Ⓓ

7   Ⓐ Ⓑ Ⓒ Ⓓ

8   Ⓐ Ⓑ Ⓒ Ⓓ

9   Ⓐ Ⓑ Ⓒ Ⓓ

10 Ⓐ Ⓑ Ⓒ Ⓓ

11 Ⓐ Ⓑ Ⓒ Ⓓ

12 Ⓐ Ⓑ Ⓒ Ⓓ

Chapter 10

Chapter Test Practice
Scoring Guide and Diagnostic Chart

Students missing Exercise . . .	Have trouble with . . .	Should review . . .
1	Metric Mass	Chapter 10, Lesson 1
2	Customary Capacity	Chapter 10, Lesson 2
3	Customary Weight	Chapter 10, Lesson 2
4	Metric Capacity	Chapter 10, Lesson 1
5	Surface Area of Rectangular Solids	Chapter 10, Lesson 3
6	Volume of Rectangular Solids	Chapter 10, Lesson 5
7	Surface Area of Rectangular Solids	Chapter 10, Lesson 3
8	Volume of Rectangular Solids	Chapter 10, Lesson 5
9	Surface Area of Rectangular Solids	Chapter 10, Lesson 3
10	Volume of Rectangular Solids	Chapter 10, Lesson 5
11	Metric Capacity	Chapter 10, Lesson 1
12	Volume of Rectangular Solids	Chapter 10, Lesson 5

Performance Assessment

1. Compare the volume and surface area of Box A and Box B below. Which box has the greater surface area? Which box has the greater volume?

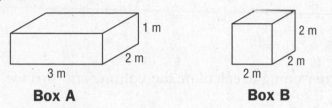

Box A   **Box B**

Checklist
☐ Write your name.
☐ Show your work.
☐ Explain your reasoning.
☐ Write the answer.

YOUR TASK: Calculate and compare the volume and surface area for both Box A and Box B.

ONE WAY:

- Calculate the surface area of Box A by using the formula
  Surface Area = 2 × length × width + 2 × length × height + 2 × width × height.

- Calculate the volume of Box A by using the formula
  Volume = length × width × height.

- Repeat for Box B.

- Compare the answers to find which box has greater volume and surface area.

ANOTHER WAY:

- Draw a sketch to show how many boxes 1 meter by 1 meter by 1 meter would fit inside of Box A.

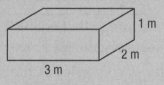

Box A

- Draw another sketch to show how many 1 meter by 1 meter squares would cover the six faces of Box A.

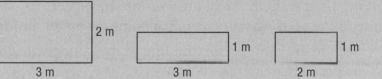

- Draw similar sketches for Box B.

- Compare the answers for Box A and Box B to find which box has greater volume and surface area.

Performance Assessment Teacher's Notes

▶ Target Skills

- Describe three-dimensional shapes and analyze their properties, including volume and surface area.

▶ Task Description

Students will use mathematical reasoning to calculate the volume and surface area of two rectangular prisms.

▶ Teacher Notes

This activity is suitable for partner work. Students can use manipulatives to model the solid figures. Kinesthetic or tactile learners may represent the two prisms with concrete physical objects. Visual learners may draw simple diagrams to represent the problem.

Box A: Surface area = 22 m^2; Volume = 6 m^3
Box B: Surface area = 24 m^2; Volume = 8 m^3

	Scoring Rubric	
Score	**Explanation**
3	Students demonstrate an efficient strategy and a thorough approach that enables them to solve the problem completely. Students will: • correctly calculate the surface area and volume for each box. • correctly compare the surface area and volume of the boxes. • explain their answer in grade-appropriate language.
2	Students demonstrate a strategy that enables them to solve the problem correctly. The strategy is disorganized or less efficient. Students may: • have some difficulty in correctly calculating surface area and volume. • incorrectly compare the volumes and surface areas. • find a solution, but have guessed for a few answers.
1	Students demonstrate a confused strategy, which leads to difficulty solving the problem. Most answers are incorrect, but students demonstrate knowledge of at least one concept being assessed. Students may: • demonstrate an understanding of the concept and a method of finding surface area and/or volume. • correctly compare the boxes' volumes and surface areas based on incorrect prior computations. • explain in grade-level language some of the concepts relevant to the problem.

NAME _____ DATE _____

Book Test

Gr.5

Convert.

1. 2 liters = _____ milliliters

   A 20   **B** 200   **C** 2,000   **D** 20,000

2. 1.5 gallons = _____ pints

   A 6   **B** 8   **C** 10   **D** 12

3. 3 pounds = _____ ounces

   A 16   **B** 30   **C** 32   **D** 48

Identify the figure.

4. **A** parallelogram   **C** rectangle

   B rhombus   **D** square

5. **A** sphere   **C** pyramid

   B cone   **D** prism

6. **A** acute triangle   **C** right triangle

   B obtuse triangle   **D** none of the above

7. A three–dimensional figure shaped like a box.

   A sphere   **B** pyramid   **C** prism   **D** cone

8. **A** square   **C** parallelogram

   B rectangle   **D** trapezoid

9. A quadrilateral with four equal sides and four right angles.

   A square   **C** rectangle

   B equilateral triangle   **D** parallelogram

Estimate the mass.

10. A banana

    A 1 gram   **B** 100 grams   **C** 3 kilograms   **D** 20 kilograms

11. 1,000 ice cubes, if one ice cube is about 0.9 grams.

    A 1 kilogram   **B** 10 kilograms   **C** 90 kilograms   **D** 100 kilograms

Book 3
Test

Answer the following questions.

12 Find the volume of the solid figure below.

A 18 cubic units   **C** 15 cubic units

B 56 cubic units   **D** 30 cubic units

13 What is the surface area of the solid figure?

A 40 square units   **C** 36 square units

B 76 square units   **D** 11 square units

14 Joshua has three identical balls that fit into one large box. Which statement below is true?

A The surface area of the large box is 3 times that of one ball.

B The volume of one ball is 3 times that of the large box.

C The surface area of one ball is three times that of the large box.

D The volume of the large box is at least 3 times that of one ball.

15 The radius of the circle below is 4.5 inches. What is the diameter?

A 2.25 inches   **C** 8 inches

B 6.5 inches   **D** 9 inches

4.5 in.

16 What is the radius of the circle at the right?

A 2.5 cm   **C** 23 cm

B 12.5 cm   **D** 50 cm

25 cm

17 **SHOPPING** A freezer compartment is shaped like a rectangular prism. It measures 4 feet long by 6 feet wide by 3 feet high. What is its volume?

A 72 ft³   **B** 72 ft²   **C** 27 ft³   **D** 22 ft²

18 **COLLEGE** A college pennant banner is triangular. It measures 12 in. wide at the base and 30 in. high. What is the area of the banner?

A 180 in.   **B** 180 in².   **C** 360 in.   **D** 360 in².

19 **CARPETING** How much carpeting is needed for a room that has a length of 25 feet and a width of 12 feet?

A 37 feet   **B** 300 feet   **C** 37 feet²   **D** 300 feet²

20 **SHIPPING** How much wrapping material is needed to send a package that is 6 cm by 12 cm by 8 cm?

A 26 cm²   **B** 216 cm²   **C** 432 cm²   **D** 576 cm²

Book Test
Scoring Guide and Diagnostic Chart

Students missing Exercise . . .	Have trouble with . . .	Should review . . .
1	Metric Capacity	Chapter 10, Lesson 1
2	Customary Capacity	Chapter 10, Lesson 2
3	Customary Weight	Chapter 10, Lesson 2
4	Quadrilaterals	Chapter 8, Lesson 1
5	Three-Dimensional Shapes	Chapter 8, Lesson 4
6	Triangles	Chapter 8, Lesson 2
7	Three-Dimensional Shapes	Chapter 8, Lesson 4
8	Quadrilaterals	Chapter 8, Lesson 1
9	Quadrilaterals	Chapter 8, Lesson 1
10	Metric Mass	Chapter 10, Lesson 1
11	Metric Mass	Chapter 10, Lesson 1
12	Volume of Rectangular Solids	Chapter 10, Lesson 5
13	Surface Area of Rectangular Solids	Chapter 10, Lesson 3
14	Concept of Volume	Chapter 10, Lesson 4
15	Circles	Chapter 8, Lesson 3
16	Circles	Chapter 8, Lesson 3
17	Volume of Rectangular Solids	Chapter 10, Lesson 5
18	Area of a Triangle	Chapter 9, Lesson 4
19	Area of a Rectangle	Chapter 9, Lesson 2
20	Surface Area of Rectangular Solids	Chapter 10, Lesson 3

NAME _____ DATE _____

Grade 5 Diagnostic and Placement Test

For each part, mark the box under the number of correctly answered questions.

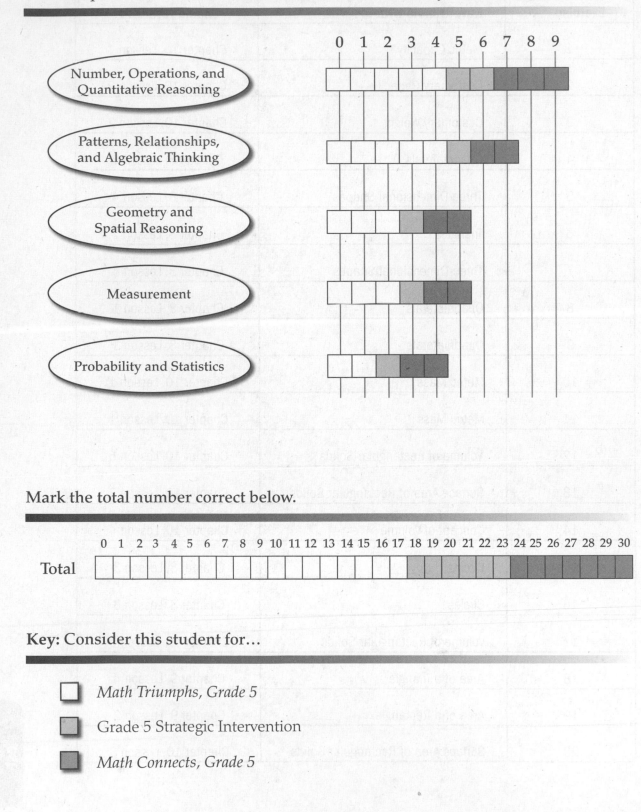

Mark the total number correct below.

Key: Consider this student for...

☐ *Math Triumphs, Grade 5*

▨ Grade 5 Strategic Intervention

▧ *Math Connects, Grade 5*

Diagnostic and Placement Test

In the column on the left, mark the questions that
the student answered *incorrectly*.

Strand	Question Number	Objective
	☐ 1	Use place value to read, write, compare and order whole numbers through 999,999,999.
	☐ 2	Use place value to read, write, compare and order decimals involving tenths and hundredths, including money, using concrete objects and pictorial models.
	☐ 3	Use concrete objects and pictorial models to generate equivalent fractions.
	☐ 4	Compare and order fractions using concrete objects and pictorial models.
Number, Operations, and Quantitative Reasoning	☐ 5	Relate decimals to fractions that name tenths and hundredths using concrete objects and pictorial models.
	☐ 6	Select appropriate methods and apply them accurately to estimate products or calculate them mentally, depending on the context and numbers involved.
	☐ 7	Add and subtract decimals to the hundredths place using concrete objects and pictorial models.
	☐ 8	Use multiplication to solve problems (no more than two digits times two digits without technology).
	☐ 9	Round whole numbers to the nearest ten, hundred, or thousand to approximate reasonable results in problem situations.
	☐ 10	Use patterns and relationships to develop strategies to remember basic multiplication and division facts (such as the patterns in related multiplication and division number sentences (fact families) such as $9 \times 9 = 81$ and $81 \div 9 = 9$).
	☐ 11	Use patterns and relationships to develop strategies to remember basic multiplication and division facts (such as the patterns in related multiplication and division number sentences (fact families) such as $9 \times 9 = 81$ and $81 \div 9 = 9$).
Patterns, Relationships, and Algebraic Reasoning	☐ 12	Use patterns to multiply by 10 and 100.
	☐ 13	Use patterns to multiply by 10 and 100.
	☐ 14	Describe the relationship between two sets of related data such as ordered pairs in a table.
	☐ 15	Describe the relationship between two sets of related data such as ordered pairs in a table.
	☐ 16	Describe the relationship between two sets of related data such as ordered pairs in a table.

Grade 5

Diagnostic and Placement Test

Strand	Question Number	Objective
Geometry and Spatial Reasoning	☐ 17	Identify and describe right, acute, and obtuse angles.
	☐ 18	Identify and describe parallel and intersecting (including perpendicular) lines using concrete objects and pictorial models.
	☐ 19	Use translations, reflections, and rotations using concrete models.
	☐ 20	Use reflections to verify that a shape has symmetry.
	☐ 21	Locate and name points on a number line using whole numbers, fractions, such as halves and fourths, and decimals, such as tenths.
Measurement	☐ 22	Estimate and use measurement tools to determine length (including perimeter), area, capacity and weight/mass using standard units (SI) and customary.
	☐ 23	Perform simple conversions between different units of length, between different units of capacity, and between different units of weight within the customary measurement system.
	☐ 24	Estimate volume in cubic units.
	☐ 25	Use a thermometer to measure temperature and changes in temperature.
	☐ 26	Quantify area by finding the total number of same-sized units of area that cover the shape without gaps or overlaps.
Probability and Statistics	☐ 27	Use concrete objects or pictures to make generalizations about determining all possible combinations of a given set of data or of objects in a problems situation.
	☐ 28	Use concrete objects or pictures to make generalizations about determining all possible combinations of a given set of data or of objects in a problems situation.
	☐ 29	Interpret bar graphs.
	☐ 30	Interpret bar graphs.

Math Triumphs

Grade 5

Diagnostic and Placement Test

Student Performance Level	Number of Questions Correct	Suggestions for Intervention and Remediation
Intensive Intervention	**0–17**	Use *Math Triumphs* to accelerate the achievement of students who are two or more years below grade level. Students should follow a personalized remediation plan. A variety of materials and instructional methods are recommended. For example, instruction and practice should be provided in print, technology, and hands-on lessons.
Strategic Intervention	**18–23**	Use the additional Intervention and Remediation materials listed on the next page. This list of materials can provide helpful resources for students who struggle in the traditional mathematics program. Strategic intervention allows students to continue to remain in the *Math Connects* program while receiving the differentiated instruction they need. Teaching Tips and other resources are also listed in the Teacher Edition.
Grade 5	**24 or more**	Use *Math Connects*. This student does not require overall intervention. However, based on the student's performance on the different sections, intervention may be required. For example, a student who missed 2 or more questions in the Measurement section may require extra assistance as you cover these skills throughout the year.

A Special Note About Intervention

When using diagnostic tests, teachers should always question the reason behind the students' scores. Students can struggle with mathematics concepts for a variety of reasons. Personalized instruction is recommended for English language learners, students with specific learning disabilities, students with certain medical conditions, or for those who struggle with traditional instructional practice. Teachers should always consider the needs of the individual student when determining the best approach for instruction and program placement.

Mathematics Chart

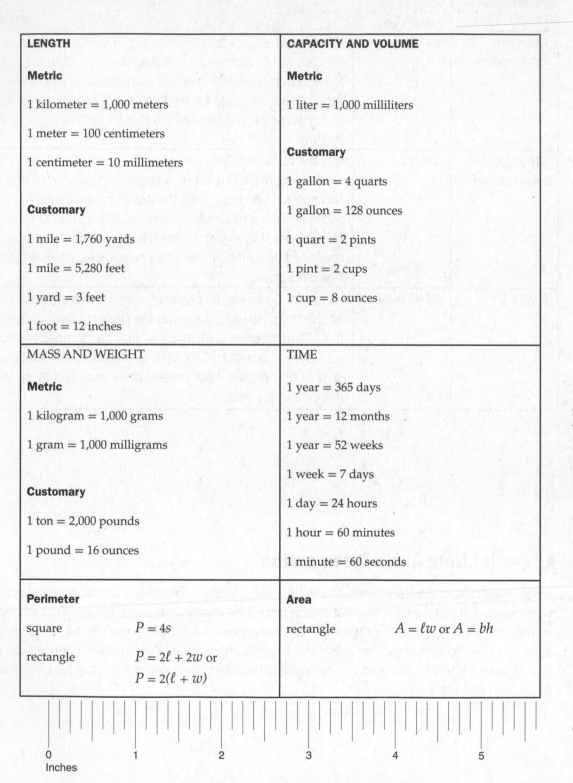

LENGTH

Metric

1 kilometer = 1,000 meters

1 meter = 100 centimeters

1 centimeter = 10 millimeters

Customary

1 mile = 1,760 yards

1 mile = 5,280 feet

1 yard = 3 feet

1 foot = 12 inches

CAPACITY AND VOLUME

Metric

1 liter = 1,000 milliliters

Customary

1 gallon = 4 quarts

1 gallon = 128 ounces

1 quart = 2 pints

1 pint = 2 cups

1 cup = 8 ounces

MASS AND WEIGHT

Metric

1 kilogram = 1,000 grams

1 gram = 1,000 milligrams

Customary

1 ton = 2,000 pounds

1 pound = 16 ounces

TIME

1 year = 365 days

1 year = 12 months

1 year = 52 weeks

1 week = 7 days

1 day = 24 hours

1 hour = 60 minutes

1 minute = 60 seconds

Perimeter

square $P = 4s$

rectangle $P = 2\ell + 2w$ or
$P = 2(\ell + w)$

Area

rectangle $A = \ell w$ or $A = bh$

Grade
5

Diagnostic and Placement Test

This test contains 30 multiple-choice questions. Work each problem in the space on this page. Select the best answer. Write the letter of the answer on the blank at the right.

1 The number 9,020,730 is read as which of the following:

    A nine billion, twenty million, seventy-three

    B nine million, two thousand, seven hundred thirty

    C nine million, twenty thousand, seven hundred thirty

    D nine hundred two thousand, seventy-three

1 _____

2 Which of the following numbers is the greatest?

    A 11.6   **B** 2.09   **C** 4.63   **D** 1.17

2 _____

3 Inali and his friends ate $\frac{1}{2}$ of a pizza.

Which fractional part of a circle below is equal to $\frac{1}{2}$?

    A

    B

    C

    D

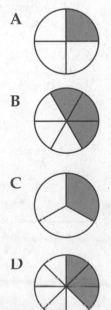

3 _____

4 During basketball practice, Michael spends time shooting free throws. The figures below are shaded to show the number of shots made compared to the number of shots attempted at each practice. What can you conclude from the data?

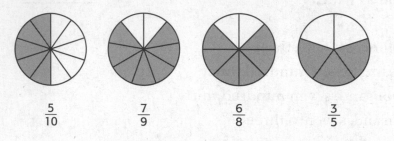

$$\frac{5}{10} \qquad \frac{7}{9} \qquad \frac{6}{8} \qquad \frac{3}{5}$$

A The fraction $\frac{5}{10}$ is greater than $\frac{3}{5}$.

B The fraction $\frac{3}{5}$ is greater than $\frac{7}{9}$.

C The fractions are all equal.

D The fraction $\frac{3}{5}$ is greater than $\frac{5}{10}$.

4 _____

5 What decimal is equivalent to $\frac{3}{4}$?

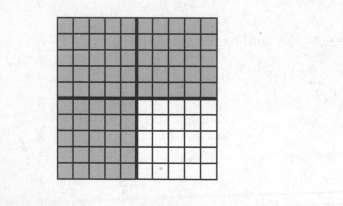

A 0.25 B 0.34 C 0.75 D 1.33

5 _____

6 Estimate to find the product of 6.12 and 4.98.

A 10

B 11

C 24

D 30

6 _____

7 The menu below shows the prices at Lunchtime Café. Lucita orders a turkey sandwich, salad, and juice. What operation should she use to determine the cost of her meal?

Lunchtime Café	
Item	**Cost**
Turkey Sandwich	$4.50
Ham Sandwich	$4.35
Salad	$2.10
Fruit Cup	$2.50
Juice	$1.90

A addition   C multiplication

B subtraction   D division

8 Each student in fifth grade donates 4 cans of food to the food bank. There are 285 fifth-grade students. Which of the following shows the number of cans donated and the correct justification for the number?

A 71 because 285 divided by 4 is approximately 71

B 289 because 285 plus 4 is 289

C 1,120 because 280 times 4 is 1,120

D 1,140 because 285 times 4 is 1,140

9 Look at the table below. Which of the following has NOT been rounded correctly to the nearest hundred?

Population in 2005		
City	**Exact Population**	**Estimated Population**
Amarillo	183,021	183,000
Austin	690,252	690,300
Corpus Christi	280,002	280,000
Fort Worth	624,067	624,000

Source: U.S. Census Bureau

A Amarillo   C Corpus Christi

B Austin   D Fort Worth

10 Which completes the fact family for the
following set of number sentences?

$$3 \times 6 = 18, 18 \div 3 = 6, 18 \div 6 = 3$$

A $3 \times 6 = 18$ **C** $6 \div 3 = 2$

B $6 \times 3 = 18$ **D** $6 \div 18 = \frac{1}{3}$

11 Raven is asked to check the answer to the
multiplication problem below. Which number
sentence could she use to check her answer?

$$8 \times 7 = 56$$

A $56 + 8 = 64$ **C** $56 \times 8 = 7$

B $56 - 8 = 48$ **D** $56 \div 8 = 7$

12 Each week, Melanie saves the same amount
of money. After the third week, she has $30.
After the fifth week, she has $50. After the
seventh week, she has $70. Which operation
could Melanie use to determine the amount
she will have saved by the tenth week?

A Add 10 to the number of weeks.

B Add 20 to the number of weeks.

C Multiply 10 times the number of weeks.

D Multiply 20 times the number of weeks.

13 Carmen created the following table
of multiplication facts for 100. If the
pattern continues, what is 100×12?

#	× 100
1	100
2	200
3	300
4	400
5	500

A 120   **C** 1,200

B 210   **D** 2,100

Math Triumphs

14 Bennett created the table below. Which operation did he perform on the numbers in the left column to find the numbers in the right column?

x	y
1	9
2	10
3	11
4	12
5	13
6	14

14 _____

A Add 8.

B Add 9.

C Multiply by 8.

D Multiply by 9.

15 Martin notices that certain pickup trucks have 6 wheels. Which table could he use to determine the number of wheels on five of these pickup trucks?

15 _____

A

Trucks	1	2	3	4	5
Wheels	4	8	12	16	20

B

Trucks	1	2	3	4	5
Wheels	6	12	18	24	30

C

Trucks	1	2	3	4	5
Wheels	4	16	64	256	1024

D

Trucks	1	2	3	4	5
Wheels	6	36	216	1296	7776

16 Tamera is 4 years younger than her brother. Which number sentence could you use to determine Tamera's age, given her brother's age b?

16 _____

A $b + 4$

B $b - 4$

C $b \times 4$

D $b \div 4$

17 Look at the four angles marked on the picture of a bicycle.

17 _____

Which angle appears to be a right angle?

A angle 1   **B** angle 2   **C** angle 3   **D** angle 4

18 The polygon below has two right angles.

18 _____

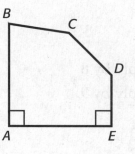

Which side of the polygon is parallel to side $\overline{AB}$?

A $\overline{BC}$ **C** $\overline{DE}$

B $\overline{CD}$ **D** $\overline{EA}$

19 On the graph below, $\triangle ABC$ has been rotated about the center to form $\triangle DEF$. Which of the following statements can be made?

19 _____

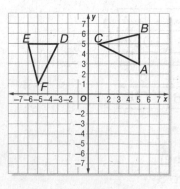

A $\triangle ABC$ is congruent to $\triangle DEF$.

B $\triangle ABC$ is a right triangle.

C $\triangle ABC$ is a reflection of $\triangle DEF$.

D $\triangle ABC$ is parallel to $\triangle DEF$.

Math Triumphs

20 Which of the following figures shows a trapezoid and its reflection line?

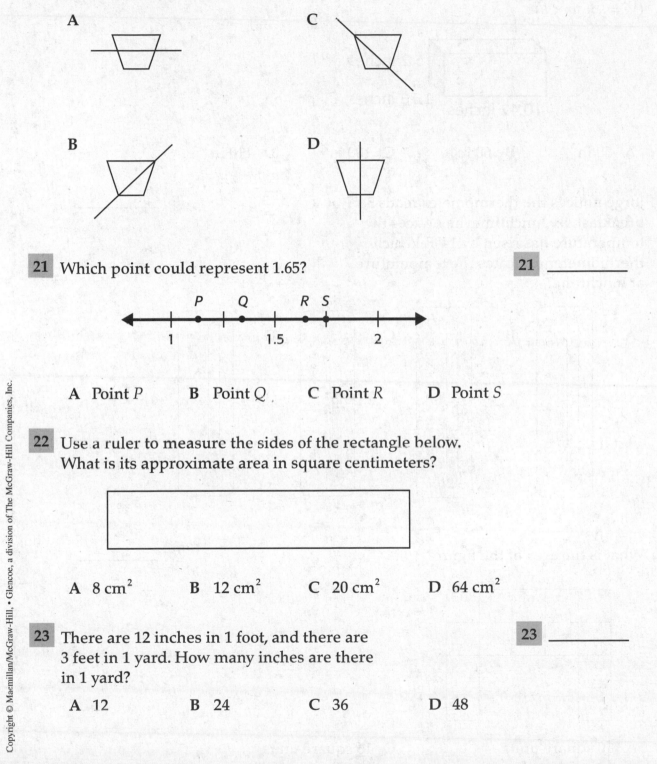

A

C

B

D

21 Which point could represent 1.65?

A Point *P*   **B** Point *Q*   **C** Point *R*   **D** Point *S*

22 Use a ruler to measure the sides of the rectangle below. What is its approximate area in square centimeters?

A 8 cm^2 **B** 12 cm^2 **C** 20 cm^2 **D** 64 cm^2

23 There are 12 inches in 1 foot, and there are 3 feet in 1 yard. How many inches are there in 1 yard?

A 12   **B** 24   **C** 36   **D** 48

24 Megan wants to estimate the volume of the box shown below. Which is the best estimate?
$(V = l \times w \times h)$

24 _____

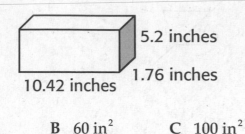

5.2 inches

1.76 inches

10.42 inches

A 50 in²   **B** 60 in²   **C** 100 in²   **D** 110 in²

25 Jorgé notices the thermometer reads 38°F at breakfast. By lunchtime, he notices the temperature has risen by 14°F. Which thermometer indicates the temperature at lunchtime?

25 _____

A 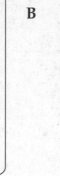 **B** 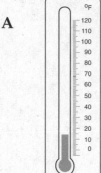 **C** 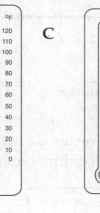 **D**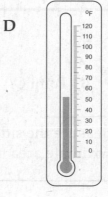

26 What is the area of the figure?

26 _____

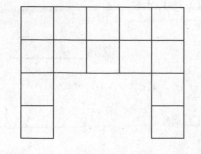

A 10 square units   **C** 16 square units

B 14 square units   **D** 28 square units

Math Triumphs

27 To win a prize, first choose a box and then choose a prize bag inside that box. There are 3 boxes and 2 prize bags in each box. There is a different prize in each bag. How many different prizes are there?

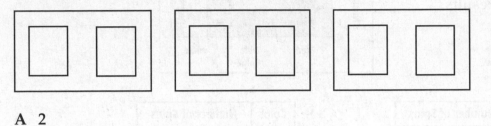

A 2

B 3

C 5

D 6

28 Kendra wears all four of the bracelets shown below at the same time. How many different ways can she arrange the bracelets on one wrist?

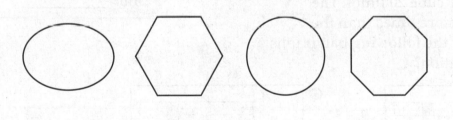

A 4

B 8

C 16

D 24

29 Adam spins a spinner 12 times. The results are shown in the bar graph below. Which tally chart shows these results?

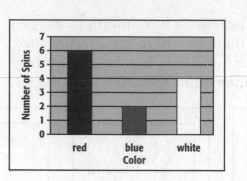

A

Color	Number of Spins
red	⫴⫴ l
blue	ll
white	llll

C

Color	Number of Spins
red	⫴⫴
blue	lll
white	lllll

B

Color	Number of Spins
red	⫴⫴ l
blue	lll
white	lll

D

Color	Number of Spins
red	⫴⫴
blue	ll
white	⫴⫴

30 Dion rolls a number cube 20 times. The number 3 is rolled more times than the number 4. Which of the following bar graphs reflects this information?

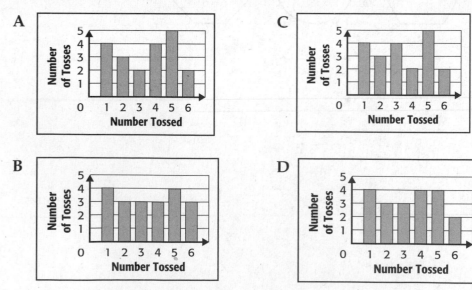

Answers (Grade 5)

Grade 5 — Intensive Intervention Placement Test

1 The number 5,371,082 is read as:

- Ⓐ five million, three hundred seventy-one thousand, eighty-two
- B five hundred thirty-seven thousand, one hundred eighty-two
- C five million, three hundred seventy-one thousand, eighty hundred twenty.
- D five million, thirty-seven thousand, one hundred eight two

2 Identify the three-dimensional figure below.

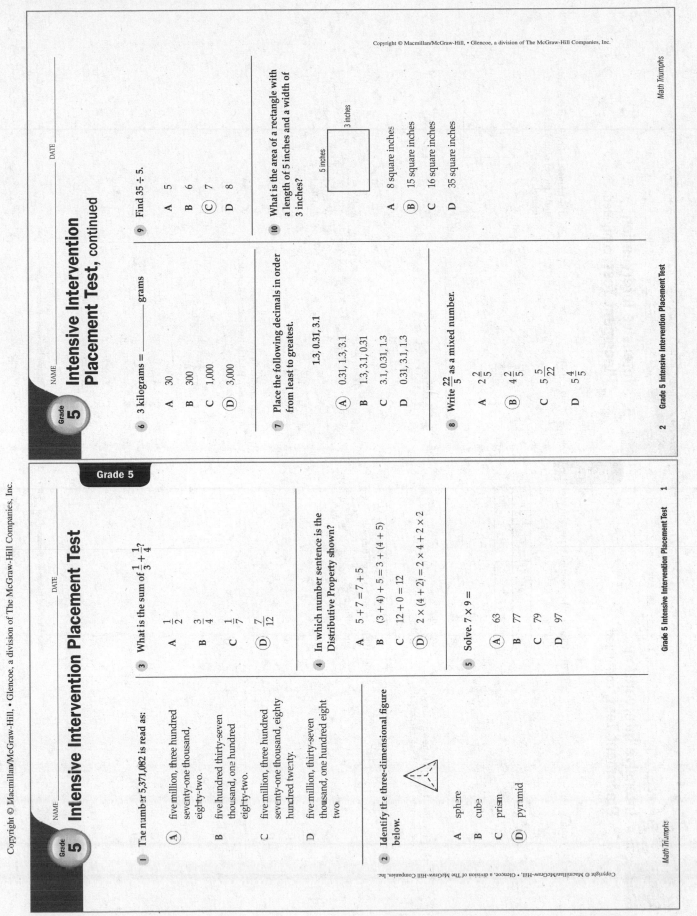

- A sphere
- B cube
- C prism
- Ⓓ pyramid

3 What is the sum of $\frac{1}{3} + \frac{1}{4}$?

- A $\frac{1}{2}$
- B $\frac{3}{4}$
- C $\frac{1}{7}$
- Ⓓ $\frac{7}{12}$

4 In which number sentence is the Distributive Property shown?

- A $5 + 7 = 7 + 5$
- B $(3 + 4) + 5 = 3 + (4 + 5)$
- C $12 + 0 = 12$
- Ⓓ $2 \times (4 + 2) = 2 \times 4 + 2 \times 2$

5 Solve. $7 \times 9 =$

- Ⓐ 63
- B 77
- C 79
- D 97

Grade 5 — Intensive Intervention Placement Test, continued

6 3 kilograms = _____ grams

- A 30
- B 300
- C 1,000
- Ⓓ 3,000

7 Place the following decimals in order from least to greatest.

1.3, 0.31, 3.1

- Ⓐ 0.31, 1.3, 3.1
- B 1.3, 3.1, 0.31
- C 3.1, 0.31, 1.3
- D 0.31, 3.1, 1.3

8 Write $\frac{22}{5}$ as a mixed number.

- A $2\frac{2}{5}$
- Ⓑ $4\frac{2}{5}$
- C $5\frac{5}{22}$
- D $5\frac{4}{5}$

9 Find $35 \div 5$.

- A 5
- B 6
- Ⓒ 7
- D 8

10 What is the area of a rectangle with a length of 5 inches and a width of 3 inches?

3 inches

5 inches

- A 8 square inches
- Ⓑ 15 square inches
- C 16 square inches
- D 35 square inches

Answers (Grade 5)

NAME _____ DATE _____

Grade 5

Intensive Intervention
Placement Test, continued

19 The triangle below is 5 inches wide and 5 inches high. What is the triangle's area?

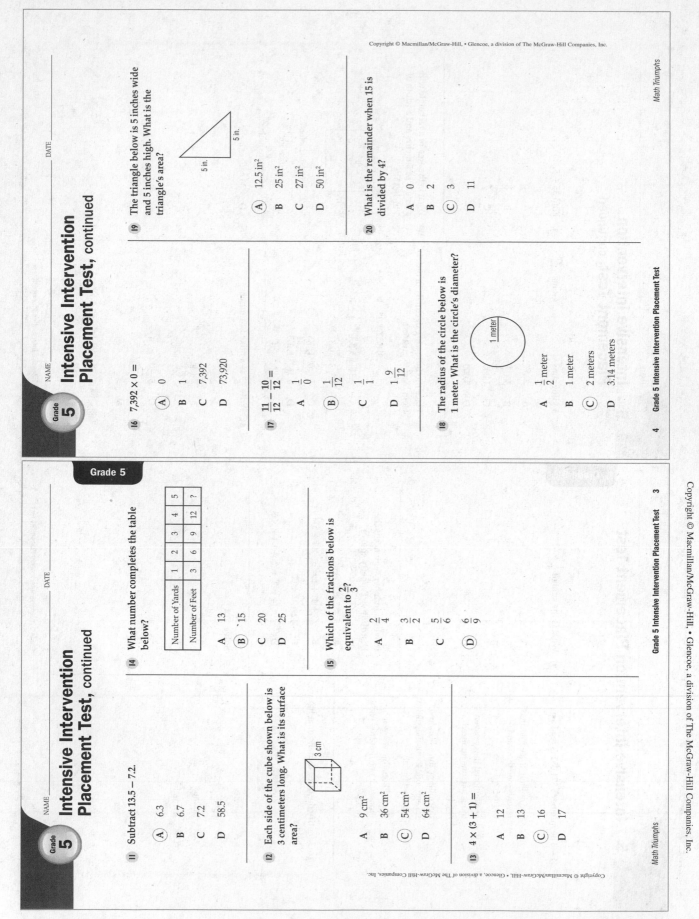

5 in.

5 in.

- Ⓐ 12.5 in²
- B 25 in²
- C 27 in²
- D 50 in²

20 What is the remainder when 15 is divided by 4?

- A 0
- B 2
- Ⓒ 3
- D 11

16 7,392 × 0 =

- Ⓐ 0
- B 1
- C 7,392
- D 73,920

17 $\frac{11}{12} - \frac{10}{12} =$

- A $\frac{1}{0}$
- Ⓑ $\frac{1}{12}$
- C $\frac{1}{1}$
- D $1\frac{9}{12}$

18 The radius of the circle below is 1 meter. What is the circle's diameter?

1 meter

- A $\frac{1}{2}$ meter
- B 1 meter
- Ⓒ 2 meters
- D 3.14 meters

NAME _____ DATE _____

Grade 5

Intensive Intervention
Placement Test, continued

14 What number completes the table below?

Number of Yards	1	2	3	4	5
Number of Feet	3	6	9	12	?

- A 13
- Ⓑ 15
- C 20
- D 25

15 Which of the fractions below is equivalent to $\frac{2}{3}$?

- A $\frac{2}{4}$
- B $\frac{3}{2}$
- C $\frac{5}{6}$
- Ⓓ $\frac{6}{9}$

11 Subtract 13.5 − 7.2.

- Ⓐ 6.3
- B 6.7
- C 7.2
- D 58.5

12 Each side of the cube shown below is 3 centimeters long. What is its surface area?

3 cm

- A 9 cm²
- B 36 cm²
- Ⓒ 54 cm²
- D 64 cm²

13 4 × (3 + 1) =

- A 12
- B 13
- Ⓒ 16
- D 17

Answers (Grade 5)

Grade 5

NAME _____ DATE _____

Intensive Intervention Placement Test, continued

26 Maria divided 78 grapes into 6 equal groups so she could share them with her friends. How many grapes did each of them get?

- A 6
- B 9
- C 11
- **(D) 13**

27 In which number sentence is the associative property shown?

- A $12 + 32 = 32 + 12$
- **(B) $(5 + 7) + 32 = 5 + (7 + 32)$**
- C $6 \times (2 + 6) = 6 \times 2 + 6 \times 6$
- D $12 + (9 - 3) = (12 - 9) + 3$

28 Which decimal is equivalent to $\frac{1}{4}$?

- A 0.2
- **(B) 0.25**
- C 0.33
- D 0.4

29 Identify the figure.

- A rectangle
- B rhombus
- C parallelogram
- **(D) trapezoid**

30 $\frac{2}{5} + \frac{5}{10} =$

- A $\frac{3}{10}$
- B $\frac{6}{20}$
- **(C) $\frac{9}{10}$**
- D $\frac{7}{20}$

Math Triumphs

Grade 5

NAME _____ DATE _____

Intensive Intervention Placement Test, continued

21 George measured a box and found it was 2 meters wide, 5 meters long, and 3 meters high. What was the volume of the box?

- **(A) 30 m³**
- B 35 m³
- C 60 m³
- D 62 m³

23 What is the fraction $\frac{15}{20}$ in simplest form?

- A $\frac{5}{20}$
- B $\frac{1}{2}$
- **(C) $\frac{3}{4}$**
- D $\frac{4}{5}$

22 The base of the parallelogram below is 8 inches long. The height of the parallelogram is 5 inches. What is its area?

8 in.   5 in.

- A 20 in²
- B 35 in²
- **(C) 40 in²**
- D 58 in²

24 $4 \times 6 =$

- A 10
- **(B) 24**
- C 46
- D 64

25 Write the next three terms in the pattern. 1, 4, 7, 10

- **(A) 13, 16, 19**
- B 14, 18, 22
- C 14, 17, 20
- D 13, 18, 23

Math Triumphs   **Grade 5**   **A3**

Answers (Grade 5)

Book 1 — Book Pretest, continued

NAME _____ DATE _____

Find each quotient.

10. $66 \div 6 =$
   A 0   B 6   C) 11   D 12

11. $60 \div 3 =$
   A) 20   B 30   C 36   D 57

12. $72 \div 6 =$
   A 10   B 11   C) 12   D 13

13. $100 \div 10 =$
   A 7   B 8   C 9   D) 10

Answer the following questions.

14. Which property is shown in the sentence below?

   $2 \times (9 + 8) = (2 \times 9) + (2 \times 8)$

   A Associative Property   C Order of Operations
   B Commutative Property   D) Distributive Property

15. Which operation is the inverse of multiplication?

   A) division   B addition   C subtraction   D multiplication

Solve.

16. $3 \times (10 + 2) =$
   A 28   B 30   C 32   D) 36

17. $(10 - 5) \times 7 + 1 =$
   A 35   B) 36   C 66   D 71

18. $7 \times (5 \times 3) =$
   A 7 × 53   B $(7 + 5) \times (7 \times 3)$ C $7 \times 5 + 7 \times 3$ D) $(7 \times 5) \times 3$

19. $124 \times 6 =$
   A $(1 \times 6) + (2 \times 6) + (4 \times 6)$ C) 6 × 124
   B 12 × 46   D $(100 \times 6) + (20 \times 4)$

Math Triumphs   Grade 5 Book 1   9

Book 1 — Book Pretest

NAME _____ DATE _____

1. What is 3,182 in expanded form?
   A) $3,000 + 100 + 80 + 2$ C $300 + 1,000 + 80 + 2$
   B $3,000 + 100 + 82$ D $3,000 + 100 + 800 + 20$

2. What is 9,450 in expanded form?
   A $9,000 + 45 + 50$ C $9,000 + 400 + 50$
   B $900 + 40 + 5$ D) $9,000 + 400 + 50$

3. What is four million, two hundred eighty-eight thousand, seven hundred three in standard form?
   A 4,288,730   C 4,208,873
   B) 4,288,703   D 428,873

4. What is the next conversion in the pattern?

Number of Feet	1	2
Number of Inches	12	24

   A 25 inches in 3 feet   C) 36 inches in 3 feet
   B 30 inches in 3 feet   D 48 inches in 3 feet

5. What is the next conversion in the pattern?

Number of Half Dozens of Apples	1	2	3
Number of Apples	6	12	18

   A 20 in 4 half dozens   C) 24 in 4 half dozens
   B 22 in 4 half dozens   D 28 in 4 half dozens

Find each product.

6. $6 \times 10 =$
   A 16   B 54   C) 60   D 61

7. $8 \times 12 =$
   A 82   B) 96   C 98   D 128

8. $22 \times 0 =$
   A) 0   B 1   C 22   D 220

9. $123 \times 5 =$
   A 128   B 515   C 605   D) 615

8   Grade 5 Book 1   *Math Triumphs*

Answers (Grade 5)

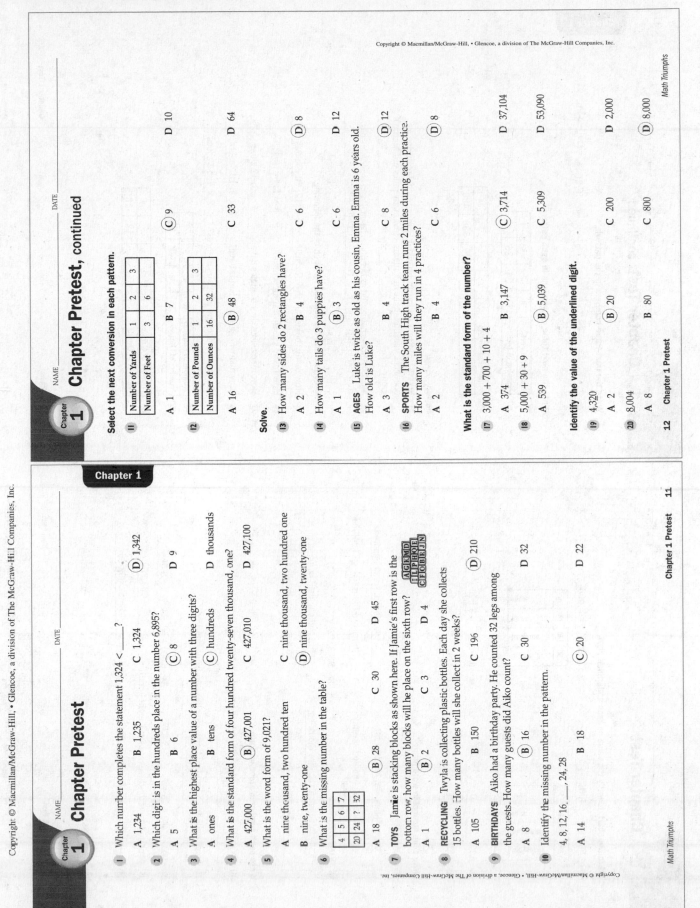

NAME _____ **DATE** _____

Chapter 1 — Chapter Pretest

1. Which number completes the statement 1,324 < _____ ?
   A 1,234 B 1,235 C 1,324 **D 1,342**

2. Which digit is in the hundreds place in the number 6,895?
   A 5 B 6 **C 8** D 9

3. What is the highest place value of a number with three digits?
   A ones B tens **C hundreds** D thousands

4. What is the standard form of four hundred twenty-seven thousand, one?
   A 427,000 **B 427,001** C 427,010 D 427,100

5. What is the word form of 9,021?
   A nine thousand, two hundred
   B nine, twenty-one
   C nine thousand, two hundred one
   D nine thousand, twenty-one

6. What is the missing number in the table?

4	5	6	7
20	24	?	32

   A 18 **B 28** C 30 D 45

7. **TOYS** Jamie is stacking blocks as shown here. If Jamie's first row is the bottom row, how many blocks will he place on the sixth row?
   A 1 **B 2** C 3 D 4

8. **RECYCLING** Twyla is collecting plastic bottles. Each day she collects 15 bottles. How many bottles will she collect in 2 weeks?
   A 105 B 150 C 196 **D 210**

9. **BIRTHDAYS** Aiko had a birthday party. He counted 32 legs among the guests. How many guests did Aiko count?
   A 8 **B 16** C 30 D 32

10. Identify the missing number in the pattern.
    4, 8, 12, 16, ____, 24, 28
    A 14 B 18 **C 20** D 22

NAME _____ **DATE** _____

Chapter 1 — Chapter Pretest, continued

Select the next conversion in each pattern.

11.

Number of Yards	1	2	3
Number of Feet	3	6	

   A 1 B 7 **C 9** D 10

12.

Number of Pounds	1	2	3
Number of Ounces	16	32	

   A 16 **B 48** C 33 D 64

Solve.

13. How many sides do 2 rectangles have?
    A 2 B 4 C 6 **D 8**

14. How many tails do 3 puppies have?
    A 1 **B 3** C 6 D 12

15. **AGES** Luke is twice as old as his cousin, Emma. Emma is 6 years old. How old is Luke?
    A 3 B 4 C 8 **D 12**

16. **SPORTS** The South High track team runs 2 miles during each practice. How many miles will they run in 4 practices?
    A 2 B 4 C 6 **D 8**

What is the standard form of the number?

17. 3,000 + 700 + 10 + 4
    A 374 B 3,147 **C 3,714** D 37,104

18. 5,000 + 30 + 9
    A 539 **B 5,039** C 5,309 D 53,090

Identify the value of the underlined digit.

19. 4,3<u>2</u>0
    A 2 **B 20** C 200 D 2,000

20. <u>8</u>,004
    A 8 B 80 C 800 **D 8,000**

Answers (Grade 5)

Chapter 1 — Chapter Test, continued

NAME _____ DATE _____

Write the next three numbers in the pattern.

17. 2, 4, 8, 16, 32, 64

18. 16, 21, 26, 31, 36, 41

Write the next three conversions in each pattern.

19.

Number of Feet	1	2	3	4
Number of Inches	12	24	36	48

20.

Number of Meters	1	2	3	4
Number of Centimeters	100	200	300	400

Solve.

21. **HIKING** Martin's hiking group hiked 12 miles each day during a one-week vacation in the mountains. How many miles did Martin's group hike? **84 miles**

22. **AGES** Alice is half as old as her uncle, Jason. Jason is 34 years old. How old is Alice? **17 years old**

Write the rule and the solution for each of the following.

23. How many cookies are in 5 dozen? 5×12; 60 cookies

24. How many legs do 8 spiders have? 8×8; 64 legs

25. How many sides do 4 triangles have? 4×3; 12 sides

26. How many fingers do 2 hands have? 2×5; 10 fingers

27. How many shoes are in 7 pairs of shoes? 2×7; 14 shoes

28.

Number of Pounds	1	2	3	4
Number of Ounces	16	32	48	64

29.

Number of Gallons	1	2	3	4
Number of Quarts	4	8	12	16

Math Triumphs

Chapter 1 — Chapter Test

NAME _____ DATE _____

Fill in the chart. Identify the value of each underlined digit.

1. 9,7<u>3</u>0   700

thousands	hundreds	tens	ones
1,000	100	10	1
9	7	3	0

2. <u>2</u>,583   2,000

thousands	hundreds	tens	ones
1,000	100	10	1
2	5	8	3

3. 6,1<u>0</u>3   0

4. <u>6</u>,090   6,000

5. 1,62<u>8</u>   8

6. 4<u>2</u>9   20

Write each number in word form.

7. 3,256,570   three million, two hundred fifty-six thousand, five hundred seventy

8. 2,732,600   two million, seven hundred thirty-two thousand, six hundred

9. 8,095,277   eight million, ninety-five thousand, two hundred seventy-seven

10. 5,803,692   five million, eight hundred three thousand, six hundred ninety-two

Write each number in standard form.

11. six million, nine hundred fifty-two thousand, six hundred three   6,952,603

12. three million, six hundred thirty-nine thousand, one hundred seventeen   3,639,117

13. 3,000 + 400 + 20 + 7   3,427

14. 8,000 + 60 + 4   8,064

15. four million, sixty-three thousand, eight hundred   4,063,800

16. eight million, three hundred nine thousand, sixty-five   8,309,065

Math Triumphs

Math Triumphs

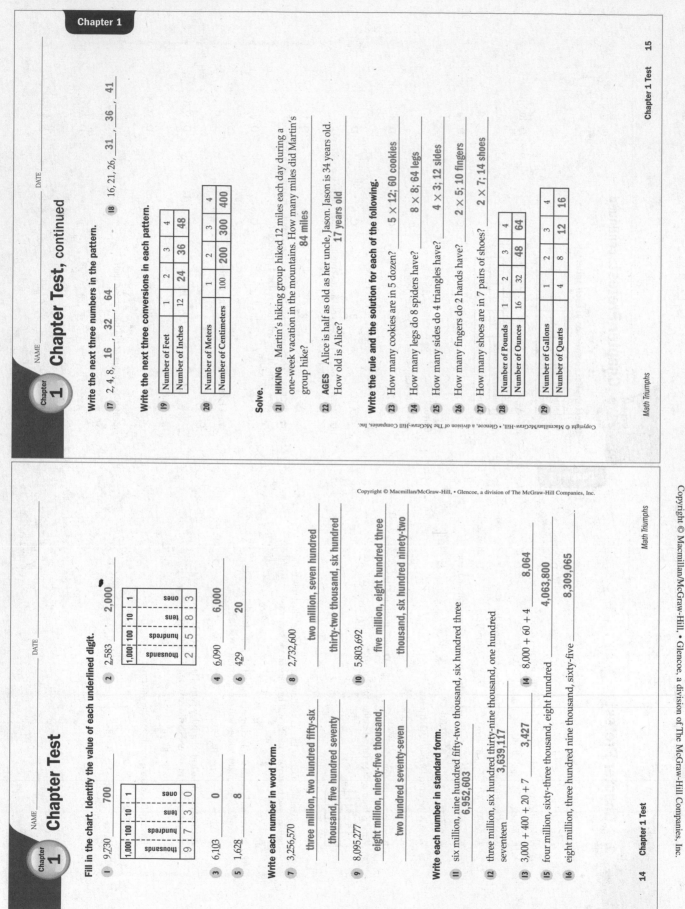

Answers (Grade 5)

NAME _____ DATE _____

Chapter 1 Test Practice

Choose the best answer and fill in the corresponding circle on the answer sheet.

1 Which number shows six hundred eight written in standard form?

(A) 608　　　C 680
B 618　　　D 688

2 5,000 + 40 + 7 =

A 547　　　C 5,407
(B) 5,047　　　D 5,447

3 Identify the value of the underlined digit.

4,091,532

A 900　　　C 900,000
B 9,000　　　(D) 90,000

4 Which digit is in the thousands place in 1,265,073?

A 1　　　(C) 5
B 2　　　D 7

5 The Cassini spacecraft travels to Saturn at 77,700 miles per hour. Identify the underlined digit.

A 700　　　C 70,000
(B) 7,000　　　D 700,000

6 Hannah's grandmother is 81 years old. Which shows her grandmother's age written in word form?

A eighteen　　　C eighty.
B eighteen-one　　(D) eighty-one

Select the next number in the pattern.

7 5, 15, 25, _____

A 26　　　(C) 35
B 30　　　D 40

8 21, 28, 35, _____

A 36　　　(C) 42
B 40　　　D 45

NAME _____ DATE _____

Chapter 1 Test Practice, continued

9 Brandon's family is gathered for a family picnic. He has a large family and a few cats. If there is a total of 44 legs at the picnic, which of the following could be an answer for how many humans and how many cats are at the picnic?

A 8 humans, 6 cats
B 15 humans, 4 cats
C 17 humans, 3 cats
(D) 18 humans, 2 cats

10 What is the next number in the sequence?

18, 24, 30, 36, 42, 48, 54, _____

(A) 60　　　C 64
B 62　　　D 70

11 What is the rule for this pattern?

15, 22, 29, 36, 43, 50

A add 9　　　C subtract 7
(B) add 7　　　D subtract 9

12 Find the missing number.

4	8	12	16
16	32	48	?

A 32　　　C 60
B 52　　　(D) 64

ANSWER SHEET
Directions: Fill in the circle of each correct answer.

1　(A) B C D
2　A B (C) D
3　A (B) C D
4　(A) B C D
5　A (B) C D
6　A (B) C D
7　(A) B C D
8　(A) B C D
9　A (B) C D
10　(A) B C D
11　A (B) C D
12　(A) B C D

Answers (Grade 5)

NAME _____ DATE _____

Chapter 2 Chapter Pretest

1. What is the product of 11 and 12?
   A 23   B 120   C 122   (D) 132

2. Which expression does the array model?
   A 3 + 5   C 15 × 1
   (B) 5 × 3   D 5 + 3

3. **PUZZLES** The grid for a square crossword puzzle has 12 squares along each of its 4 sides. How many smaller squares are in the crossword puzzle?
   A 24   B 100   C 121   (D) 144

4. What is 9 × 8?
   (A) 72   B 74   C 81   D 82

5. **KNITTING** Tara is knitting scarves to sell. Each scarf uses 95 yards of yarn. If she knits 23 scarves, how many yards of yarn will Tara use?
   A 218   B 1,955   (C) 2,185   D 3,040

6. Which is a multiple of 7?
   A 27   B 47   (C) 77   D 97

7. What missing factor makes the equation true?
   5 × ____ = 75
   A 3   (B) 15   C 20   D 25

8. **FOOD** On a strip of button candy there are 3 pieces in each row and 12 rows. How many pieces of button candy are on the strip?
   A 15   B 30   (C) 36   D 39

9. Which fact belongs to the same fact family as 4 × 3 = 12?
   (A) 12 ÷ 3 = 4   B 4 + 3 = 7   C 6 × 2 = 12   D 12 ÷ 1 = 12

10. **SHOPPING** Marion bought 8 packs of the light bulbs. If there are 4 light bulbs in each pack, how many light bulbs did he buy?
    A 12   B 28   C 30   (D) 32

11. What is another way to write the product 24 × 7?
    A 20 + 7 + 7   (B) 20 × 7 + 4 × 7   C 24 × 7 + 20 × 7   D 20 × 7 + 7

NAME _____ DATE _____

Chapter 2 Chapter Pretest, continued

Use the Distributive Property of Multiplication to find the product.

12. 18 × 31 =
    A 72   B 234   (C) 558   D 725

13. 27 × 52 =
    A 189   B 675   C 1,304   (D) 1,404

14. 33 × 34 =
    A 231   (B) 1,122   C 1,452   D 3,334

Select the appropriate property.

15. Which property is shown by 120 × 0 = 0?
    A Distributive Property of Multiplication   C Identity Property of Multiplication
    (B) Zero Property of Multiplication   D Associative Property of Multiplication

16. Which property is shown by 14 × 82 = 82 × 14?
    A Distributive Property   (C) Commutative Property of Multiplication
    B Zero Property of Multiplication   D Associative Property of Multiplication

Find each product.

17. 24 × 1 = ____
    A 0   B 1   (C) 24   D 25

18. 10 × 62 = ____
    A 72   B 602   C 612   (D) 620

19. 9 × 11 = ____
    A 20   B 91   (C) 99   D 109

20. **SCHOOL** Each student in a class has 7 textbooks. There are 18 students in the class. How many textbooks do they have altogether?
    A 78   B 116   (C) 126   D 216

21. **FINANCE** Amelia's grandmother gives her $3 every Saturday. If there are 52 Saturdays this year, how much will her grandmother give her in the year?
    A $55   B $152   C $153   (D) $156

Math Triumphs

Math Triumphs

Answers (Grade 5)

NAME _____ DATE _____

Chapter 2 Chapter Test

Draw an array to model the expression. Then write and model the commutative fact.

1. 6×4 ___ 4×6

Find each product.

2. 6×0 ___ **0**
3. 2×11 ___ **22**
4. 5×10 ___ **50**

5. 0×6 ___ **0**
6. 5×3 ___ **15**
7. 12×4 ___ **48**

8. 3×9 ___ **27**
9. 5×6 ___ **30**
10. 9×7 ___ **63**

11. 7×6 ___ **42**
12. 12×7 ___ **84**
13. 2×6 ___ **12**

Draw an array to model each expression. Find the product.

14. 4×8 ___ **32**

15. 6×12 ___ **72**

Find each product.

16. 38×6 ___ **228**
17. 42×8 ___ **336**

18. 206×3 ___ **618**
19. 418×4 ___ **1,672**

20. 542×5 ___ **2,710**
21. 490×7 ___ **3,430**

Find the missing number that makes the equation true.

22. $7 \times$ ___ $= 63$ ___ **9**
23. $8 \times$ ___ $= 32$ ___ **4**

NAME _____ DATE _____

Chapter 2 Chapter Test, continued

Write each product in distributive form.

24. 11×4 __40 + 4__
25. 22×7 __140 + 14__
26. 5×43 __200 + 15__

Solve.

27. **LIBRARY** Brownsville County Library has 5 shelves in each bookcase. Each shelf holds 24 paperback books. What is the maximum number of paperback books that each bookcase holds?

120 paperback books

28. **MOVING** When Andrea moved to a new house or apartment room, she packed her belongings into 6 boxes. Each box weighed 25 pounds. How many pounds did her boxes weigh in all?

150 pounds

29. **FINANCE** Mr. Raul wants to buy a big-screen TV that costs about $1,765. He has been saving $150 a month for an entire year. At the end of one year, how much money will he have saved? Is that enough money for the big screen TV? (There are 12 months in a year.)

$1,800; yes

30. **SCHOOL** Beth is bringing 10 books home from school in her backpack. Each book weighs 3 pounds. How many pounds of books does she have in her backpack?

30 pounds

Correct the mistakes.

31. Carlos told Julius that he knows a shortcut for multiplying by 100. He said, "You add one zero to the factor." Julius told Carlos that his shortcut was not right. What is the correct shortcut?

add two zeros to the factor

Answers (Grade 5)

NAME _____ DATE _____

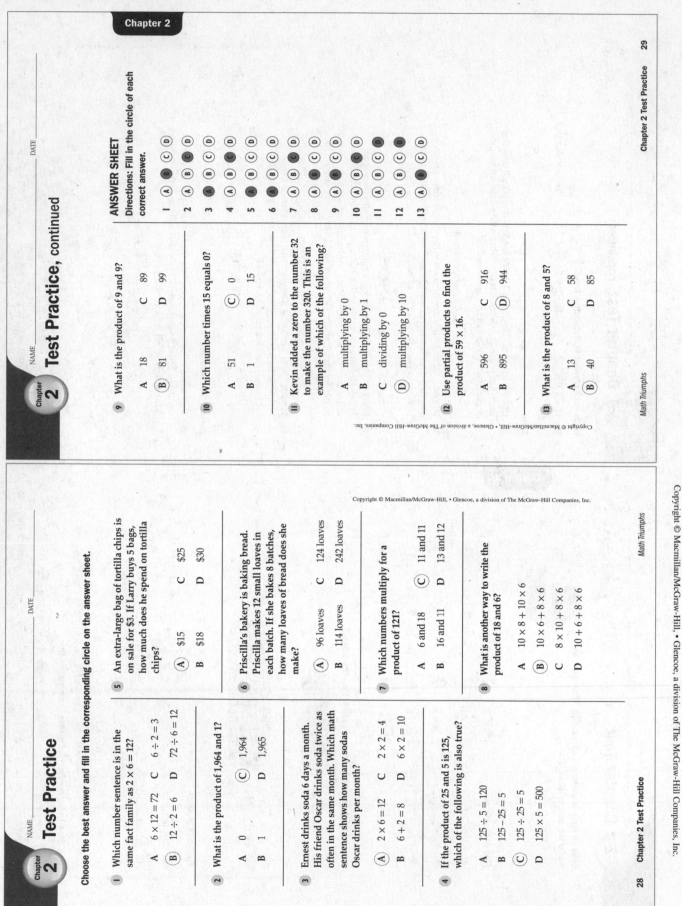

Chapter 2 Test Practice

Choose the best answer and fill in the corresponding circle on the answer sheet.

1 Which number sentence is in the same fact family as $2 \times 6 = 12$?

A $6 \times 12 = 72$ C $6 \div 2 = 3$

(B) $12 \div 2 = 6$ D $72 \div 6 = 12$

2 What is the product of 1,964 and 1?

A 0   (C) 1,964

B 1   D 1,965

3 Ernest drinks soda 6 days a month. His friend Oscar drinks soda twice as often in the same month. Which math sentence shows how many sodas Oscar drinks per month?

(A) $2 \times 6 = 12$ C $2 \times 2 = 4$

B $6 + 2 = 8$ D $6 \times 2 = 10$

4 If the product of 25 and 5 is 125, which of the following is also true?

A $125 \div 5 = 120$

B $125 - 25 = 5$

(C) $125 \div 25 = 5$

D $125 \times 5 = 500$

5 An extra-large bag of tortilla chips is on sale for $3. If Larry buys 5 bags, how much does he spend on tortilla chips?

(A) $15   C $25

B $18   D $30

6 Priscilla's bakery is baking bread. Priscilla makes 12 small loaves in each batch. If she bakes 8 batches, how many loaves of bread does she make?

(A) 96 loaves   C 124 loaves

B 114 loaves   D 242 loaves

7 Which numbers multiply for a product of 121?

A 6 and 18   (C) 11 and 11

B 16 and 11   D 13 and 12

8 What is another way to write the product of 18 and 6?

A $10 \times 8 + 10 \times 6$

(B) $10 \times 6 + 8 \times 6$

C $8 \times 10 + 8 \times 6$

D $10 + 6 + 8 \times 6$

28   Chapter 2 Test Practice   *Math Triumphs*

NAME _____ DATE _____

Chapter 2 Test Practice, continued

9 What is the product of 9 and 9?

A 18   C 89

(B) 81   D 99

10 Which number times 15 equals 0?

A 51   (C) 0

B 1   D 15

11 Kevin added a zero to the number 32 to make the number 320. This is an example of which of the following?

A multiplying by 0

B multiplying by 1

C dividing by 0

(D) multiplying by 10

12 Use partial products to find the product of 59×16.

A 596   C 916

B 895   (D) 944

13 What is the product of 8 and 5?

A 13   C 58

(B) 40   D 85

ANSWER SHEET

Directions: Fill in the circle of each correct answer.

1 (A) B C D
2 A B C D
3 (A) B C D
4 A B C D
5 A B C D
6 A B C D
7 A B C D
8 A B C D
9 A B C D
10 A B C D
11 A B C D
12 A B C D
13 A B C D

Math Triumphs   Chapter 2 Test Practice   29

A10   Grade 5 Chapter 2   *Math Triumphs*

Answers (Grade 5)

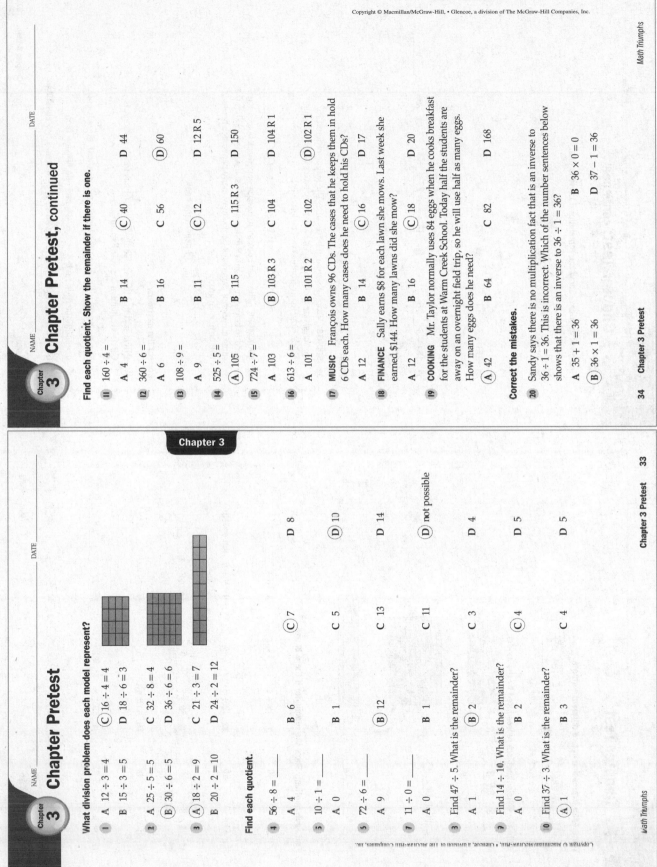

NAME _____ DATE _____

Chapter 3 — Chapter Pretest

What division problem does each model represent?

1. A 12 ÷ 3 = 4   **C** 16 ÷ 4 = 4
   B 15 ÷ 3 = 5   D 18 ÷ 6 = 3

2. A 25 ÷ 5 = 5   C 32 ÷ 8 = 4
   B 30 ÷ 6 = 5   D 36 ÷ 6 = 6

3. **A** 18 ÷ 2 = 9   C 21 ÷ 3 = 7
   B 20 ÷ 2 = 10   D 24 ÷ 2 = 12

Find each quotient.

4. 56 ÷ 8 = _____
   A 4   B 6   **C** 7   D 8

5. 10 ÷ 1 = _____
   A 0   B 1   C 5   **D** 10

6. 72 ÷ 6 = _____
   A 9   **B** 12   C 13   D 14

7. 11 ÷ 0 = _____
   A 0   B 1   C 11   **D** not possible

8. Find 47 ÷ 5. What is the remainder?
   A 1   **B** 2   C 3   D 4

9. Find 14 ÷ 10. What is the remainder?
   A 0   B 2   **C** 4   D 5

10. Find 37 ÷ 3. What is the remainder?
    A 1   B 3   C 4   D 5

NAME _____ DATE _____

Chapter 3 — Chapter Pretest, continued

Find each quotient. Show the remainder if there is one.

11. 160 ÷ 4 =
    A 4   B 14   **C** 40   D 44

12. 360 ÷ 6 =
    A 6   B 16   C 56   **D** 60

13. 108 ÷ 9 =
    A 9   B 11   **C** 12   D 12 R 5

14. 525 ÷ 5 =
    A 105   B 115   C 115 R 3   D 150

15. 724 ÷ 7 =
    A 103   **B** 103 R 3   C 104   D 104 R 1

16. 613 ÷ 6 =
    A 101   B 101 R 2   C 102   **D** 102 R 1

17. **MUSIC** François owns 96 CDs. The cases that he keeps them in hold 6 CDs each. How many cases does he need to hold his CDs?
    A 12   B 14   **C** 16   D 17

18. **FINANCE** Sally earns $8 for each lawn she mows. Last week she earned $144. How many lawns did she mow?
    A 12   B 16   **C** 18   D 20

19. **COOKING** Mr. Taylor normally uses 84 eggs when he cooks breakfast for the students at Warm Creek School. Today half the students are away on an overnight field trip, so he will use half as many eggs. How many eggs does he need?
    A 42   B 64   C 82   D 168

Correct the mistakes.

20. Sandy says there is no multiplication fact that is an inverse to 36 ÷ 1 = 36. This is incorrect. Which of the number sentences below shows that there is an inverse to 36 ÷ 1 = 36?
    A 35 + 1 = 36   B 36 × 0 = 0
    B 36 × 1 = 36   D 37 − 1 = 36

Answers (Grade 5)

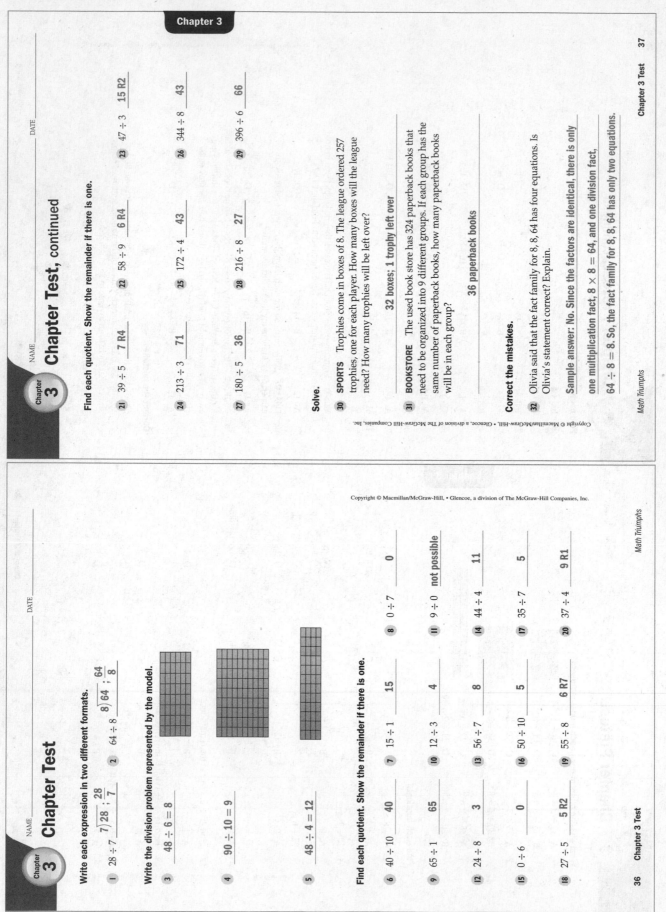

Chapter Test

NAME _____ DATE _____

Write each expression in two different formats.

1. $28 \div 7$ $7\overline{)28}$; $\dfrac{28}{7}$

2. $64 \div 8$ $8\overline{)64}$; $\dfrac{64}{8}$

Write the division problem represented by the model.

3. $48 \div 6 = 8$

4. $90 \div 10 = 9$

5. $48 \div 4 = 12$

Find each quotient. Show the remainder if there is one.

6. $40 \div 10$ **40**

7. $15 \div 1$ **15**

8. $0 \div 7$ **0**

9. $65 \div 1$ **65**

10. $12 \div 3$ **4**

11. $9 \div 0$ **not possible**

12. $24 \div 8$ **3**

13. $56 \div 7$ **8**

14. $44 \div 4$ **11**

15. $0 \div 6$ **0**

16. $50 \div 10$ **5**

17. $35 \div 7$ **5**

18. $27 \div 5$ **5 R2**

19. $55 \div 8$ **6 R7**

20. $37 \div 4$ **9 R1**

36   Chapter 3 Test

Math Triumphs

NAME _____ DATE _____

3 Chapter Test, continued

Find each quotient. Show the remainder if there is one.

21. $39 \div 5$ **7 R4**

22. $58 \div 9$ **6 R4**

23. $47 \div 3$ **15 R2**

24. $213 \div 3$ **71**

25. $172 \div 4$ **43**

26. $344 \div 8$ **43**

27. $180 \div 5$ **36**

28. $216 \div 8$ **27**

29. $396 \div 6$ **66**

Solve.

30. **SPORTS** Trophies come in boxes of 8. The league ordered 257 trophies, one for each player. How many boxes will the league need? How many trophies will be left over?

32 boxes; 1 trophy left over

31. **BOOKSTORE** The used book store has 324 paperback books that need to be organized into 9 different groups. If each group has the same number of paperback books, how many paperback books will be in each group?

36 paperback books

Correct the mistakes.

32. Olivia said that the fact family for 8, 8, 64 has four equations. Is Olivia's statement correct? Explain.

Sample answer: No. Since the factors are identical, there is only one multiplication fact, $8 \times 8 = 64$, and one division fact, $64 \div 8 = 8$. So, the fact family for 8, 8, 64 has only two equations.

Math Triumphs   Chapter 3 Test   37

Math Triumphs

Answers (Grade 5)

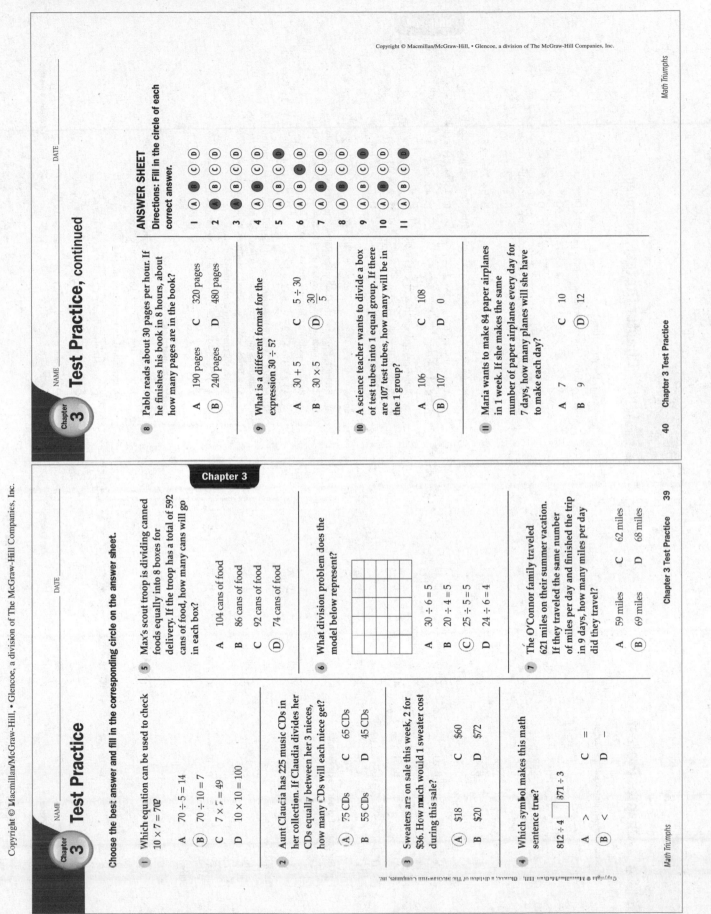

NAME _____ DATE _____

Chapter 3 Test Practice

Choose the best answer and fill in the corresponding circle on the answer sheet.

1 Which equation can be used to check
$10 \times 7 = 70$?

A $70 \div 5 = 14$

(B) $70 \div 10 = 7$

C $7 \times 7 = 49$

D $10 \times 10 = 100$

2 Max's scout troop is dividing canned foods equally into 8 boxes for delivery. If the troop has a total of 592 cans of food, how many cans will go in each box?

A 104 cans of food

B 86 cans of food

C 92 cans of food

(D) 74 cans of food

2 Aunt Claudia has 225 music CDs in her collection. If Claudia divides her CDs equally between her 3 nieces, how many CDs will each niece get?

(A) 75 CDs

B 55 CDs

C 65 CDs

D 45 CDs

3 Sweaters are on sale this week, 2 for $36. How much would 1 sweater cost during this sale?

(A) $18

B $20

C $60

D $72

4 Which symbol makes this math sentence true?

$812 \div 4 \ \boxed{} \ 371 \div 3$

A $>$

(B) $<$

C $=$

D $-$

5 What division problem does the model below represent?

A $30 \div 6 = 5$

B $20 \div 4 = 5$

(C) $25 \div 5 = 5$

D $24 \div 6 = 4$

6 What division problem does the model below represent?

A $30 \div 6 = 5$

B $20 \div 4 = 5$

(C) $25 \div 5 = 5$

D $24 \div 6 = 4$

7 The O'Connor family traveled 621 miles on their summer vacation. If they traveled the same number of miles per day and finished the trip in 9 days, how many miles per day did they travel?

A 59 miles

(B) 69 miles

C 62 miles

D 68 miles

NAME _____ DATE _____

Chapter 3 Test Practice, continued

8 Pablo reads about 30 pages per hour. If he finishes his book in 8 hours, about how many pages are in the book?

A 190 pages

(B) 240 pages

C 320 pages

D 480 pages

9 What is a different format for the expression $30 \div 5$?

A $30 + 5$

B 30×5

C $5 \div 30$

(D) $\dfrac{30}{5}$

10 A science teacher wants to divide a box of test tubes into 1 equal group. If there are 107 test tubes, how many will be in the 1 group?

A 106

(B) 107

C 108

D 0

11 Maria wants to make 84 paper airplanes in 1 week. If she makes the same number of paper airplanes every day for 7 days, how many planes will she have to make each day?

A 7

B 9

C 10

(D) 12

ANSWER SHEET
Directions: Fill in the circle of each correct answer.

1 (A) **(B)** (C) (D)
2 (A) **(B)** (C) (D)
3 **(A)** (B) (C) (D)
4 (A) **(B)** (C) (D)
5 **(A)** (B) (C) (D)
6 (A) (B) (C) **(D)**
7 **(A)** (B) (C) (D)
8 (A) **(B)** (C) (D)
9 (A) (B) (C) **(D)**
10 (A) **(B)** (C) (D)
11 (A) (B) (C) **(D)**

Answers (Grade 5)

Chapter 4 — Chapter Pretest, continued

NAME _____ DATE _____

Identify the properties.

13. Which number sentence is an example of the Distributive Property?
   A) $8 \times (3 + 10) = (8 \times 3) + (8 \times 10)$ *(circled)*
   B) $8 \times 0 = 0$
   C) $8 \times (3 \times 10) = (8 \times 3) \times 10$
   D) $8 \times 3 = 3 \times 8$

14. Which number sentence is an example of the Associative Property?
   A) $5 \times 7 + 5 \times 2 = 5 \times 9$
   B) $5 \times 1 = 5$
   C) $5 \times (7 \times 2) = (5 \times 7) \times 2$ *(circled)*
   D) $5 \times 7 = 7 \times 5$

15. Which number sentence is an example of the Commutative Property?
   A) $4 \times 9 + 4 \times 6 = 4 \times 15$
   B) $4 \times 1 = 4$
   C) $4 \times (9 \times 6) = (4 \times 9) \times 6$
   D) $4 \times 9 = 9 \times 4$ *(circled)*

16. Make the equation true. $26 \times (13 \times 58) =$
   A) $26 \times (10 \times 58 + 3 \times 50)$
   B) $(26 \times 13) \times 58$ *(circled)*
   C) $26 \times (13 + 58)$
   D) $(13 \times 20 + 6) \times 58$

Solve.

17. **FINANCE** To buy school supplies, Randy's mother will give him either $2 each week for 4 weeks or $4 each week for 2 weeks. Which number sentence compares the two choices?
   A) $2 \times 4 = 4 \times 2$ *(circled)*
   B) $2 \times 4 < 4 \times 2$
   C) $2 \times 4 > 4 \times 2$
   D) $2 \times 2 > 4 \times 2$

18. **SCHOOL** Mrs. Jefferson's class had 18 students. The first month, 2 students moved to a different school. For each of the next 2 months, Mrs. Jefferson's class gained 3 students. Which number sentence shows the change in students in her class?
   A) $18 \times (3 - 2) + 2 = 20$
   B) $18 - 2 + 2 \times 3 = 22$ *(circled)*
   C) $18 - (2 + 2) \times 3 = 18$
   D) $(18 - 2 + 2) \times 3 = 56$

Correct the mistakes.

19. Maria says that the Associative Property allows her to rewrite 15×7 as $10 \times 7 + 5 \times 7$. Did she make a mistake?
   A) No, she didn't make any mistake.
   B) Yes, she used the wrong order of operations.
   C) Yes, she is actually using the Distributive Property. *(circled)*
   D) Yes, she is actually using the Commutative Property.

Math Triumphs
Chapter 4 Pretest   45

Chapter 4 — Chapter Pretest

NAME _____ DATE _____

Which number completes each equation?

1. $6 + 9 = \underline{\quad} + 6$
   A) 3 B) 6 C) 9 *(circled)* D) 15

2. $5 \times 4 = \underline{\quad} \times 5$
   A) 4 *(circled)* B) 5 C) 9 D) 20

3. $(9 \times 3) \times 2 = 9 \times (\underline{\quad} \times 2)$
   A) 2 B) 3 *(circled)* C) 6 D) 9

4. $3 \times 14 = \underline{\quad} \times 3$
   A) 3 B) 11 C) 14 *(circled)* D) 17

5. $19 + 8 = \underline{\quad} + 19$
   A) 8 *(circled)* B) 11 C) 19 D) 27

6. $(17 + 16) + 4 = 17 + (16 + \underline{\quad})$
   A) 4 *(circled)* B) 16 C) 17 D) 20

Find the product of each expression.

7. $2 \times 7 \times 5$
   A) 14 B) 35 C) 60 D) 70 *(circled)*

8. $8 \times (10 + 6)$
   A) 96 B) 128 *(circled)* C) 140 D) 148

9. $7 \times (6 + 8)$
   A) 98 *(circled)* B) 100 C) 196 D) 336

Solve.

10. $17 - (7 - 4) \times 2 + 3 \times 5$
   A) 16 B) 23 C) 26 *(circled)* D) 55

11. $6 + 8 \times 2 - (10 - 7)$
   A) 15 B) 16 C) 19 *(circled)* D) 24

12. $9 + (2 + 1) \times 3 + 8 \times 10 \div 2$
   A) 49 B) 57 C) 58 *(circled)* D) 76

44   Chapter 4 Pretest

Math Triumphs

A14   Grade 5 Chapter 4

Answers (Grade 5)

NAME _____ DATE _____

Chapter 4 — Chapter Test

Use the Commutative Properties of Addition and Multiplication to fill in each blank with the correct value. Check your answer.

1. $5 \times 7 = \underline{} \times 5$ **7**
   $35 = \underline{}$ **35**

2. $\underline{} + 6 = 6 + 12$ **12**
   $\underline{} = \underline{}$ **18; 18**

3. $8 + 7 = \underline{} + \underline{}$ **7; 8**
   $\underline{} = \underline{}$ **15; 15**

4. $12 \times 4 = \underline{} \times \underline{}$ **4; 12**
   $\underline{} = \underline{}$ **48; 48**

5. Give an example of the Commutative Property of Addition. Check your example.
   Sample answer: $6 + 5 = 5 + 6$; $11 = 11$

Use the Associative Property to fill in each blank. Check your answer.

6. $5 \times (5 \times 10)$
   $= (\underline{} \times 5) \times 10$ **5**
   $= \underline{} \times 10$ **25**
   $= \underline{}$ **250**

7. $8 + (13 + 2)$
   $= (\underline{} + 2) + 13$ **8**
   $= \underline{} + 13$ **10**
   $= \underline{}$ **23**

8. $3 + (15 + 17)$
   $= (\underline{} + \underline{}) + \underline{}$ **3; 15; 17**
   $= \underline{} + \underline{}$ **18; 17**
   $= \underline{}$ **35**

9. $4 \times (6 \times 5)$
   $= (\underline{} \times \underline{}) \times \underline{}$ **4; 6; 5**
   $= \underline{} \times \underline{}$ **24; 5**
   $= \underline{}$ **120**

10. Give an example of the Associative Property of Multiplication. Check your answer.
    Sample answer: $(5 \times 4) \times 5 = 5 \times (4 \times 5)$; $20 \times 5 = 5 \times 20$; $100 = 100$

Use the Distributive Property of Multiplication to find each product.

11. $7 \times (3 + 4)$
    _____ **49**

12. $3 \times (15 - 7)$
    _____ **24**

Find the value of each expression.

13. $15 \div 3 + 3 \times 7 - (14 - 6)$
    _____ **14**

14. $((15 - 5) \div 5) \div 2 + (12 + 8)$
    _____ **21**

NAME _____ DATE _____

Chapter 4 — Chapter Test, continued

Solve.

15. **JUICE** Lionel wants to make 2 gallons of punch for a party at school. Each gallon requires 2 cans of juice, and each can of juice costs $2.50. How much will the punch cost?   **$10.00**

16. **PACKAGING** Mrs. Lopez bought 4 packages of hot dogs with 8 hot dogs in each package. Mr. Ruiz bought 5 packages of hamburgers with 6 hamburgers in each package. Who bought more food?
    $4 \times 8 = 32$ hot dogs; $5 \times 6 = 30$ hamburgers; Mrs. Lopez bought more food.

17. **MOVIES** Anna watched two 50-minute history videos last week and three 40-minute science videos this week. How many minutes did she spend watching videos during both weeks?   **220 minutes**

18. **BASEBALL** The baseball team stored their baseballs in boxes. Five boxes had 3 baseballs in each box, and two boxes had 4 baseballs in each box. For one game they used 11 baseballs. What is the total number of baseballs left?
    12 baseballs

Correct the mistakes.

19. **LIGHTBULBS** Rita went to the hardware store and purchased 6 boxes of the lightbulbs labeled "box A." Her friend Ava went to the discount store and purchased 4 boxes of the lightbulbs labeled "box B." Rita told Ava that she bought more lightbulbs because she bought more boxes. What mistake did Rita make?
    They actually bought the same number of lightbulbs. Rita was only counting the number of boxes. She needed to also consider the number of lightbulbs in each box; $6 \times 4 = 4 \times 6$.

20. **BAKERY** At the Bake Shop, the baker had 7 dozen rolls in a case. Two customers purchased 2 dozen rolls each, and 3 dozen more went to another customer. The baker then brought out 4 more dozen rolls but dropped 1 dozen on the floor, so they had to be thrown away. The baker exclaimed, "Now we only have 5 dozen rolls to sell." Was the baker correct? Explain.
    No. They have 3 dozen rolls left to sell.
    $7 - (2 \times 2) - 3 + 4 - 1 = 3$

48   Chapter 4 Test

Answers (Grade 5)

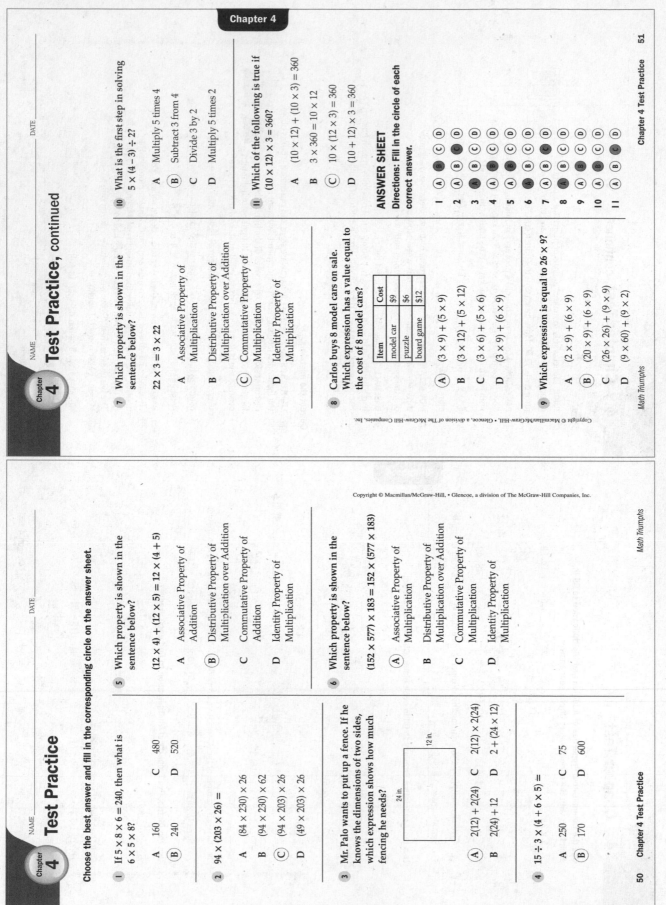

Chapter 4

NAME _____ DATE _____

Chapter 4 Test Practice

Choose the best answer and fill in the corresponding circle on the answer sheet.

1. If $5 \times 8 \times 6 = 240$, then what is $6 \times 5 \times 8$?

- A 160
- **B 240**
- C 480
- D 520

2. $94 \times (203 \times 26) =$

- A $(84 \times 230) \times 26$
- B $(94 \times 230) \times 62$
- **C $(94 \times 203) \times 26$**
- D $(49 \times 203) \times 26$

3. Mr. Palo wants to put up a fence. If he knows the dimensions of two sides, which expression shows how much fencing he needs?

24 in.
12 in.

- **A $2(12) + 2(24)$**
- B $2(24) + 12$
- C $2(12) \times 2(24)$
- D $2 + (24 \times 12)$

4. $15 \div 3 \times (4 + 6 \times 5) =$

- A 250
- **B 170**
- C 75
- D 600

5. Which property is shown in the sentence below?

$(12 \times 4) + (12 \times 5) = 12 \times (4 + 5)$

- A Associative Property of Addition
- **B Distributive Property of Multiplication over Addition**
- C Commutative Property of Addition
- D Identity Property of Multiplication

6. Which property is shown in the sentence below?

$(152 \times 577) \times 183 = 152 \times (577 \times 183)$

- **A Associative Property of Multiplication**
- B Distributive Property of Multiplication over Addition
- C Commutative Property of Multiplication
- D Identity Property of Multiplication

NAME _____ DATE _____

Test Practice, continued

7. Which property is shown in the sentence below?

$22 \times 3 = 3 \times 22$

- A Associative Property of Multiplication
- B Distributive Property of Multiplication over Addition
- **C Commutative Property of Multiplication**
- D Identity Property of Multiplication

8. Carlos buys 8 model cars on sale. Which expression has a value equal to the cost of 8 model cars?

Item	Cost
model car	$9
puzzle	$6
board game	$12

- **A $(3 \times 9) + (5 \times 9)$**
- B $(3 \times 12) + (5 \times 12)$
- C $(3 \times 6) + (5 \times 6)$
- D $(3 \times 9) + (6 \times 9)$

9. Which expression is equal to 26×9?

- A $(2 \times 9) + (6 \times 9)$
- **B $(20 \times 9) + (6 \times 9)$**
- C $(26 \times 26) + (9 \times 9)$
- D $(9 \times 60) + (9 \times 2)$

10. What is the first step in solving $5 \times (4 - 3) \div 2$?

- A Multiply 5 times 4
- **B Subtract 3 from 4**
- C Divide 3 by 2
- D Multiply 5 times 2

11. Which of the following is true if $(10 \times 12) \times 3 = 360$?

- A $(10 \times 12) + (10 \times 3) = 360$
- B $3 \times 360 = 10 \times 12$
- **C $10 \times (12 \times 3) = 360$**
- D $(10 + 12) \times 3 = 360$

ANSWER SHEET
Directions: Fill in the circle of each correct answer.

1. (A) **(B)** (C) (D)
2. (A) (B) (C) **(D)**
3. **(A)** (B) (C) (D)
4. (A) (B) **(C)** (D)
5. (A) **(B)** (C) (D)
6. **(A)** (B) (C) (D)
7. (A) (B) **(C)** (D)
8. **(A)** (B) (C) (D)
9. (A) **(B)** (C) (D)
10. (A) **(B)** (C) (D)
11. (A) (B) **(C)** (D)

Answers (Grade 5)

Book 1

Book Test

Identify the place of each underlined digit. Fill in the chart to help you.

1. 9,012

thousands	hundreds	ones	tens
1,000	100	10	1

A ones   C hundreds
B tens   (D) thousands

2. 7,413

thousands	hundreds	ones	tens
1,000	100	10	1

(A) ones   C hundreds
B tens   D thousands

Answer the following questions.

3. What is 5,412,091 in word form?
A five million, four hundred twelve thousand, nine hundred ten
B fifty-four million, twelve thousand, ninety-one
(C) five million, four hundred twelve thousand, ninety-one
D five million, forty-one thousand, two hundred ninety-one

4. What are the next two numbers in the pattern below?

Number of Liters	1	2	3	4
Number of Milliliters	1,000	2,000		

A 1,100; 1,200   C 2,000; 4,000
B 2,000; 3,000   (D) 3,000; 4,000

5. How many cookies are in 3 dozen?
A 30   B 32   (C) 36   D 38

Find each product.

5. 8 × 9 =
(A) 72   B 78   C 89   D 98

7. 11 × 12 =
A 110   B 120   C 130   (D) 132

8. 13 × 0 =
A 13   B 1,300   (C) 0   D 130

9. 145 × 2 =
A 147   B 245   (C) 290   D 1,452

Book 1 Test

Book 1

Book Test, continued

Find each quotient.

10. 145 ÷ 29 =
A 0   B 3   (C) 5   D 10

11. 72 ÷ 9 =
A 7   (B) 8   C 9   D 10

12. 60 ÷ 3 =
(A) 20   B 30   C 36   D 57

13. 72 ÷ 6 =
A 10   B 11   (C) 12   D 13

Answer the following questions below.

14. Which operation is the inverse of division?
A division   B addition   C subtraction   (D) multiplication

15. 3 × (4 − 1) =
A 8   (B) 9   C 11   D 15

16. (15 − 15) × 6 + 3 =
A 0   (B) 3   C 78   D 93

17. Which property is shown in the sentence below?
3 + (17 + 1) = (3 + 17) + 1
(A) Associative Property   B Commutative Property   C Order of Operations   D Distributive Property

18. 12 × (5 + 9) =
A (10 × 5) + (2 × 9)   B 12 × 5 × 9   C 5 × 12 + 5 × 9   (D) 12 × 5 + 12 × 9

19. 139 × 47 =
A 139 + 47   B (100 + 39) × (40 − 7)   (C) 47 × 139   D (139 × 1) + (47 × 0)

Answers (Grade 5)

Book 2 — Book Pretest, continued

NAME _____ DATE _____

Answer the following questions.

11. Which fraction does the shaded part of the model represent?

    A $\frac{9}{14}$ B $\frac{8}{14}$ C $\frac{7}{14}$ D $\frac{5}{14}$

12. Which number in the fraction $\frac{13}{24}$ represents the number of equal parts into which an object is divided?

    A 1   B 2   C 13   (D) 24

13. The least common multiple of the denominators of two or more fractions is referred to as the _____.

    A least common multiple   C greatest common factor
    B least common denominator   D equivalent fraction

14. Write $4\frac{1}{6}$ as an improper fraction.

    (A) $\frac{25}{6}$ B $\frac{24}{6}$ C $\frac{11}{6}$ D $\frac{10}{6}$

15. Which fraction is equal to 1?

    A $\frac{26}{27}$ (B) $\frac{27}{27}$ C $\frac{28}{27}$ D $\frac{27}{1}$

16. Write $\frac{19}{7}$ as a mixed number.

    A $2\frac{4}{7}$ (B) $2\frac{5}{7}$ C $5\frac{2}{7}$ D $7\frac{2}{5}$

17. Select the equivalent decimal and mixed number for six and four tenths.

    A $6.04; 6\frac{4}{100}$ B $6.04; 6\frac{1}{25}$ C $6.04; 6\frac{2}{50}$ (D) $6.64; 6\frac{4}{10}$

18. **PAINTING** Javon, Nissa, Lulu, and Marcus each painted an unfinished wooden toy. Javon used $\frac{2}{3}$ of his paint, Nissa used $\frac{1}{4}$ of her paint, Lulu used $\frac{1}{6}$ of her paint, and Marcus used $\frac{1}{2}$ of his paint. Who used the greatest amount of paint?

    (A) Javon   B Nissa   C Lulu   D Marcus

19. **LANDSCAPING** Samantha needs mulch for her gardens. She usually needs $\frac{1}{2}$ bag for the front gardens and $\frac{2}{3}$ bag for the back gardens. How many total bags of mulch does she need?

    A $\frac{3}{5}$ B $\frac{4}{5}$ C $\frac{5}{6}$ (D) $1\frac{1}{6}$

Math Triumphs

Book 2 — Book Pretest

NAME _____ DATE _____

Solve.

1. $\frac{3}{7} - \frac{1}{14} =$

   A $\frac{3}{14}$ (B) $\frac{5}{14}$ C $\frac{7}{14}$ D $\frac{5}{7}$

2. $\frac{4}{5} - \frac{2}{3} =$

   A $\frac{1}{15}$ (B) $\frac{2}{15}$ C $\frac{1}{3}$ D $\frac{4}{15}$

3. $\frac{5}{11} + \frac{3}{11} =$

   A $\frac{2}{11}$ B $\frac{4}{11}$ C $\frac{6}{11}$ (D) $\frac{8}{11}$

4. $\frac{5}{8} - \frac{3}{8} =$

   A 2   B $\frac{8}{8}$ C 1   (D) $\frac{1}{4}$

5. Add. Write the sum in simplest form.

   $\frac{3}{8} + \frac{5}{12} =$

   A $\frac{3}{4}$ (B) $\frac{19}{24}$ C $\frac{5}{6}$ D $\frac{7}{8}$

6. $0.67 - 0.4 =$

   (A) 0.27   B 0.37   C 0.63   D 1.07

7. $5.94 + 3.82 =$

   A 8.66   B 8.76   (C) 9.76   D 9.86

Order the following numbers from least to greatest.

8. $\frac{2}{5}, \frac{1}{7}, \frac{3}{2}$

   A $\frac{2}{5}, \frac{1}{7}, \frac{3}{2}$ B $\frac{1}{2}, \frac{3}{7}, \frac{2}{5}$ (C) $\frac{2}{5}, \frac{3}{7}, \frac{1}{2}$ D $\frac{3}{7}, \frac{1}{2}, \frac{2}{5}$

9. $\frac{3}{4}, \frac{4}{5}, \frac{2}{3}, \frac{1}{2}$

   A $\frac{4}{5}, \frac{3}{4}, \frac{2}{3}, \frac{1}{2}$ C $\frac{1}{2}, \frac{3}{4}, \frac{4}{5}, \frac{2}{3}$
   (B) $\frac{1}{2}, \frac{2}{3}, \frac{3}{4}, \frac{4}{5}$ D $\frac{2}{3}, \frac{1}{2}, \frac{3}{4}, \frac{4}{5}$

10. 0.25, 0.05, 0.52

    A 0.52, 0.05, 0.25   B 0.05, 0.52, 0.25   C 0.25, 0.05, 0.52   (D) 0.05, 0.25, 0.52

Math Triumphs

Math Triumphs

Answers (Grade 5)

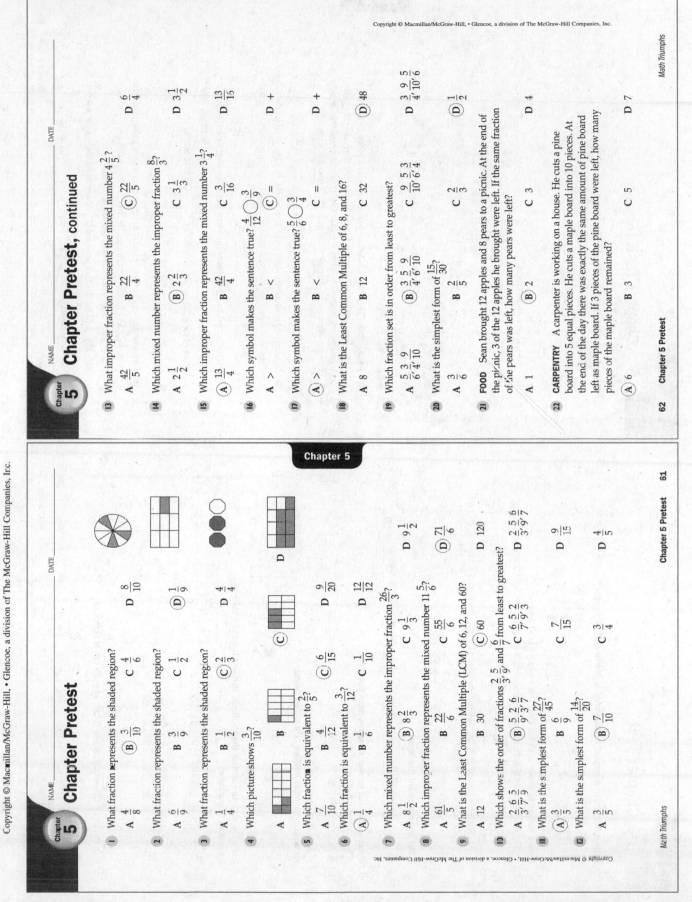

NAME _____ DATE _____

Chapter 5 — Chapter Pretest, continued

13. What improper fraction represents the mixed number $4\frac{2}{5}$?
A $\frac{42}{5}$ B $\frac{22}{4}$ C $\frac{22}{5}$ D $\frac{6}{4}$

14. Which mixed number represents the improper fraction $\frac{8}{3}$?
A $2\frac{1}{2}$ B $2\frac{2}{3}$ C $3\frac{1}{3}$ D $3\frac{1}{2}$

15. Which improper fraction represents the mixed number $3\frac{1}{4}$?
A $\frac{13}{4}$ B $\frac{42}{4}$ C $\frac{3}{16}$ D $\frac{13}{15}$

16. Which symbol makes the sentence true? $\frac{4}{12} \bigcirc \frac{3}{9}$
A > B < C = D +

17. Which symbol makes the sentence true? $\frac{5}{6} \bigcirc \frac{3}{4}$
A > B < C = D +

18. What is the Least Common Multiple of 6, 8, and 16?
A 8 B 12 C 32 D 48

19. Which fraction set is in order from least to greatest?
A $\frac{5}{6}, \frac{3}{4}, \frac{9}{10}$ B $\frac{3}{4}, \frac{5}{6}, \frac{9}{10}$ C $\frac{9}{10}, \frac{5}{6}, \frac{3}{4}$ D $\frac{3}{4}, \frac{9}{10}, \frac{5}{6}$

20. What is the simplest form of $\frac{15}{30}$?
A $\frac{3}{6}$ B $\frac{2}{5}$ C $\frac{2}{3}$ D $\frac{1}{2}$

21. FOOD Sean brought 12 apples and 8 pears to a picnic. At the end of the picnic, 3 of the 12 apples he brought were left. If the same fraction of the pears was left, how many pears were left?
A 1 B 2 C 3 D 4

22. CARPENTRY A carpenter is working on a house. He cuts a pine board into 5 equal pieces. He cuts a maple board into 10 pieces. At the end of the day there was exactly the same amount of pine board left as maple board. If 3 pieces of the pine board were left, how many pieces of the maple board remained?
A 6 B 3 C 5 D 7

NAME _____ DATE _____

Chapter 5 — Chapter Pretest

1. What fraction represents the shaded region?
A $\frac{4}{8}$ B $\frac{3}{10}$ C $\frac{4}{6}$ D $\frac{8}{10}$

2. What fraction represents the shaded region?
A $\frac{6}{9}$ B $\frac{3}{9}$ C $\frac{1}{2}$ D $\frac{1}{9}$

3. What fraction represents the shaded region?
A $\frac{1}{4}$ B $\frac{1}{2}$ C $\frac{2}{3}$ D $\frac{4}{4}$

4. Which picture shows $\frac{3}{10}$?

5. Which fraction is equivalent to $\frac{2}{5}$?
A $\frac{7}{10}$ B $\frac{4}{12}$ C $\frac{6}{15}$ D $\frac{9}{20}$

6. Which fraction is equivalent to $\frac{3}{12}$?
A $\frac{1}{4}$ B $\frac{1}{6}$ C $\frac{1}{10}$ D $\frac{12}{12}$

7. Which mixed number represents the improper fraction $\frac{26}{3}$?
A $8\frac{1}{2}$ B $8\frac{2}{3}$ C $9\frac{1}{3}$ D $9\frac{1}{2}$

8. Which improper fraction represents the mixed number $11\frac{5}{6}$?
A $\frac{61}{5}$ B $\frac{22}{6}$ C $\frac{55}{6}$ D $\frac{71}{6}$

9. What is the Least Common Multiple (LCM) of 6, 12, and 60?
A 12 B 30 C 60 D 120

10. Which shows the order of fractions $\frac{2}{3}, \frac{5}{9}$, and $\frac{6}{7}$ from least to greatest?
A $\frac{2}{3}, \frac{6}{9}, \frac{5}{7}$ B $\frac{5}{9}, \frac{2}{3}, \frac{6}{7}$ C $\frac{6}{7}, \frac{5}{9}, \frac{2}{3}$ D $\frac{2}{3}, \frac{5}{9}, \frac{6}{7}$

11. What is the simplest form of $\frac{27}{45}$?
A $\frac{3}{5}$ B $\frac{6}{9}$ C $\frac{7}{15}$ D $\frac{9}{15}$

12. What is the simplest form of $\frac{14}{20}$?
A $\frac{3}{5}$ B $\frac{7}{10}$ C $\frac{3}{4}$ D $\frac{4}{5}$

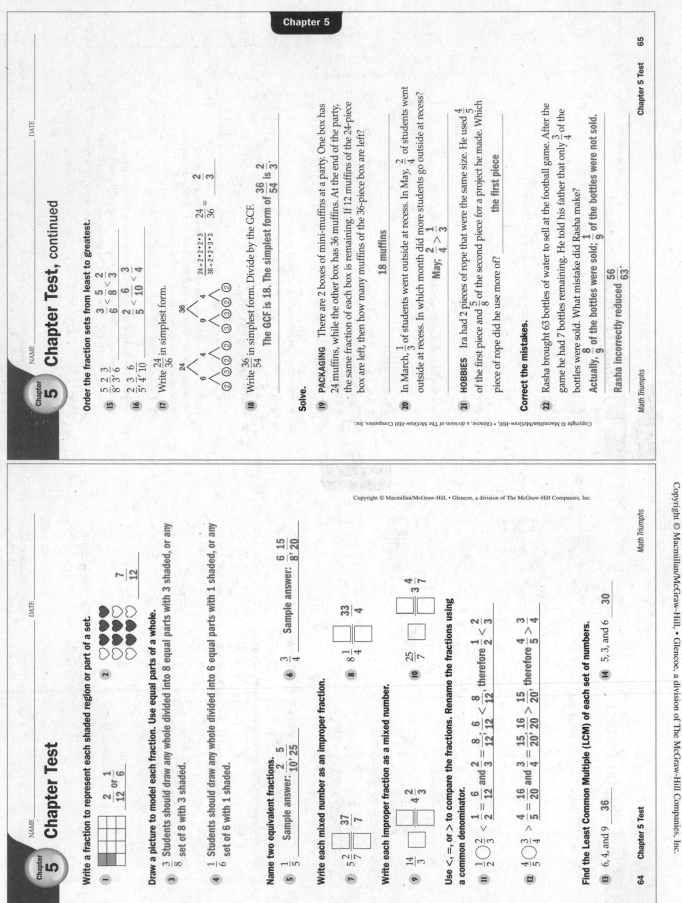

Chapter 5

NAME _____ DATE _____

Chapter 5 Chapter Test, continued

Order the fraction sets from least to greatest.

15. $\frac{5}{8}, \frac{5}{3}, \frac{3}{6}$ $\frac{3}{6} < \frac{5}{8} < \frac{2}{3}$

16. $\frac{2}{5}, \frac{3}{4}, \frac{6}{10}$ $\frac{2}{5} < \frac{6}{10} < \frac{3}{4}$

17. Write $\frac{24}{36}$ in simplest form.

$24 = 2 \cdot 2 \cdot 2 \cdot 3$
$36 = 2 \cdot 2 \cdot 3 \cdot 3$
$\frac{24}{36} = \frac{2}{3}$

18. Write $\frac{36}{54}$ in simplest form. Divide by the GCF.

The GCF is 18. The simplest form of $\frac{36}{54}$ is $\frac{2}{3}$.

Solve.

19. **PACKAGING** There are 2 boxes of mini-muffins at a party. One box has 24 muffins, while the other box has 36 muffins. At the end of the party, the same fraction of each box is remaining. If 12 muffins of the 24-piece box are left, then how many muffins of the 36-piece box are left?

18 muffins

20. In March, $\frac{1}{3}$ of students went outside at recess. In May, $\frac{2}{4}$ of students went outside at recess. In which month did more students go outside at recess?

May; $\frac{2}{4} > \frac{1}{3}$

21. **HOBBIES** Ira had 2 pieces of rope that were the same size. He used $\frac{4}{5}$ of the first piece and $\frac{5}{8}$ of the second piece for a project he made. Which piece of rope did he use more of?

the first piece

Correct the mistakes.

22. Rasha brought 63 bottles of water to sell at the football game. After the game he had 7 bottles remaining. He told his father that only $\frac{3}{4}$ of the bottles were sold. What mistake did Rasha make?

Actually, $\frac{8}{9}$ of the bottles were sold; $\frac{1}{9}$ of the bottles were not sold.

Rasha incorrectly reduced $\frac{56}{63}$.

Math Triumphs   Chapter 5 Test   65

NAME _____ DATE _____

Chapter 5 Chapter Test

Write a fraction to represent each shaded region or part of a set. Use equal parts of a whole.

1. $\frac{2}{12}$ or $\frac{1}{6}$

2. $\frac{7}{12}$

Draw a picture to model each fraction.

3. $\frac{3}{8}$ Students should draw any whole divided into 8 equal parts with 3 shaded, or any set of 8 with 3 shaded.

4. $\frac{1}{6}$ Students should draw any whole divided into 6 equal parts with 1 shaded, or any set of 6 with 1 shaded.

Name two equivalent fractions.

5. $\frac{1}{5}$ Sample answer: $\frac{2}{10}, \frac{5}{25}$

6. $\frac{3}{4}$ Sample answer: $\frac{6}{8}, \frac{15}{20}$

Write each mixed number as an improper fraction.

7. $5\frac{2}{7}$ $\frac{37}{7}$

8. $8\frac{1}{4}$ $\frac{33}{4}$

Write each improper fraction as a mixed number.

9. $\frac{14}{3}$ $4\frac{2}{3}$

10. $\frac{25}{7}$ $3\frac{4}{7}$

Use <, =, or > to compare the fractions. Rename the fractions using a common denominator.

11. $\frac{1}{2} \bigcirc \frac{2}{3}$ $\frac{1}{2} = \frac{6}{12}$ and $\frac{2}{3} = \frac{8}{12}, \frac{6}{12} < \frac{8}{12}$, therefore $\frac{1}{2} < \frac{2}{3}$

12. $\frac{4}{5} \bigcirc \frac{3}{4}$ $\frac{4}{5} = \frac{16}{20}$ and $\frac{3}{4} = \frac{15}{20}, \frac{16}{20} > \frac{15}{20}$, therefore $\frac{4}{5} > \frac{3}{4}$

Find the Least Common Multiple (LCM) of each set of numbers.

13. 6, 4, and 9   36

14. 5, 3, and 6   30

64   Chapter 5 Test

Math Triumphs

Answers (Grade 5)

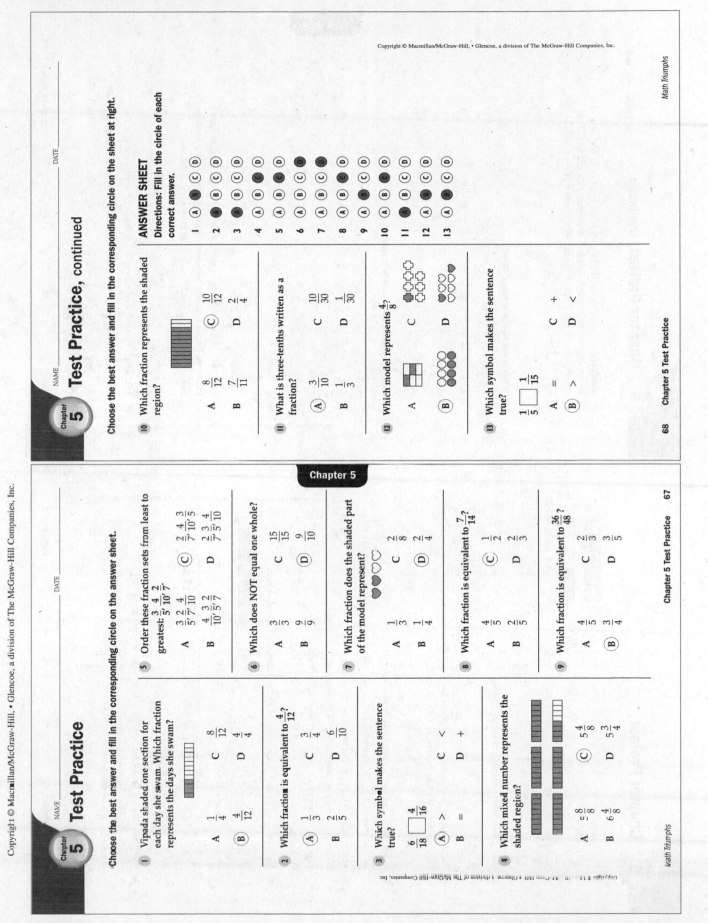

Answers (Grade 5)

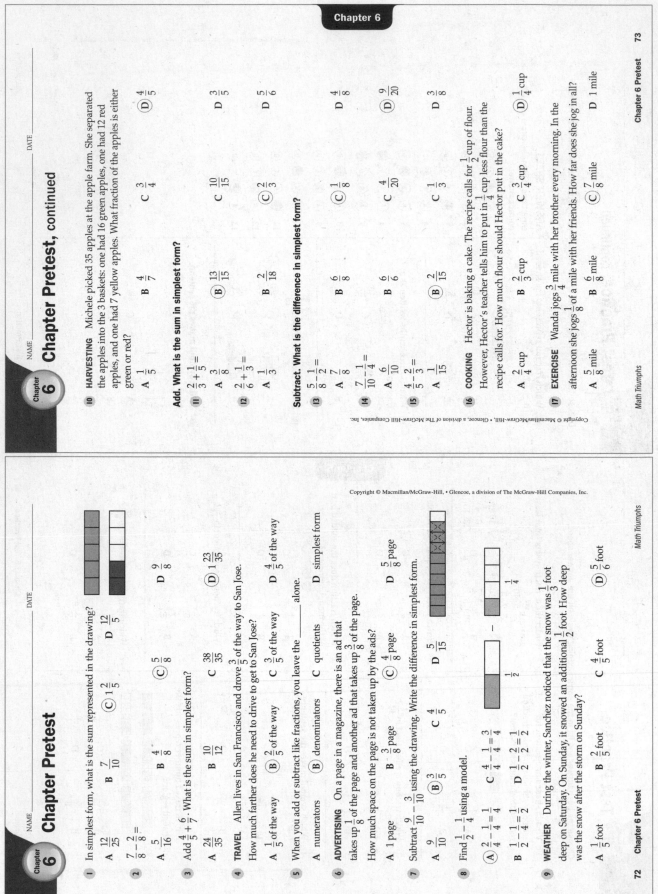

Chapter 6 — Chapter Pretest

NAME _____ DATE _____

1. In simplest form, what is the sum represented in the drawing?

A $\frac{12}{25}$ B $\frac{7}{10}$ **C** $1\frac{2}{5}$ D $\frac{12}{5}$

2. $\frac{7}{8} - \frac{2}{8} =$

A $\frac{5}{16}$ B $\frac{4}{8}$ **C** $\frac{5}{8}$ D $\frac{9}{8}$

3. Add $\frac{4}{5} + \frac{6}{7}$. What is the sum in simplest form?

A $\frac{24}{35}$ B $\frac{10}{12}$ C $\frac{38}{35}$ **D** $1\frac{23}{35}$

4. TRAVEL Allen lives in San Francisco and drove $\frac{2}{5}$ of the way to San Jose. How much farther does he need to drive to get to San Jose?

A $\frac{1}{5}$ of the way   **B** $\frac{2}{5}$ of the way   C $\frac{3}{5}$ of the way   D $\frac{4}{5}$ of the way

5. When you add or subtract like fractions, you leave the _____ alone.

A numerators   **B** denominators   C quotients   D simplest form

6. ADVERTISING On a page in a magazine, there is an ad that takes up $\frac{1}{8}$ of the page and another ad that takes up $\frac{3}{8}$ of the page. How much space on the page is not taken up by the ads?

A 1 page   B $\frac{3}{8}$ page   **C** $\frac{4}{8}$ page   D $\frac{5}{8}$ page

7. Subtract $\frac{9}{10} - \frac{3}{10}$ using the drawing. Write the difference in simplest form.

A $\frac{9}{10}$ **B** $\frac{3}{5}$ C $\frac{4}{5}$ D $\frac{5}{15}$

8. Find $\frac{1}{2} - \frac{1}{4}$ using a model.

A $\frac{2}{4} - \frac{1}{4} = \frac{1}{4}$ B $\frac{1}{2} - \frac{1}{4} = \frac{1}{2}$ C $\frac{4}{4} - \frac{4}{4} = \frac{3}{4}$ D $\frac{2}{2} - \frac{2}{2} = \frac{1}{2}$

9. WEATHER During the winter, Sanchez noticed that the snow was $\frac{1}{3}$ foot deep on Saturday. On Sunday, it snowed an additional $\frac{1}{2}$ foot. How deep was the snow after the storm on Sunday?

A $\frac{1}{5}$ foot   B $\frac{2}{5}$ foot   C $\frac{4}{5}$ foot   **D** $\frac{5}{6}$ foot

72   Chapter 6 Pretest   *Math Triumphs*

Chapter 6 — Chapter Pretest, continued

NAME _____ DATE _____

10. HARVESTING Michele picked 35 apples at the apple farm. She separated the apples into the 3 baskets: one had 16 green apples, one had 12 red apples, and one had 7 yellow apples. What fraction of the apples is either green or red?

A $\frac{1}{5}$ B $\frac{4}{7}$ C $\frac{3}{4}$ **D** $\frac{4}{5}$

Add. What is the sum in simplest form?

11. $\frac{2}{3} + \frac{1}{5} =$

A $\frac{3}{8}$ **B** $\frac{13}{15}$ C $\frac{10}{15}$ D $\frac{3}{5}$

12. $\frac{2}{6} + \frac{1}{3} =$

A $\frac{1}{3}$ B $\frac{2}{18}$ **C** $\frac{2}{3}$ D $\frac{5}{6}$

Subtract. What is the difference in simplest form?

13. $\frac{5}{8} - \frac{1}{2} =$

A $\frac{7}{8}$ B $\frac{6}{8}$ **C** $\frac{1}{8}$ D $\frac{4}{8}$

14. $\frac{7}{10} - \frac{1}{4} =$

A $\frac{6}{10}$ B $\frac{6}{6}$ C $\frac{4}{20}$ **D** $\frac{9}{20}$

15. $\frac{4}{5} - \frac{2}{3} =$

A $\frac{1}{15}$ **B** $\frac{2}{15}$ C $\frac{1}{3}$ D $\frac{3}{8}$

16. COOKING Hector is baking a cake. The recipe calls for $\frac{1}{2}$ cup of flour. However, Hector's teacher tells him to put in $\frac{1}{4}$ cup less flour than the recipe calls for. How much flour should Hector put in the cake?

A $\frac{2}{4}$ cup   B $\frac{2}{3}$ cup   C $\frac{3}{4}$ cup   **D** $\frac{1}{4}$ cup

17. EXERCISE Wanda jogs $\frac{3}{4}$ mile with her brother every morning. In the afternoon she jogs $\frac{1}{8}$ of a mile with her friends. How far does she jog in all?

A $\frac{5}{8}$ mile   B $\frac{6}{8}$ mile   **C** $\frac{7}{8}$ mile   D 1 mile

Math Triumphs   Chapter 6 Pretest   73

Math Triumphs

Answers (Grade 5)

Chapter 6 — Chapter Test

NAME _____ DATE _____

Add. Write each sum in simplest form.

1. $\frac{4}{8} + \frac{2}{8} = \frac{6}{8} = \frac{3}{4}$

2. $\frac{3}{9} + \frac{3}{9} = \frac{6}{9} = \frac{2}{3}$

3. $\frac{3}{4} + \frac{1}{3} = \frac{9}{12} + \frac{4}{12} = \frac{13}{12} = 1\frac{1}{12}$

4. $\frac{2}{7} + \frac{4}{14} = \frac{4}{14} + \frac{4}{14} = \frac{8}{14} = \frac{4}{7}$

Subtract. Write each difference in simplest form.

5. $\frac{7}{8} - \frac{5}{8} = \frac{2}{8} = \frac{1}{4}$

6. $\frac{5}{10} - \frac{2}{10} = \frac{3}{10}$

7. $\frac{6}{12} - \frac{4}{12} = \frac{2}{12} = \frac{1}{6}$

8. $\frac{8}{20} - \frac{4}{20} = \frac{4}{20} = \frac{2}{10} = \frac{1}{5}$

Add or subtract. Write each answer in simplest form.

9. $\frac{9}{10} - \frac{3}{10} = \frac{3}{5}$

10. $\frac{2}{5} + \frac{1}{10} = \frac{1}{2}$

11. $\frac{1}{4} + \frac{2}{4} = \frac{3}{4}$

12. $\frac{5}{8} - \frac{1}{8} = \frac{1}{2}$

Solve.

13. **DESSERT** Grace's mother has a cookie recipe that calls for $\frac{1}{3}$ cup sugar, and her grandma has a cookie recipe that calls for $\frac{1}{2}$ cup sugar. How much sugar is needed altogether for both recipes?

$\frac{5}{6}$ cup

14. **TRAVEL** Harry is driving to the store from his house. He stops along the way at Luis's house, which is $\frac{1}{2}$ mile from his house. How much farther does Harry have to drive to get to the store?

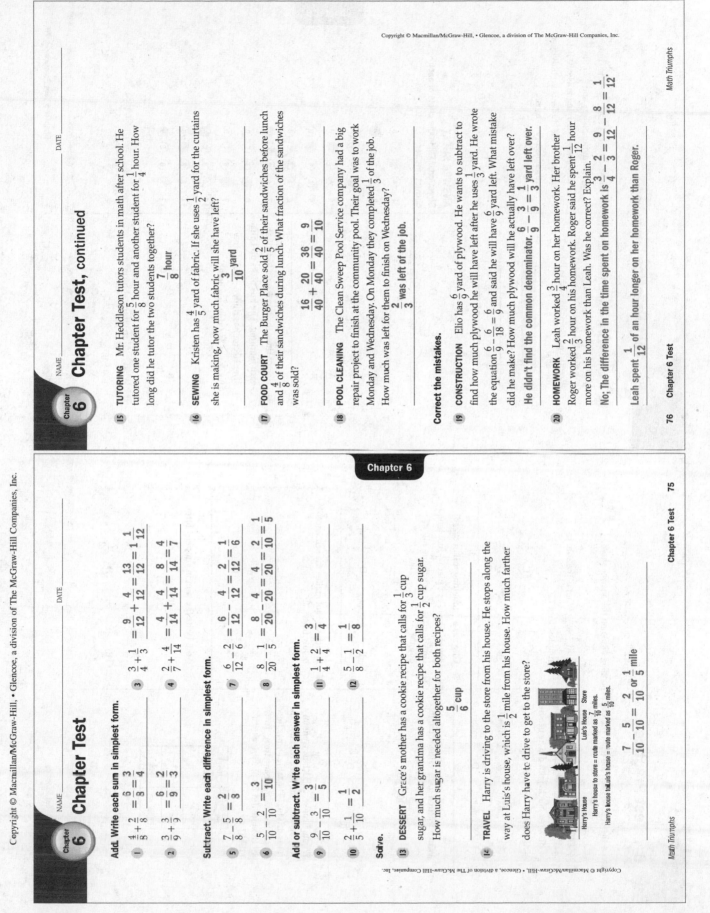

Harry's House — Luis's House — Store
Harry's house to store = route marked as $\frac{7}{10}$ miles.
Harry's house to Luis's house = route marked as $\frac{5}{10}$ miles.

$\frac{7}{10} - \frac{5}{10} = \frac{2}{10}$ or $\frac{1}{5}$ mile

---

Chapter 6 — Chapter Test, continued

NAME _____ DATE _____

15. **TUTORING** Mr. Heddleson tutors students in math after school. He tutored one student for $\frac{5}{8}$ hour and another student for $\frac{1}{4}$ hour. How long did he tutor the two students together?

$\frac{7}{8}$ hour

16. **SEWING** Kristen has $\frac{4}{5}$ yard of fabric. If she uses $\frac{1}{2}$ yard for the curtains she is making, how much fabric will she have left?

$\frac{3}{10}$ yard

17. **FOOD COURT** The Burger Place sold $\frac{2}{5}$ of their sandwiches before lunch and $\frac{4}{8}$ of their sandwiches during lunch. What fraction of the sandwiches was sold?

$\frac{16}{40} + \frac{20}{40} = \frac{36}{40} = \frac{9}{10}$

18. **POOL CLEANING** The Clean Sweep Pool Service company had a big repair project to finish at the community pool. Their goal was to work Monday and Wednesday. On Monday they completed $\frac{1}{3}$ of the job. How much was left for them to finish on Wednesday?

$\frac{2}{3}$ was left of the job.

Correct the mistakes.

19. **CONSTRUCTION** Elio has $\frac{6}{9}$ yard of plywood. He wants to subtract to find how much plywood he will have left after he uses $\frac{1}{3}$ yard. He wrote the equation $\frac{6}{9} - \frac{6}{18} = \frac{6}{9}$ and said he will have $\frac{6}{9}$ yard left. What mistake did he make? How much plywood will he actually have left over?

He didn't find the common denominator: $\frac{6}{9} - \frac{3}{9} = \frac{3}{9}$ yard left over.

20. **HOMEWORK** Leah worked $\frac{3}{4}$ hour on her homework. Her brother Roger worked $\frac{2}{3}$ hour on his homework. Roger said he spent $\frac{1}{12}$ hour more on his homework than Leah. Was he correct? Explain.

No; The difference in the time spent on homework is $\frac{3}{4} - \frac{2}{3} = \frac{9}{12} - \frac{8}{12} = \frac{1}{12}$. Leah spent $\frac{1}{12}$ of an hour longer on her homework than Roger.

Chapter 6

Chapter 6 — Test Practice

Choose the best answer and fill in the corresponding circle on the answer sheet.

1. Logan used $\frac{2}{8}$ gallon of paint for one wall and $\frac{4}{8}$ gallon of paint for another wall. How much paint did he use for both walls?

A $\frac{6}{16}$ gallon   C $\frac{1}{2}$ gallon

(B) $\frac{3}{4}$ gallon   D $\frac{2}{8}$ gallon

2. Which fraction has a value equal to $\frac{5}{10} - \frac{3}{10}$?

A $\frac{2}{0}$ C $\frac{2}{20}$

B $\frac{8}{10}$ (D) $\frac{1}{5}$

3. Elijah, Brooke, and Klaus went on a trip together. The three friends took turns driving. The table shows how much time each person drove. How much more did Brooke drive than Elijah?

Name	Drive Time
Brooke	$\frac{7}{14}$
Klaus	$\frac{4}{14}$
Elijah	$\frac{3}{14}$

(A) $\frac{4}{14}$ or $\frac{2}{7}$ C $\frac{5}{14}$

B $\frac{1}{14}$ D $\frac{7}{14}$ or $\frac{1}{2}$

4. Add $\frac{2}{3} + \frac{1}{4}$. What is the sum in simplest form?

A $\frac{3}{7}$ (C) $\frac{11}{12}$

B $\frac{5}{6}$ D $\frac{3}{12}$

5. Gita has a $\frac{3}{4}$ foot long roll of bread dough. She uses a piece $\frac{1}{4}$ foot long. How long is the remaining roll of dough?

A $\frac{4}{4}$ or 1 foot   (C) $\frac{2}{4}$ or $\frac{1}{2}$ foot

B $\frac{3}{4}$ foot   D $\frac{1}{4}$ foot

6. Which symbol makes the sentence below true?

$$\frac{3}{5} - \frac{2}{5} \;\square\; \frac{4}{5} - \frac{3}{5}$$

A <   C >

(B) =   D +

7. Add. Write the sum in simplest form.

$$\frac{10}{24} + \frac{4}{24}$$

A $\frac{6}{32}$ C $\frac{6}{16}$

B $\frac{3}{4}$ (D) $\frac{7}{12}$

Chapter 6 — Test Practice, continued

8. Employees at Brentwood Farms harvest part of their fields in September and October. What part of the fields did Brentwood Farms harvest in those 2 months?

Months	Harvested
September	$\frac{1}{4}$
October	$\frac{3}{8}$

(A) $\frac{5}{8}$ C $\frac{4}{8}$ or $\frac{1}{2}$

B $\frac{6}{8}$ or $\frac{3}{4}$ D $\frac{5}{16}$

9. Which symbol makes this sentence true?

$$\frac{5}{6} \;\square\; \frac{20}{24}$$

(A) =   C <

B >   D +

10. Hector rides the bus $\frac{2}{3}$ mile to school each morning. The bus picks up Gina after Hector has ridden $\frac{1}{2}$ mile. How far does Gina ride to school?

A $\frac{1}{2}$ mile   C $\frac{1}{4}$ mile

B $\frac{1}{3}$ mile   (D) $\frac{1}{6}$ mile

11. What is $\frac{24}{48}$ in simplest form?

A $\frac{3}{4}$ (C) $\frac{1}{2}$

B $\frac{1}{3}$ D $\frac{3}{8}$

12. In Ms. Roger's class, $\frac{1}{3}$ of the students are studying history and $\frac{1}{3}$ of the students are studying music. What fraction of the students is studying either history or music?

A $\frac{1}{6}$ C $\frac{1}{2}$

B $\frac{1}{3}$ (D) $\frac{2}{3}$

ANSWER SHEET

Directions: Fill in the circle of each correct answer.

1. (A) **B** (C) (D) — B filled
2. (A) (B) (C) **D** — D filled
3. **A** (B) (C) (D) — A filled
4. (A) (B) **C** (D) — C filled
5. (A) (B) (C) (D)
6. **A** (B) (C) (D) — A filled
7. (A) (B) (C) **D** — D filled
8. **A** (B) (C) (D) — A filled
9. **A** (B) (C) (D) — A filled
10. (A) (B) (C) **D** — D filled
11. (A) (B) **C** (D) — C filled
12. (A) (B) (C) **D** — D filled

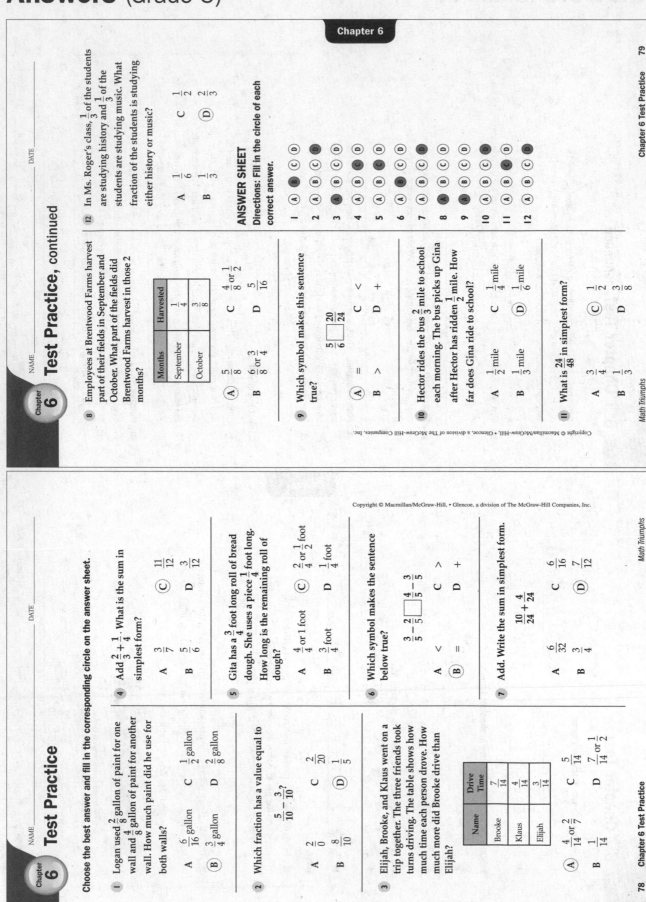

Answers (Grade 5)

NAME _____ DATE _____

Chapter 7 Chapter Pretest

1. What is the equivalent decimal of the grid?
   A 0.86   C 0.75 (circled)
   B 0.33   D 0.34

2. What fraction is equivalent to 0.4?
   A 4/10 (circled)   C 2/7
   B 1/4   D 6/10

3. What is the equivalent decimal for seventy and two hundredths?
   A 0.72   B 70.2   C 70.02 (circled)   D 72.00

4. Which decimal is represented on the number line?
   0 0.5 1 1.5 2 2.5 3 3.5 4 4.5 5
   A 2.2   B 2.8 (circled)   C 3.4   D 5.5

5. GAMES Lorenzo spent two dollars and a quarter at the arcade. What is the amount he spent written in decimal form?
   A $2.14   B $2.24   C $2.25 (circled)   D $2.41

6. Compare the decimals below. Which symbol makes the statement true?
   5.07 ○ 5.7
   A +   B =   C >   D < (circled)

7. Add. 13.5 + 8 =
   A 13.58   B 14.3   C 21.5 (circled)   D 93.5

8. Subtract. 40.17 − 18.2 =
   A 21.97 (circled)   B 38.17   C 38.35   D 41.75

9. Add. 1.21 + 2.46 =
   A 1.25   B 3.57   C 3.67 (circled)   D 14.56

10. Subtract. 8.54 − 3.13 =
    A 5.41 (circled)   B 5.67   C 8.23   D 11.67

NAME _____ DATE _____

Chapter 7 Chapter Pretest, continued

11. Which set of numbers is in order from least to greatest?
    A 1.4, 1.05, 1.45   B 1.05, 1.4, 1.45 (circled)   C 1.4, 1.45, 1.05   D 1.45, 1.05, 1.4

12. Which decimal represents 7 tenths plus 5 hundredths?
    A 0.57   B 0.705   C 0.75 (circled)   D 57.0

13. Which decimal represents seven thousandths?
    A 0.007 (circled)   B 0.070   C 0.07   D 0.700

14. Which decimal is equivalent to 6.2?
    A 06.002   B 6.02   C 6.20 (circled)   D 6.2

15. Add. 12.62 + 5.7 =
    A 17.32   B 17.69   C 18.32 (circled)   D 18.69

16. Subtract. 34.89 − 25.27 =
    A 9.62 (circled)   B 10.16   C 19.62   D 32.37

17. Subtract. 5.06 − 4.66 =
    A 0.4 (circled)   B 0.61   C 1.49   D 1.61

18. Add. 13.72 + 3.6 =
    A 16.12   B 16.32   C 17.12   D 17.32 (circled)

19. Estimate the sum of 1.75 and 2.32.
    A 2   B 3   C 4 (circled)   D 5

20. SCHOOL Ellen's average grade in music class was 93.2 points. Her teacher added 4.5 bonus points to her grade. To the nearest whole number, what is Ellen's grade now?
    A 96   B 97   C 98 (circled)   D 99

21. MEASUREMENT Frank measured his pencil to be 5.3 inches long one month ago. Yesterday, he measured it again and found it was 1.9 inches long. To the nearest inch, how much shorter was his pencil yesterday than it was one month ago?
    A 1 inch   B 2 inches   C 3 inches (circled)   D 4 inches

22. TRAVEL Sam spent thirty-five hundredths of an hour on the bus when he went to visit his grandmother. How is thirty-five hundredths written as a decimal?
    A $3\frac{1}{2}$ B $\frac{35}{10}$ C $\frac{3}{5}$ D $\frac{7}{20}$ (circled)

Answers (Grade 5)

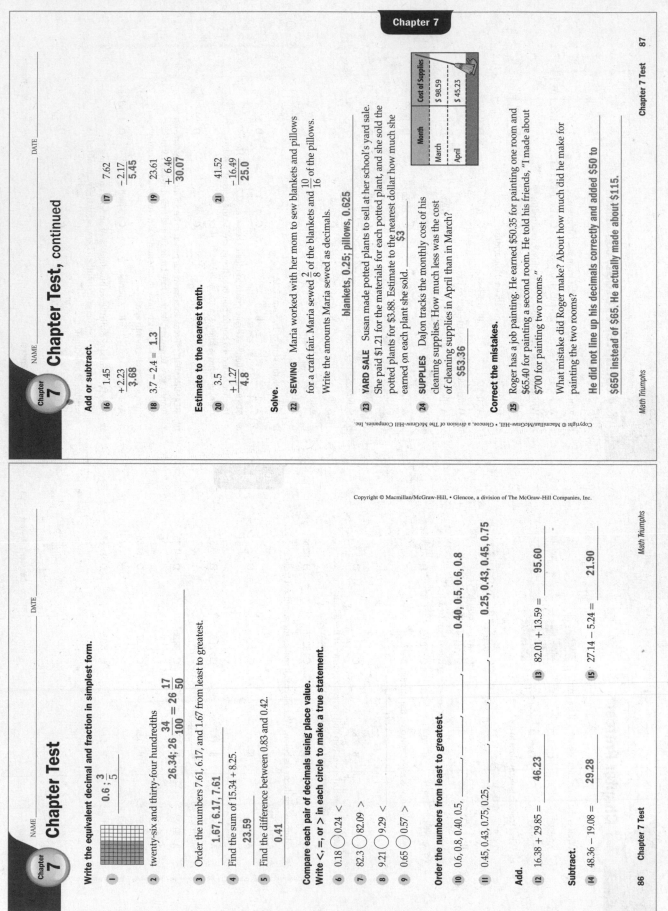

NAME _____ DATE _____

Chapter Test

7

Write the equivalent decimal and fraction in simplest form.

1. $0.6 ; \dfrac{3}{5}$

2. twenty-six and thirty-four hundredths
$26.34 ; 26\dfrac{34}{100} = 26\dfrac{17}{50}$

3. Order the numbers 7.61, 6.17, and 1.67 from least to greatest.
$1.67, 6.17, 7.61$

4. Find the sum of 15.34 + 8.25.
23.59

5. Find the difference between 0.83 and 0.42.
0.41

Compare each pair of decimals using place value.
Write <, =, or > in each circle to make a true statement.

6. 0.18 ◯ 0.24 **<**

7. 82.3 ◯ 82.09 **>**

8. 9.21 ◯ 9.29 **<**

9. 0.65 ◯ 0.57 **>**

Order the numbers from least to greatest.

10. 0.6, 0.8, 0.40, 0.5,
$0.40, 0.5, 0.6, 0.8$

11. 0.45, 0.43, 0.75, 0.25,
$0.25, 0.43, 0.45, 0.75$

Add.

12. 16.38 + 29.85 = **46.23**

13. 82.01 + 13.59 = **95.60**

Subtract.

14. 48.36 − 19.08 = **29.28**

15. 27.14 − 5.24 = **21.90**

Math Triumphs

NAME _____ DATE _____

Chapter Test, continued

7

Add or subtract.

16.
```
  1.45
+ 2.23
------
  3.68
```

17.
```
  7.62
- 2.17
------
  5.45
```

18. 3.7 − 2.4 = **1.3**

19.
```
  23.61
+  6.46
-------
 30.07
```

Estimate to the nearest tenth.

20.
```
  3.5
+ 1.27
------
  4.8
```

21.
```
  41.52
- 16.49
-------
  25.0
```

Solve.

22. **SEWING** Maria worked with her mom to sew blankets and pillows for a craft fair. Maria sewed $\dfrac{2}{8}$ of the blankets and $\dfrac{10}{16}$ of the pillows. Write the amounts Maria sewed as decimals.
blankets, 0.25; pillows, 0.625

23. **YARD SALE** Susan made potted plants to sell at her school's yard sale. She paid $1.21 for the materials for each potted plant, and she sold the potted plants for $3.88. Estimate to the nearest dollar how much she earned on each plant she sold. **$3**

24. **SUPPLIES** DaJon tracks the monthly cost of his cleaning supplies. How much less was the cost of cleaning supplies in April than in March?
$53.36

Month	Cost of Supplies
March	$ 98.59
April	$ 45.23

Correct the mistakes.

25. Roger has a job painting. He earned $50.35 for painting one room and $65.40 for painting a second room. He told his friends, "I made about $700 for painting two rooms."

What mistake did Roger make? About how much did he make for painting the two rooms?
He did not line up his decimals correctly and added $50 to
$650 instead of $65. He actually made about $115.

Math Triumphs

Answers (Grade 5)

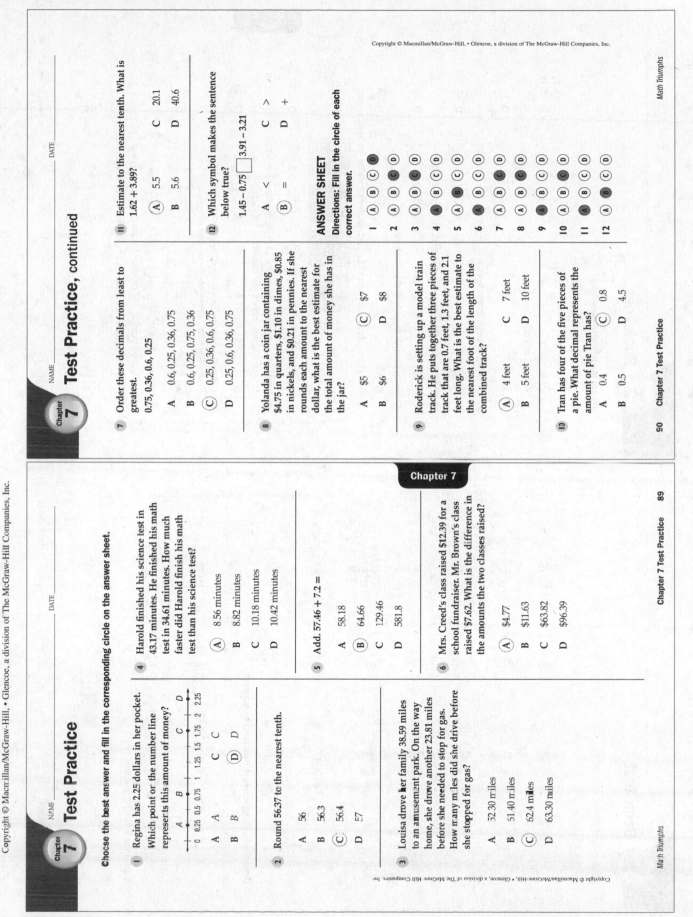

NAME _____ DATE _____

Chapter 7 Test Practice

Choose the best answer and fill in the corresponding circle on the answer sheet.

1 Regina has 2.25 dollars in her pocket. Which point or the number line represents this amount of money?

```
   A    B       C    C         D
0 0.25 0.5 0.75 1 1.25 1.5 1.75 2 2.25
```

- A A
- B (B)
- C C
- (D) D

2 Round 56.37 to the nearest tenth.

- A 56
- B 56.3
- (C) 56.4
- D 57

3 Louisa drove her family 38.59 miles to an amusement park. On the way home, she drove another 23.81 miles before she needed to stop for gas. How many miles did she drive before she stopped for gas?

- A 52.30 miles
- B 51.40 miles
- (C) 62.4 miles
- D 63.30 miles

4 Harold finished his science test in 43.17 minutes. He finished his math test in 34.61 minutes. How much faster did Harold finish his math test than his science test?

- (A) 8.56 minutes
- B 8.82 minutes
- C 10.18 minutes
- D 10.42 minutes

5 Add. 57.46 + 7.2 =

- A 58.18
- (B) 64.66
- C 129.46
- D 581.8

6 Mrs. Creed's class raised $12.39 for a school fundraiser. Mr. Brown's class raised $7.62. What is the difference in the amounts the two classes raised?

- (A) $4.77
- B $11.63
- C $63.82
- D $96.39

NAME _____ DATE _____

Chapter 7 Test Practice, continued

7 Order these decimals from least to greatest.

0.75, 0.36, 0.6, 0.25

- A 0.6, 0.25, 0.36, 0.75
- B 0.6, 0.25, 0.75, 0.36
- (C) 0.25, 0.36, 0.6, 0.75
- D 0.25, 0.6, 0.36, 0.75

8 Yolanda has a coin jar containing $4.75 in quarters, $1.10 in dimes, $0.85 in nickels, and $0.21 in pennies. If she rounds each amount to the nearest dollar, what is the best estimate for the total amount of money she has in the jar?

- A $5
- B $6
- (C) $7
- D $8

9 Roderick is setting up a model train track. He puts together three pieces of track that are 0.7 feet, 1.3 feet, and 2.1 feet long. What is the best estimate to the nearest foot of the length of the combined track?

- (A) 4 feet
- B 5 feet
- C 7 feet
- D 10 feet

10 Tran has four of the five pieces of a pie. What decimal represents the amount of pie Tran has?

- A 0.4
- B 0.5
- (C) 0.8
- D 4.5

11 Estimate to the nearest tenth. What is 1.62 + 3.89?

- (A) 5.5
- B 5.6
- C 20.1
- D 40.6

12 Which symbol makes the sentence below true?

1.45 − 0.75 [ ] 3.91 − 3.21

- A <
- (B) =
- C >
- D +

ANSWER SHEET

Directions: Fill in the circle of each correct answer.

1	A	B	C	●
2	A	●	C	D
3	A	●	C	D
4	A	B	C	D
5	●	B	C	D
6	A	B	C	D
7	A	B	●	D
8	A	B	●	D
9	●	B	C	D
10	A	B	●	D
11	A	●	C	D
12	●	B	C	D

Answers (Grade 5)

Book 2 — Book Test

NAME _____ **DATE** _____

Solve.

1. $\frac{2}{3} - \frac{1}{5} =$ A ⓐ $\frac{7}{15}$ B $\frac{1}{15}$ C $\frac{1}{8}$ D $\frac{13}{15}$

2. $\frac{6}{13} + \frac{1}{2} =$ A $\frac{11}{13}$ B $\frac{23}{26}$ C ⓒ $\frac{25}{26}$ D $1\frac{1}{13}$

3. $\frac{9}{11} - \frac{3}{11} =$ A $\frac{2}{8}$ B $\frac{12}{11}$ C ⓒ $\frac{6}{11}$ D 1

4. $\frac{1}{6} + \frac{2}{5} =$ A $\frac{1}{10}$ B ⓑ $\frac{17}{30}$ C $\frac{12}{30}$ D $\frac{2}{3}$

5. $\frac{2}{3} - \frac{6}{15} =$ A $\frac{1}{5}$ B ⓑ $\frac{4}{15}$ C $\frac{2}{5}$ D $\frac{1}{2}$

6. $\frac{2}{7} + \frac{4}{7} - \frac{3}{7} =$ A $\frac{2}{7}$ B ⓑ $\frac{3}{7}$ C $\frac{4}{7}$ D $\frac{9}{7}$

7. $\frac{2}{7} + \frac{4}{7} =$ A $\frac{7}{6}$ B ⓑ $\frac{6}{7}$ C $\frac{6}{14}$ D $\frac{8}{49}$

Order the following numbers from least to greatest.

8. $\frac{3}{5}, \frac{1}{3}, 0.65, 0.24$ A $\frac{3}{5}, \frac{1}{3}, 0.65, 0.24$ B $0.24, \frac{1}{3}, 0.65, \frac{3}{5}$ C $\frac{1}{3}, 0.24, 0.65, \frac{3}{5}$ D ⓓ $0.24, \frac{1}{3}, \frac{3}{5}, 0.65$

9. $0.9, 0.65, \frac{2}{3}, 1\frac{1}{8}$ A ⓐ $0.65, \frac{2}{3}, 0.9, 1\frac{1}{8}$ B $\frac{2}{3}, 0.65, 0.9, 1\frac{1}{8}$ C $1\frac{1}{8}, \frac{2}{3}, 0.65, 0.9$ D $0.9, 1\frac{1}{8}, 0.65, \frac{2}{3}$

Answer the following question.

10. Which fraction does the shaded part of the model represent?

    A $\frac{1}{5}$ B $\frac{7}{15}$ C $\frac{8}{15}$ D ⓓ $\frac{2}{5}$

Math Triumphs

Book 2 — Book Test

NAME _____ **DATE** _____

Answer the following questions.

11. What are the equivalent fractions for $\frac{4}{5}$ and $\frac{7}{8}$? A $\frac{16}{40}, \frac{32}{40}$ B $\frac{9}{10}, \frac{14}{20}$ C $\frac{7}{15}, \frac{8}{9}$ D ⓓ $\frac{12}{15}, \frac{14}{16}$

12. Write $\frac{12}{5}$ as a mixed number. A ⓐ $2\frac{2}{5}$ B $5\frac{2}{5}$ C $7\frac{2}{5}$ D $2\frac{3}{5}$

13. Write $4\frac{3}{7}$ as an improper fraction. A $\frac{29}{28}$ B $\frac{30}{28}$ C ⓒ $\frac{31}{7}$ D $\frac{32}{28}$

14. What is the least common multiple (LCM) of 5, 7, and 10? A 350 B 35 C ⓒ 70 D 50

15. What decimal is equivalent to the fraction $\frac{3}{5}$? A 0.3 B 0.5 C ⓒ 0.6 D 0.8

16. Select the equivalent decimal and mixed number which the model represents.

    A $332; 3\frac{32}{100}$ B $3.33; 3\frac{33}{100}$ C ⓒ $3.32; 3\frac{8}{25}$ D $332; 3\frac{16}{50}$

17. **TOYS** A basket held 62 marbles. 27 of the marbles were red. What fraction represents the number of red marbles? A $\frac{18}{62}$ B $\frac{17}{62}$ C ⓒ $\frac{27}{62}$ D $\frac{28}{62}$

18. **COOKING** Alyssa uses 8 of the 12 eggs in the carton. Which fraction, in simplest form, represents the number of eggs used? A $\frac{8}{12}$ B $\frac{4}{6}$ C ⓒ $\frac{2}{3}$ D $\frac{10}{15}$

19. **CHORUS** Mrs. Waller is preparing for the spring concert. For today's practice $\frac{1}{4}$ of the choir members are out sick, and $\frac{1}{3}$ of the choir members are away on a field trip. What fraction of the members is missing? A $\frac{1}{2}$ B ⓑ $\frac{7}{12}$ C $\frac{3}{4}$ D $\frac{5}{6}$

Math Triumphs

Math Triumphs

Answers (Grade 5)

Book 3

Book Pretest

Convert.

1. 3 gallons = ____ quarts
   A 4   **B 12**   C 24   D 30

2. 7 L = ____ mL
   A 0.07   B 0.7   C 700   **D 7,000**

3. 2.5 kilograms = ____ grams
   A 200.5 grams   B 250 grams   C 2,000 grams   **D 2,500 grams**

Find the surface area of the following figures.

4. A 13 square units   B 56 square units   **C 100 square units**   D 30 square units

5. A 4 ft²   B 8 ft²   C 16 ft²   **D 24 ft²**

Identify the figure.

6. A square   B rectangle   **C parallelogram**   D trapezoid

7. A sphere   B cone   **C pyramid**   D prism

8. A square   **B rectangle**   C parallelogram   D trapezoid

9. A triangle with two sides that are 4 centimeters long, and one side that is 4.5 centimeters long.
   A equilateral   B scalene   C right   **D isosceles**

Book 3 Pretest

Book 3

Book Pretest, continued

Answer the following questions.

10. Which three-dimensional figure is shaped like a ball?
    A cube   **B sphere**   C prism   D pyramid

11. What is the best estimate for the weight of one apple?
    A 1 ounce   **B 6 ounces**   C 10 pounds   D ½ ton

Find the area.

12. A 8 in.   B 8 sq in.   C 15 in.   **D 15 sq in.**

13. A 152 m   B 152 sq m   C 76 m   **D 76 sq m**

14. A rectangle with length 3 inches and width 2 inches.
    A 5 in²   **B 6 in²**   C 10 in²   D 12 in²

Answer the following questions.

15. What is the volume of the solid figure?
    A 13 cubic units   B 32 cubic units   **C 60 cubic units**   D 17 cubic units

16. Which of the following measures the number of cubic units a solid figure contains?
    A perimeter   B surface area   **C volume**   D diameter

17. A grape weighs about 1 ounce. About how much do 100 grapes weigh?
    A 1 pound   **B 6 pounds**   C 16 pounds   D 25 pounds

18. **FARMING** A potato farmer wants to put netting over his potato crop. The potato patch is 20 feet in length and 45 feet wide. What is the area of the potato crop that he will have to net?
    A 65 ft   B 130 sq ft   **C 900 sq ft**   D 900 ft

19. **SPORTS** The radius of a certain flying disk is 7 centimeters. What is the disk's diameter?
    A 7 cm   B 9 cm   **C 14 cm**   D 21.9 cm

Answers (Grade 5)

NAME _____ DATE _____

Chapter 8 Chapter Pretest, continued

Choose the correct name of each three-dimensional figure.

11. A triangular prism   C cube
    B sphere   **(D)** triangular pyramid

12. **(A)** cube   C rectangular pyramid
    B sphere   D triangular prism

13. A cube   C prism
    B cone   **(D)** sphere

14. A cube   **(C)** prism
    B cone   D sphere

15. **(A)** cube   C prism
    (B) cone   D sphere

16. Choose the correct diameter measure of the circle.

    $r = 5$
    $d = ?$

    A 2.5   B 5   C 7.5   **(D)** 10

Solve.

17. **GAMES** Jess's sister said she was thinking of a three-dimensional figure with four faces. What figure could she be thinking about?

    A cube   **(B)** pyramid   C sphere   D prism

18. **SPORTS** Alice's pen pal from Ghana asked Alice what shape a bowling ball is. Which name can she use to describe a bowling ball?

    A prism   B cube   **(C)** sphere   D cylinder

Math Triumphs   **Chapter 8 Pretest**   101

NAME _____ DATE _____

Chapter 8 Chapter Pretest

Choose the correct name of each figure.

1. A square   C parallelogram
   B rhombus   **(D)** rectangle

2. A scalene triangle   **(C)** equilateral triangle
   B right triangle   D obtuse triangle

3. A parallelogram   C rectangle
   B rhombus   **(D)** trapezoid

4. A isosceles triangle   C equilateral triangle
   (B) right triangle   D obtuse triangle

5. A rhombus   C rectangle
   (B) parallelogram   D trapezoid

6. A rhombus   C square
   (B) parallelogram   D trapezoid

7. **(A)** rhombus   C square
   B parallelogram   D trapezoid

Answer the following questions.

8. The diameter of a circle is 4 feet. What is the circle's radius?

   A 1 foot   **(B)** 2 feet   C 4 feet   D 8 feet

9. A box is 12 inches long, 5 inches wide, and 3 inches high. What is the box's shape?

   A pyramid   B cube   **(C)** prism   D cone

10. Mrs. Jacobs draws a line from one corner of a square to the opposite corner. What are the two new figures?

    A rectangles   C equilateral triangles
    B trapezoids   **(D)** right triangles

100   **Chapter 8 Pretest**   *Math Triumphs*

Answers (Grade 5)

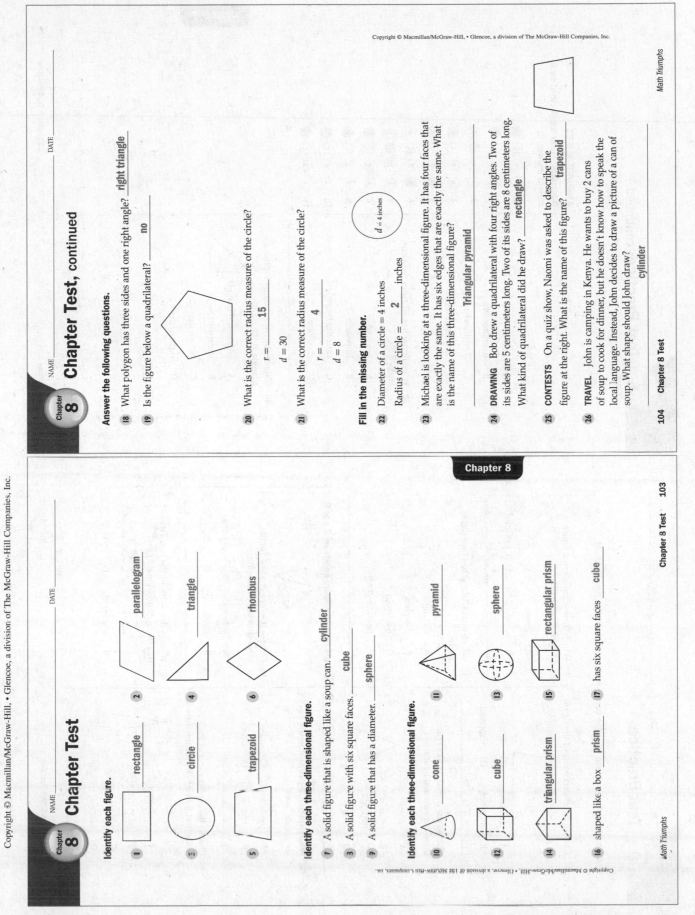

NAME _____ DATE _____

Chapter 8 Chapter Test, continued

Answer the following questions.

18. What polygon has three sides and one right angle? __right triangle__

19. Is the figure below a quadrilateral? __no__

20. What is the correct radius measure of the circle?

$r =$ __15__

$d = 30$

21. What is the correct radius measure of the circle?

$r =$ __4__

$d = 8$

$d = 4$ inches

Fill in the missing number.

22. Diameter of a circle = 4 inches

Radius of a circle = __2__ inches

23. Michael is looking at a three-dimensional figure. It has four faces that are exactly the same. It has six edges that are exactly the same. What is the name of this three-dimensional figure?

__Triangular pyramid__

24. **DRAWING** Bob drew a quadrilateral with four right angles. Two of its sides are 5 centimeters long. Two of its sides are 8 centimeters long. What kind of quadrilateral did he draw? __rectangle__

25. **CONTESTS** On a quiz show, Naomi was asked to describe the figure at the right. What is the name of this figure? __trapezoid__

26. **TRAVEL** John is camping in Kenya. He wants to buy 2 cans of soup to cook for dinner, but he doesn't know how to speak the local language. Instead, John decides to draw a picture of a can of soup. What shape should John draw? __cylinder__

104 **Chapter 8 Test**

Math Triumphs

NAME _____ DATE _____

Chapter 8 Chapter Test

Identify each figure.

1. __rectangle__

2. __parallelogram__

3. __circle__

4. __triangle__

5. __trapezoid__

6. __rhombus__

Identify each three-dimensional figure.

7. A solid figure that is shaped like a soup can. __cylinder__

3. A solid figure with six square faces. __cube__

9. A solid figure that has a diameter. __sphere__

Identify each three-dimensional figure.

10. __cone__

11. __pyramid__

12. __cube__

13. __sphere__

14. __triangular prism__

15. __rectangular prism__

16. shaped like a box __prism__

17. has six square faces __cube__

Math Triumphs **Chapter 8 Test** 103

Chapter 8

Answers (Grade 5)

NAME _____ DATE _____

Chapter 8

Test Practice, continued

9 Choose the correct diameter.

$r = 6$ centimeters

$d = ?$

A 3 centimeters

B 6 centimeters

C 9 centimeters

(D) 12 centimeters

10 What figure has all sides the same length?

A rectangle

B trapezoid

C isosceles triangle

(D) rhombus

11 Choose the correct name for the triangle at the right.

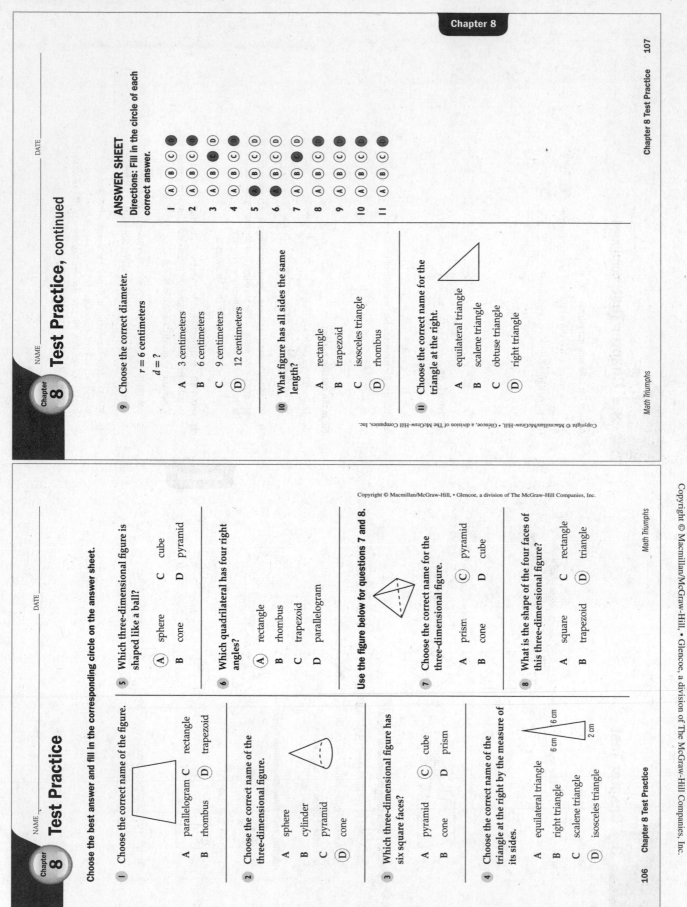

A equilateral triangle

B scalene triangle

C obtuse triangle

(D) right triangle

ANSWER SHEET

Directions: Fill in the circle of each correct answer.

1	(A)	(B)	C	●
2	(A)	(B)	C	●
3	(A)	●	C	D
4	(A)	(B)	C	●
5	(A)	(B)	C	●
6	●	(B)	C	D
7	(A)	(B)	C	●
8	(A)	(B)	C	●
9	(A)	(B)	C	●
10	(A)	(B)	C	●
11	(A)	(B)	C	●

Math Triumphs

NAME _____ DATE _____

Test Practice

Choose the best answer and fill in the corresponding circle on the answer sheet.

1 Choose the correct name of the figure.

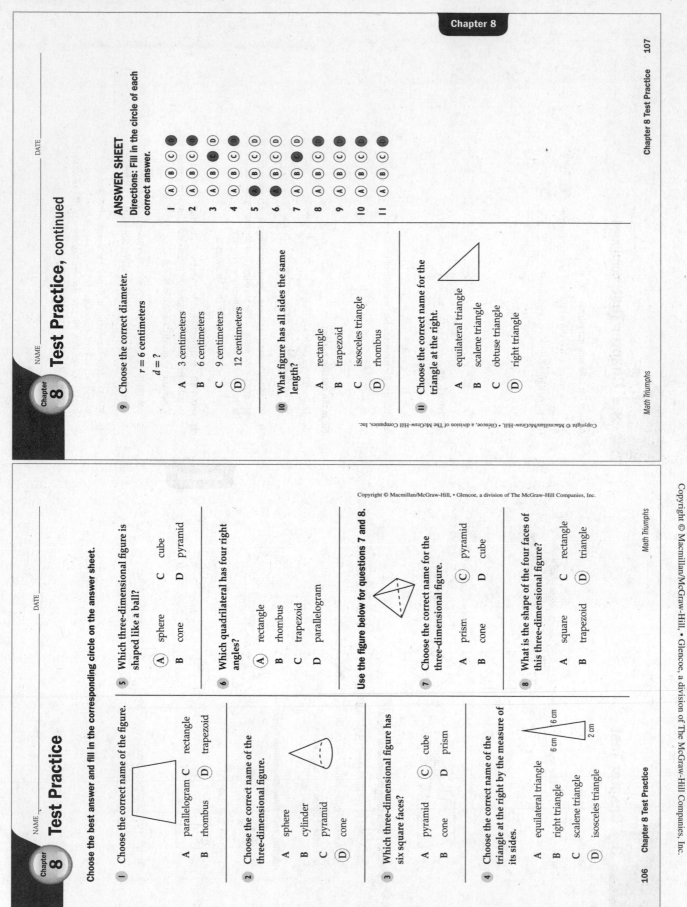

A parallelogram C rectangle

B rhombus **(D)** trapezoid

2 Choose the correct name of the three-dimensional figure.

A sphere

B cylinder

C pyramid

(D) cone

3 Which three-dimensional figure has six square faces?

A pyramid **(C)** cube

B cone D prism

4 Choose the correct name of the triangle at the right by the measure of its sides.

A equilateral triangle

B right triangle

C scalene triangle

(D) isosceles triangle

6 cm 6 cm

2 cm

5 Which three-dimensional figure is shaped like a ball?

(A) sphere C cube

B cone D pyramid

6 Which quadrilateral has four right angles?

(A) rectangle

B rhombus

C trapezoid

D parallelogram

Use the figure below for questions 7 and 8.

7 Choose the correct name for the three-dimensional figure.

A prism **(C)** pyramid

B cone D cube

8 What is the shape of the four faces of this three-dimensional figure?

A square C rectangle

B trapezoid **(D)** triangle

Math Triumphs

Math Triumphs

Answers (Grade 5)

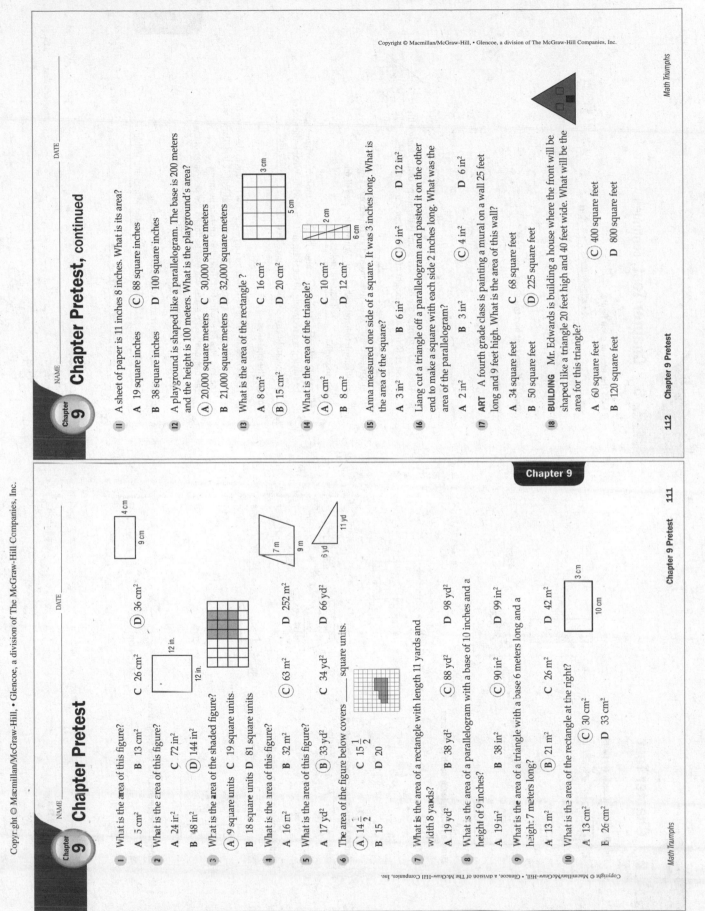

NAME _____ DATE _____

Chapter 9 — Chapter Pretest

1. What is the area of this figure? [4 cm × 9 cm]
   A 5 cm² B 13 cm² C 26 cm² (D) 36 cm²

2. What is the area of this figure? [12 in. × 12 in.]
   A 24 in² B 48 in² C 72 in² (D) 144 in²

3. What is the area of the shaded figure?
   (A) 9 square units C 19 square units
   B 18 square units D 81 square units

4. What is the area of this figure? [7 m, 9 m]
   A 16 m² B 32 m² (C) 63 m² D 252 m²

5. What is the area of this figure? [6 yd, 11 yd]
   A 17 yd² (B) 33 yd² C 34 yd² D 66 yd²

6. The area of the figure below covers _____ square units.
   (A) $14\frac{1}{2}$ C $15\frac{1}{2}$
   B 15 D 20

7. What is the area of a rectangle with length 11 yards and width 8 yards?
   A 19 yd² B 38 yd² (C) 88 yd² D 98 yd²

8. What is the area of a parallelogram with a base of 10 inches and a height of 9 inches?
   A 19 in² B 38 in² (C) 90 in² D 99 in²

9. What is the area of a triangle with a base 6 meters long and a height 7 meters long?
   A 13 m² (B) 21 m² C 26 m² D 42 m²

10. What is the area of the rectangle at the right? [3 cm × 10 cm]
    A 13 cm² (C) 30 cm²
    B 26 cm² D 33 cm²

NAME _____ DATE _____

Chapter 9 — Chapter Pretest, continued

11. A sheet of paper is 11 inches 8 inches. What is its area?
    A 19 square inches (C) 88 square inches
    B 38 square inches D 100 square inches

12. A playground is shaped like a parallelogram. The base is 200 meters and the height is 100 meters. What is the playground's area?
    (A) 20,000 square meters C 30,000 square meters
    B 21,000 square meters D 32,000 square meters

13. What is the area of the rectangle? [3 cm × 5 cm]
    A 8 cm² C 16 cm²
    (B) 15 cm² D 20 cm²

14. What is the area of the triangle? [2 cm, 6 cm]
    (A) 6 cm² C 10 cm²
    B 8 cm² D 12 cm²

15. Anna measured one side of a square. It was 3 inches long. What is the area of the square?
    A 3 in² B 6 in² (C) 9 in² D 12 in²

16. Liang cut a triangle off a parallelogram and pasted it on the other end to make a square with each side 2 inches long. What was the area of the parallelogram?
    A 2 in² B 3 in² (C) 4 in² D 6 in²

17. ART A fourth grade class is painting a mural on a wall 25 feet long and 9 feet high. What is the area of this wall?
    A 34 square feet C 68 square feet
    B 50 square feet (D) 225 square feet

18. BUILDING Mr. Edwards is building a house where the front will be shaped like a triangle 20 feet high and 40 feet wide. What will be the area for this triangle?
    A 60 square feet (C) 400 square feet
    B 120 square feet D 800 square feet

Answers (Grade 5)

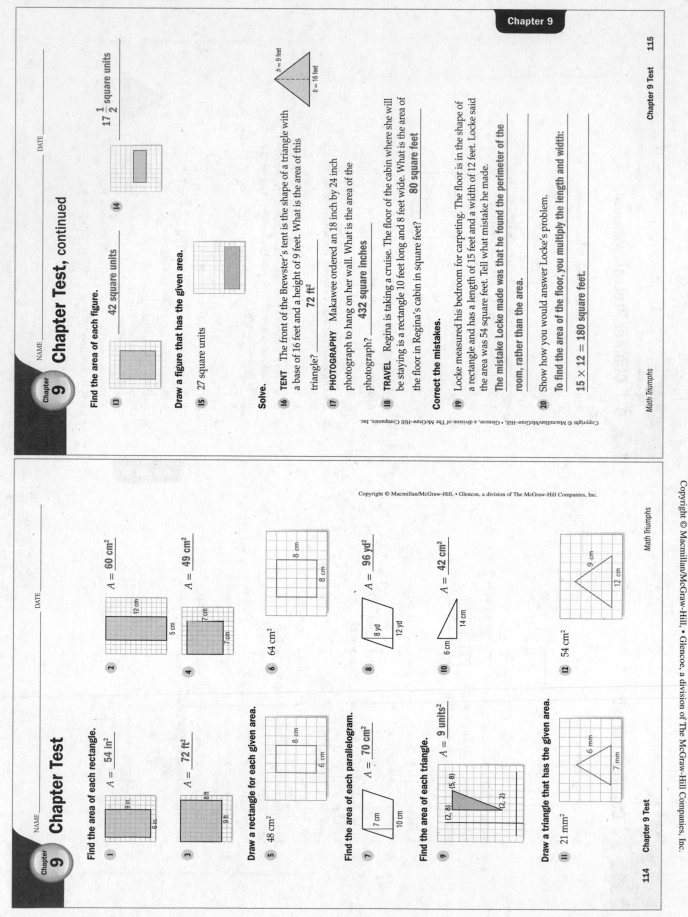

NAME _____ DATE _____

Chapter 9 — Chapter Test, continued

Find the area of each figure.

13. 42 square units

14. $17\frac{1}{2}$ square units

Draw a figure that has the given area.

15. 27 square units

Solve.

16. **TENT** The front of the Brewster's tent is the shape of a triangle with a base of 16 feet and a height of 9 feet. What is the area of this triangle? ____ **72 ft²**

$h = 9$ feet
$b = 16$ feet

17. **PHOTOGRAPHY** Makawee ordered an 18 inch by 24 inch photograph to hang on her wall. What is the area of the photograph? ____ **432 square inches**

18. **TRAVEL** Regina is taking a cruise. The floor of the cabin where she will be staying is a rectangle 10 feet long and 8 feet wide. What is the area of the floor in Regina's cabin in square feet? ____ **80 square feet**

Correct the mistakes.

19. Locke measured his bedroom for carpeting. The floor is in the shape of a rectangle and has a length of 15 feet and a width of 12 feet. Locke said the area was 54 square feet. Tell what mistake he made. **The mistake Locke made was that he found the perimeter of the room, rather than the area.**

20. Show how you would answer Locke's problem. **To find the area of the floor, you multiply the length and width:** **15 × 12 = 180 square feet.**

Math Triumphs   Chapter 9 Test   115

NAME _____ DATE _____

Chapter 9 — Chapter Test

Find the area of each rectangle.

1. $A = $ **54 in²**
   9 in.
   6 in.

2. $A = $ **60 cm²**
   12 cm
   5 cm

3. $A = $ **72 ft²**
   8 ft
   9 ft

4. $A = $ **49 cm²**
   7 cm
   7 cm

Draw a rectangle for each given area.

5. 48 cm²
   8 cm
   6 cm

6. 64 cm²
   8 cm
   8 cm

Find the area of each parallelogram.

7. $A = $ **70 cm²**
   7 cm
   10 cm

8. $A = $ **96 yd²**
   8 yd
   12 yd

Find the area of each triangle.

9. $A = $ **9 units²**
   (2, 8) (5, 8)
   (2, 2)

10. $A = $ **42 cm²**
    6 cm
    14 cm

Draw a triangle that has the given area.

11. 21 mm²
    6 mm
    7 mm

12. 54 cm²
    9 cm
    12 cm

114   Chapter 9 Test   *Math Triumphs*

A34   Grade 5 Chapter 9

Answers (Grade 5)

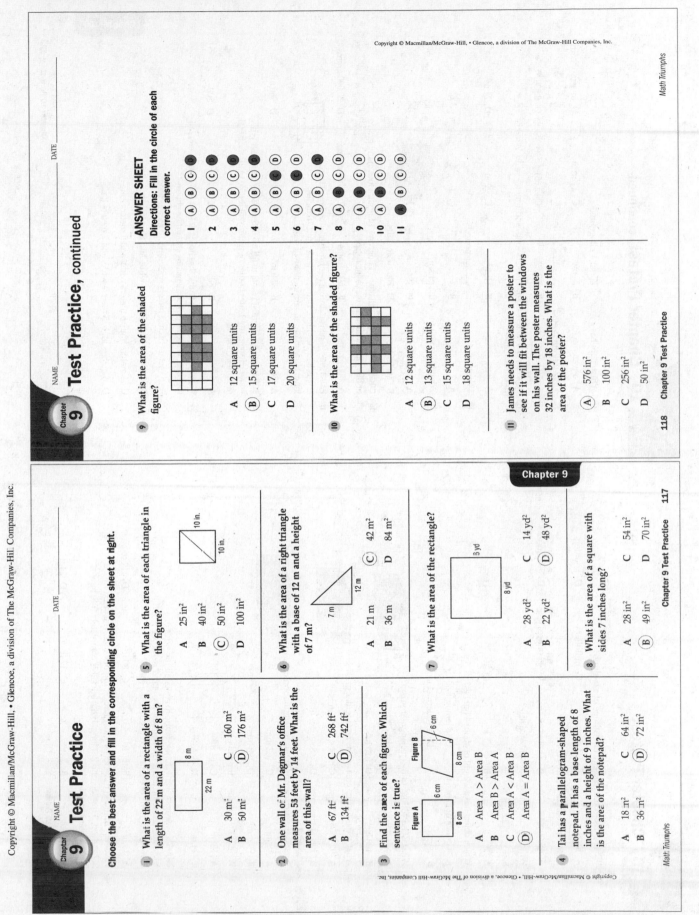

NAME _____ DATE _____

Chapter 9 Test Practice

Choose the best answer and fill in the corresponding circle on the sheet at right.

1 What is the area of a rectangle with a length of 22 m and a width of 8 m?

8 m, 22 m

A 30 m²   C 160 m²
B 50 m²   D 176 m²

2 One wall of Mr. Dagmar's office measures 53 feet by 14 feet. What is the area of this wall?

A 67 ft²   C 268 ft²
B 134 ft²   D 742 ft²

3 Find the area of each figure. Which sentence is true?

Figure A   6 cm, 6 cm, 8 cm
Figure B   6 cm, 8 cm

A Area A > Area B
B Area B > Area A
C Area A < Area B
D Area A = Area B

4 Tai has a parallelogram-shaped notepad. It has a base length of 8 inches and a height of 9 inches. What is the area of the notepad?

A 18 in²   C 64 in²
B 36 in²   D 72 in²

5 What is the area of each triangle in the figure?

10 in., 10 in.

A 25 in²
B 40 in²
C 50 in²
D 100 in²

6 What is the area of a right triangle with a base of 12 m and a height of 7 m?

7 m, 12 m

A 21 m   C 42 m²
B 36 m   D 84 m²

7 What is the area of the rectangle?

8 yd, 6 yd

A 28 yd²   C 14 yd²
B 22 yd²   D 48 yd²

8 What is the area of a square with sides 7 inches long?

A 28 in²   C 54 in²
B 49 in²   D 70 in²

NAME _____ DATE _____

Chapter 9 Test Practice, continued

9 What is the area of the shaded figure?

A 12 square units
B 15 square units
C 17 square units
D 20 square units

10 What is the area of the shaded figure?

A 12 square units
B 13 square units
C 15 square units
D 18 square units

11 James needs to measure a poster to see if it will fit between the windows on his wall. The poster measures 32 inches by 18 inches. What is the area of the poster?

A 576 in²
B 100 in²
C 256 in²
D 50 in²

ANSWER SHEET
Directions: Fill in the circle of each correct answer.

1 A B C D
2 A B C D
3 A B C D
4 A B C D
5 A B C D
6 A B C D
7 A B C D
8 A B C D
9 A B C D
10 A B C D
11 A B C D

Answers (Grade 5)

Chapter 10 — Chapter Pretest

1. What units would measure the volume of a bathtub?
   (A) liters   B kilograms   C milliliters   D kiloliters

2. How many ounces are in 5 pounds?
   A 13 ounces   B 21 ounces   C 40 ounces   **(D)** 80 ounces

3. Which symbol makes the sentence true?
   8 qt _____ 2.5 gal
   A >   **(B)** <   C =   D −

4. Which object has a weight of about 4 ounces?
   A a bunch of bananas   **(C)** a lemon
   B a grape   D a watermelon

5. What is the volume of this rectangular prism?
   A 21 in^3 C 288 in^3
   B 160 in^3 **(D)** 320 in^3

6. What is the surface area of this rectangular prism?
   A 92 square units   **(C)** 184 square units
   B 120 square units   D 368 square units

7. What is the surface area of this rectangular prism?
   A 18 mm^2 C 162 mm^2
   B 99 mm^2 **(D)** 198 mm^2

8. What is the volume of this cube?
   A 12 m^3 **(C)** 64 m^3
   B 24 m^3 D 384 m^3

9. **CRAFTS** Meagan wants to use fabric to cover all the sides of a television stand including the bottom. The stand is 4 ft × 4 ft × 5 ft. How much fabric does she need to cover the stand?
   A 13 ft^2 B 56 ft^2 C 80 ft^2 **(D)** 112 ft^2

10. **VOLUME** Brandon has a rectangular bucket full of water. The bucket is 2 ft deep, 3 ft wide, and 2 ft long. If the bucket is completely full, how much water is inside?
    A 6 ft^3 B 7 ft^3 **(C)** 12 ft^3 D 24 ft^3

Chapter 10 — Chapter Pretest, continued

11. Which item has a mass of about 4 kilograms?
    (A) a watermelon   B a cow   C a carrot   D an ear of corn

12. 5,302 milliliters = _____ liters
    A 10.604   **(B)** 5.302   C 2.651   D 0.5302

13. A prism is 3 meters high, 2 meters long, and 1 meter wide. What is its surface area?
    A 6 m^2 B 11 m^2 **(C)** 22 m^2 D 24 m^2

14. 48 ounces = _____ pounds
    A 2   **(B)** 3   C 4   D 6

15. What is the volume of the prism?
    A 60 cubic units   C 184 cubic units
    (B) 160 cubic units   D 200 cubic units

16. **COOKING** A recipe calls for 3 kilograms of flour. How many grams of flour are needed to make the recipe?
    A 300 grams   B 600 grams   **(C)** 3,000 grams   D 30,000 grams

17. **PAINTING** Jane is painting her brother's toy box. The toy box is 8 inches high, 10 inches wide, and 16 inches long. How many square inches will she paint?
    A 368 in^2 B 480 in^2 **(C)** 736 in^2 D 960 in^2

18. **SCIENCE** An scientist wants to fill a 5,000 milliliter container with water. How many 1-liter bottles of water will it take to fill the 5,000 milliliter container?
    (A) 5   B 50   C 100   D 500

19. **TRAVEL** Isaac needs a trunk that holds at least 300 cubic meters of luggage. Which trunk dimensions should he choose?
    A 5 meters high, 3 meters wide, and 10 meters long
    (B) 6 meters high, 7 meters wide, and 8 meters long
    C 4 meters high, 8 meters wide, and 9 meters long
    D 6 meters high, 5 meters wide, and 7 meters long

Answers (Grade 5)

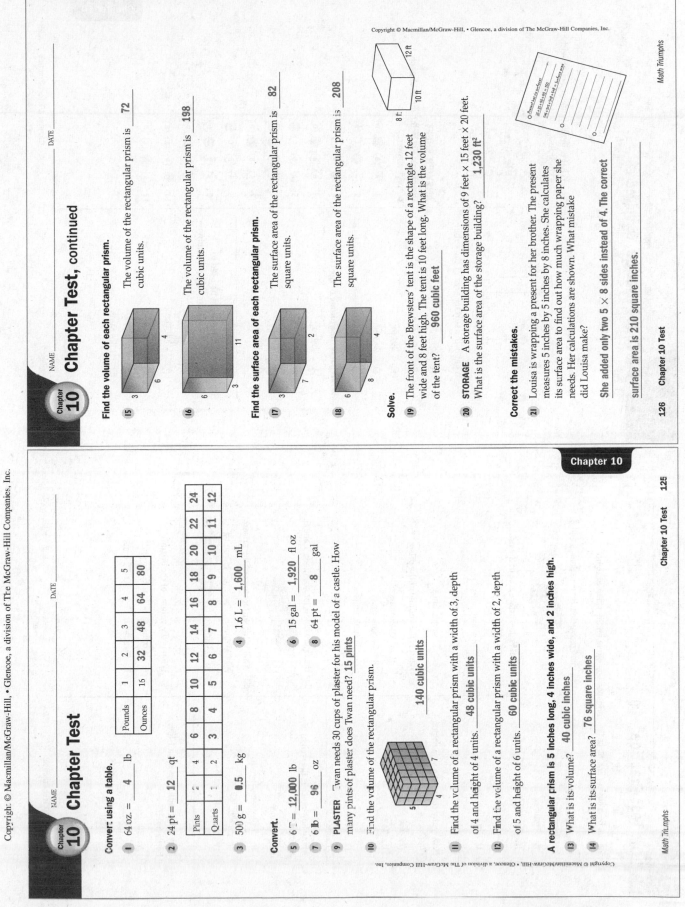

NAME _____ DATE _____

Chapter 10 Chapter Test

Convert using a table.

1. 64 oz. = __4__ lb

Pounds	1	2	3	4	5
Ounces	16	32	48	64	80

2. 24 pt = __12__ qt

Pints	2	4	6	8	10	12	14	16	18	20	22	24
Quarts	1	2	3	4	5	6	7	8	9	10	11	12

3. 500 g = __0.5__ kg

4. 1.6 L = __1,600__ mL

Convert.

5. 6 T = __12,000__ lb

6. 15 gal = __1,920__ fl oz

7. 6 lb = __96__ oz

8. 64 pt = __8__ gal

9. **PLASTER** Twan needs 30 cups of plaster for his model of a castle. How many pints of plaster does Twan need? __15 pints__

10. Find the volume of the rectangular prism.

__140 cubic units__

11. Find the volume of a rectangular prism with a width of 3, depth of 4 and height of 4 units. __48 cubic units__

12. Find the volume of a rectangular prism with a width of 2, depth of 5 and height of 6 units. __60 cubic units__

A rectangular prism is 5 inches long, 4 inches wide, and 2 inches high.

13. What is its volume? __40 cubic inches__

14. What is its surface area? __76 square inches__

NAME _____ DATE _____

Chapter 10 Chapter Test, continued

Find the volume of each rectangular prism.

15. The volume of the rectangular prism is __72__ cubic units.

16. The volume of the rectangular prism is __198__ cubic units.

Find the surface area of each rectangular prism.

17. The surface area of the rectangular prism is __82__ square units.

18. The surface area of the rectangular prism is __208__ square units.

Solve.

19. The front of the Brewsters' tent is the shape of a rectangle 12 feet wide and 8 feet high. The tent is 10 feet long. What is the volume of the tent? __960 cubic feet__

20. **STORAGE** A storage building has dimensions of 9 feet × 15 feet × 20 feet. What is the surface area of the storage building? __1,230 ft²__

Correct the mistakes.

21. Louisa is wrapping a present for her brother. The present measures 5 inches by 5 inches by 8 inches. She calculates its surface area to find out how much wrapping paper she needs. Her calculations are shown. What mistake did Louisa make?

__She added only two 5 × 8 sides instead of 4. The correct surface area is 210 square inches.__

Answers (Grade 5)

NAME _____ DATE _____

Test Practice

Choose the best answer and fill in the corresponding circle on the sheet at right.

1 About how much is the mass of 1 watermelon?
- A 2 grams
- B 2 milligrams
- Ⓒ 4 kilograms
- D 20 kilograms

2 How many cups can a 6-quart pot hold?
- A 12
- Ⓑ 24
- C 36
- D 48

3 About how much is the weight of a button?
- Ⓐ 1 ounce
- B 5 kilograms
- C 2 pounds
- D 1 ton

4 How many milliliters can a 1-liter bottle hold?
- A 10
- B 100
- Ⓒ 1,000
- D 10,000

Use the figure below for questions 5 and 6.

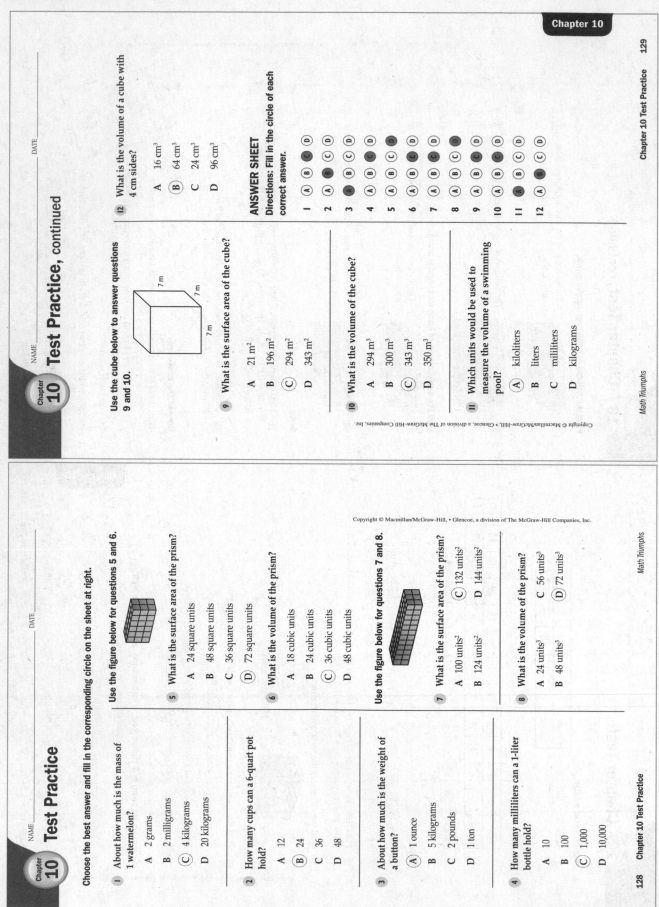

5 What is the surface area of the prism?
- A 24 square units
- B 48 square units
- C 36 square units
- Ⓓ 72 square units

6 What is the volume of the prism?
- A 18 cubic units
- B 24 cubic units
- Ⓒ 36 cubic units
- D 48 cubic units

Use the figure below for questions 7 and 8.

7 What is the surface area of the prism?
- A 100 units²
- B 124 units²
- Ⓒ 132 units²
- D 144 units²

8 What is the volume of the prism?
- A 24 units³
- B 48 units³
- C 56 units³
- Ⓓ 72 units³

NAME _____ DATE _____

Test Practice, continued

Use the cube below to answer questions 9 and 10.

7 m   7 m   7 m

9 What is the surface area of the cube?
- A 21 m²
- B 196 m²
- Ⓒ 294 m²
- D 343 m²

10 What is the volume of the cube?
- A 294 m³
- B 300 m³
- Ⓒ 343 m³
- D 350 m³

11 Which units would be used to measure the volume of a swimming pool?
- Ⓐ kiloliters
- B liters
- C milliliters
- D kilograms

12 What is the volume of a cube with 4 cm sides?
- A 16 cm³
- Ⓑ 64 cm³
- C 24 cm³
- D 96 cm³

ANSWER SHEET

Directions: Fill in the circle of each correct answer.

#	A	B	C	D
1	A	B	●	D
2	A	B	●	D
3	●	B	C	D
4	A	B	●	D
5	A	B	C	●
6	A	B	●	D
7	A	B	●	D
8	A	B	C	●
9	A	B	●	D
10	A	B	C	●
11	●	B	C	D
12	A	●	C	D

Answers (Grade 5)

Book 3 — Book Test

NAME _____ DATE _____

Book 3 — **Book Test**

Convert.

1. 2 liters = _____ milliliters
   - A 20
   - B 200
   - **C 2,000**
   - D 20,000

2. 1.5 gallons = _____ pints
   - A 5
   - B 8
   - C 10
   - **D 12**

3. 3 pounds = _____ ounces
   - A 16
   - B 30
   - C 32
   - **D 48**

Identify the figure.

4. [parallelogram]
   - A parallelogram
   - **B rhombus**
   - C rectangle
   - D square

5. [cone]
   - A sphere
   - **B cone**
   - C pyramid
   - D prism

6. [right triangle, 9 and 7]
   - A acute triangle
   - B obtuse triangle
   - **C right triangle**
   - D none of the above

7. A three-dimensional figure shaped like a box.
   - A sphere
   - B pyramid
   - **C prism**
   - D cone

8. [trapezoid]
   - A square
   - B rectangle
   - C parallelogram
   - **D trapezoid**

9. A quadrilateral with four equal sides and four right angles.
   - **A square**
   - B equilateral triangle
   - C rectangle
   - D parallelogram

Estimate the mass.

10. A banana
    - A 1 gram
    - **B 100 grams**
    - C 3 kilograms
    - D 20 kilograms

11. 1,000 ice cubes, if one ice cube is about 0.9 grams.
    - **A 1 kilogram**
    - B 10 kilograms
    - C 90 kilograms
    - D 100 kilograms

Book 3 Test

NAME _____ DATE _____

Book 3 — **Book Test, continued**

Answer the following questions.

12. Find the volume of the solid figure below. [7 × 2 × 4]
    - A 18 cubic units
    - **B 56 cubic units**
    - C 15 cubic units
    - D 30 cubic units

13. What is the surface area of the solid figure? [4 × 5 × 2]
    - A 40 square units
    - **B 76 square units**
    - C 36 square units
    - D 11 square units

14. Joshua has three identical balls that fit into one large box. Which statement below is true?
    - A The surface area of the large box is 3 times that of one ball.
    - B The volume of one ball is 3 times that of the large box.
    - C The surface area of one ball is three times that of the large box.
    - **D The volume of the large box is at least 3 times that of one ball.**

15. The radius of the circle below is 4.5 inches. What is the diameter? [4.5 in.]
    - A 2.25 inches
    - B 6.5 inches
    - C 8 inches
    - **D 9 inches**

16. What is the radius of the circle at the right? [23 cm]
    - A 2.5 cm
    - **B 12.5 cm**
    - C 23 cm
    - D 50 cm

17. **SHOPPING** A freezer compartment is shaped like a rectangular prism. It measures 4 feet long by 6 feet wide by 3 feet high. What is its volume?
    - **A 72 ft³**
    - B 72 ft²
    - C 27 ft³
    - D 22 ft²

18. **COLLEGE** A college pennant banner is triangular. It measures 12 in. wide at the base and 30 in. high. What is the area of the banner?
    - A 180 in.
    - **B 180 in².**
    - C 360 in.
    - D 360 in².

19. **CARPETING** How much carpeting is needed for a room that has a length of 25 feet and a width of 12 feet?
    - A 37 feet
    - B 300 feet
    - C 37 feet²
    - **D 300 feet²**

20. **SHIPPING** How much wrapping material is needed to send a package that is 6 cm by 12 cm by 8 cm?
    - A 26 cm²
    - B 216 cm²
    - **C 432 cm²**
    - D 576 cm²

Answers (Grade 5)

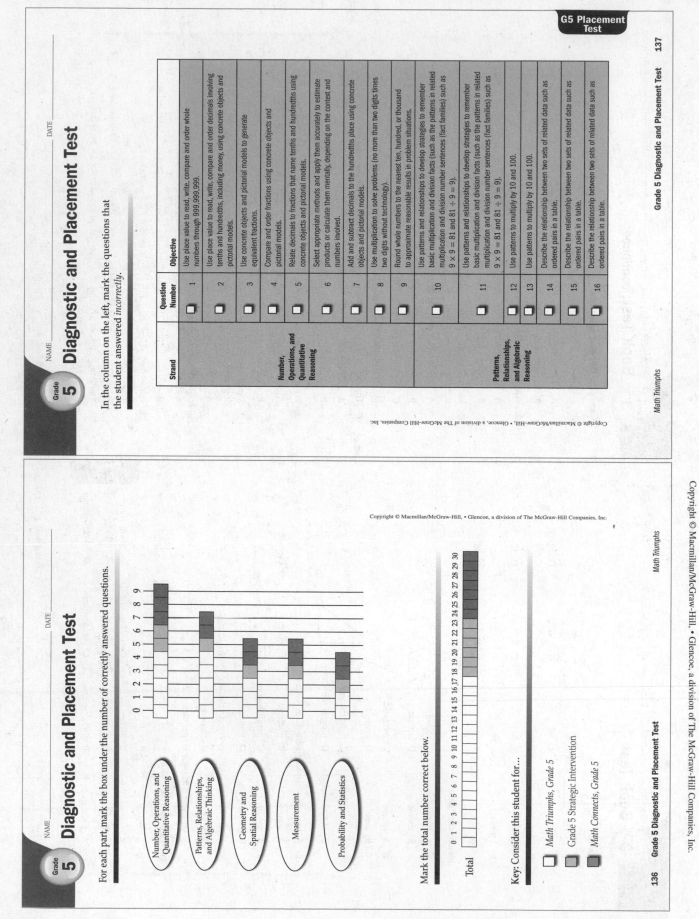

NAME _____ DATE _____

Diagnostic and Placement Test

In the column on the left, mark the questions that the student answered *incorrectly*.

Strand	Question Number	Objective
	1	Use place value to read, write, compare and order whole numbers through 999,999,999.
	2	Use place value to read, write, compare and order decimals involving tenths and hundredths, including money, using concrete objects and pictorial models.
	3	Use concrete objects and pictorial models to generate equivalent fractions.
Number, Operations, and Quantitative Reasoning	4	Compare and order fractions using concrete objects and pictorial models.
	5	Relate decimals to fractions that name tenths and hundredths using concrete objects and pictorial models.
	6	Select appropriate methods and apply them accurately to estimate products or calculate them mentally, depending on the context and numbers involved.
	7	Add and subtract decimals to the hundredths place using concrete objects and pictorial models.
	8	Use multiplication to solve problems (no more than two digits times two digits without technology).
	9	Round whole numbers to the nearest ten, hundred, or thousand to approximate reasonable results in problem situations.
	10	Use patterns and relationships to develop strategies to remember basic multiplication and division facts (such as the patterns in related multiplication and division number sentences (fact families) such as $9 \times 9 = 81$ and $81 \div 9 = 9$).
Patterns, Relationships, and Algebraic Reasoning	11	Use patterns and relationships to develop strategies to remember basic multiplication and division facts (such as the patterns in related multiplication and division number sentences (fact families) such as $9 \times 9 = 81$ and $81 \div 9 = 9$).
	12	Use patterns to multiply by 10 and 100.
	13	Use patterns to multiply by 10 and 100.
	14	Describe the relationship between two sets of related data such as ordered pairs in a table.
	15	Describe the relationship between two sets of related data such as ordered pairs in a table.
	16	Describe the relationship between two sets of related data such as ordered pairs in a table.

Math Triumphs   Grade 5 Diagnostic and Placement Test   137

NAME _____ DATE _____

Diagnostic and Placement Test

For each part, mark the box under the number of correctly answered questions.

- Number, Operations, and Quantitative Reasoning
- Patterns, Relationships, and Algebraic Thinking
- Geometry and Spatial Reasoning
- Measurement
- Probability and Statistics

Mark the total number correct below.

Total   0 1 2 3 4 5 6 7 8 9 10 11 12 13 14 15 16 17 18 19 20 21 22 23 24 25 26 27 28 29 30

Key: Consider this student for…

- ☐ *Math Triumphs, Grade 5*
- ☐ Grade 5 Strategic Intervention
- ☐ *Math Connects, Grade 5*

136   Grade 5 Diagnostic and Placement Test   *Math Triumphs*

Answers (Grade 5)

Grade 5 — Diagnostic and Placement Test

Strand	Question Number	Objective
Geometry and Spatial Reasoning	☐ 17	Identify and describe right, acute, and obtuse angles.
	☐ 18	Identify and describe parallel and intersecting (including perpendicular) lines using concrete objects and pictorial models.
	☐ 19	Use translations, reflections, and rotations using concrete models.
	☐ 20	Use reflections to verify that a shape has symmetry.
	☐ 21	Locate and name points on a number line using whole numbers, fractions, such as halves and fourths, and decimals, such as tenths.
	☐ 22	Estimate and use measurement tools to determine length (including perimeter), area, capacity and weight/mass using standard units (SI) and customary.
	☐ 23	Perform simple conversions between different units of length, between different units of capacity, and between different units of weight within the customary measurement system.
Measurement	☐ 24	Estimate volume in cubic units.
	☐ 25	Use a thermometer to measure temperature and changes in temperature.
	☐ 26	Quantify area by finding the total number of same-sized units of area that cover the shape without gaps or overlaps.
	☐ 27	Use concrete objects or pictures to make generalizations about determining all possible combinations of a given set of data or of objects in a problems situation.
Probability and Statistics	☐ 28	Use concrete objects or pictures to make generalizations about determining all possible combinations of a given set of data or of objects in a problems situation.
	☐ 29	Interpret bar graphs.
	☐ 30	Interpret bar graphs.

Grade 5 — Diagnostic and Placement Test

Student Performance Level	Number of Questions Correct	Suggestions for Intervention and Remediation
Intensive Intervention	0–17	Use *Math Triumphs* to accelerate the achievement of students who are two or more years below grade level. Students should follow a personalized remediation plan. A variety of materials and instructional methods are recommended. For example, instruction and practice should be provided in print, technology, and hands-on lessons.
Strategic Intervention	18–23	Use the additional Intervention and Remediation materials listed on the next page. This list of materials can provide helpful resources for students who struggle in the traditional mathematics program. Strategic intervention allows students to continue to remain in the *Math Connects* program while receiving the differentiated instruction they need. Teaching Tips and other resources are also listed in the Teacher Edition.
Grade 5	24 or more	Use *Math Connects*. This student does not require overall intervention. However, based on the student's performance on the different sections, intervention may be required. For example, a student who missed 2 or more questions in the Measurement section may require extra assistance as you cover these skills throughout the year.

A Special Note About Intervention

When using diagnostic tests, teachers should always question the reason behind the students' scores. Students can struggle with mathematics concepts for a variety of reasons. Personalized instruction is recommended for English language learners, students with specific learning disabilities, students with certain medical conditions, or for those who struggle with traditional instructional practice. Teachers should always consider the needs of the individual student when determining the best approach for instruction and program placement.

Answers (Grade 5)

Grade 5 — Diagnostic and Placement Test

This test contains 30 multiple-choice questions. Work each problem in the space on this page. Select the best answer. Write the letter of the answer on the blank at the right.

1. The number 9,020,730 is read as which of the following:

   A nine billion, twenty million, seventy-three

   B nine million, two thousand, seven hundred thirty

   C nine million, twenty thousand, seven hundred thirty

   D nine hundred two thousand, seventy-three

   1 ___C___

2. Which of the following numbers is the greatest?

   A 11.6   B 2.09   C 4.63   D 1.17

   2 ___A___

3. Inali and his friends ate $\frac{1}{2}$ of a pizza.

   Which fractional part of a circle below is equal to $\frac{1}{2}$?

   A

   B

   C

   D

   3 ___B___

Math Triumphs

Mathematics Chart

LENGTH	
Metric	
1 kilometer = 1,000 meters	
1 meter = 100 centimeters	
1 centimeter = 10 millimeters	
Customary	
1 mile = 1,760 yards	
1 mile = 5,280 feet	
1 yard = 3 feet	
1 foot = 12 inches	

MASS AND WEIGHT
Metric
1 kilogram = 1,000 grams
1 gram = 1,000 milligrams
Customary
1 ton = 2,000 pounds
1 pound = 16 ounces

CAPACITY AND VOLUME
Metric
1 liter = 1,000 milliliters
Customary
1 gallon = 4 quarts
1 gallon = 128 ounces
1 quart = 2 pints
1 pint = 2 cups
1 cup = 8 ounces

TIME
1 year = 365 days
1 year = 12 months
1 year = 52 weeks
1 week = 7 days
1 day = 24 hours
1 hour = 60 minutes
1 minute = 60 seconds

Perimeter	
square	$P = 4s$
rectangle	$P = 2l + 2w$ or $P = 2(l + w)$

Area	
rectangle	$A = lw$ or $A = bh$

Math Triumphs

Math Triumphs

Answers (Grade 5)

Grade 5

7 ____ **A**

7. The menu below shows the prices at Lunchtime Café. Lucita orders a turkey sandwich, salad, and juice. What operation should she use to determine the cost of her meal?

Lunchtime Café	
Item	Cost
Turkey Sandwich	$4.50
Ham Sandwich	$4.35
Salad	$2.10
Fruit Cup	$2.50
Juice	$1.90

A addition   C multiplication
B subtraction   D division

8 ____ **D**

8. Each student in fifth grade donates 4 cans of food to the food bank. There are 285 fifth-grade students. Which of the following shows the number of cans donated and the correct justification for the number?

A 71 because 285 divided by 4 is approximately 71
B 289 because 285 plus 4 is 289
C 1,120 because 280 times 4 is 1,120
D 1,140 because 285 times 4 is 1,140

9 ____ **D**

9. Look at the table below. Which of the following has NOT been rounded correctly to the nearest hundred?

Population in 2005		
City	Exact Population	Estimated Population
Amarillo	183,021	183,000
Austin	690,252	690,300
Corpus Christi	280,002	280,000
Fort Worth	624,067	624,000

Source: U.S. Census Bureau

A Amarillo   C Corpus Christi
B Austin   D Fort Worth

Grade 5

4 ____ **D**

4. During basketball practice, Michael spends time shooting free throws. The figures below are shaded to show the number of shots made compared to the number of shots attempted at each practice. What can you conclude from the data?

$\frac{5}{10}$ $\frac{7}{9}$ $\frac{6}{8}$ $\frac{3}{5}$

A The fraction $\frac{5}{10}$ is greater than $\frac{3}{5}$.
B The fraction $\frac{3}{5}$ is greater than $\frac{7}{9}$.
C The fractions are all equal.
D The fraction $\frac{3}{5}$ is greater than $\frac{5}{10}$.

5 ____ **C**

5. What decimal is equivalent to $\frac{3}{4}$?

A 0.25   B 0.34   C 0.75   D 1.33

6 ____ **D**

6. Estimate to find the product of 6.12 and 4.98.

A 10
B 11
C 24
D 30

Answers (Grade 5)

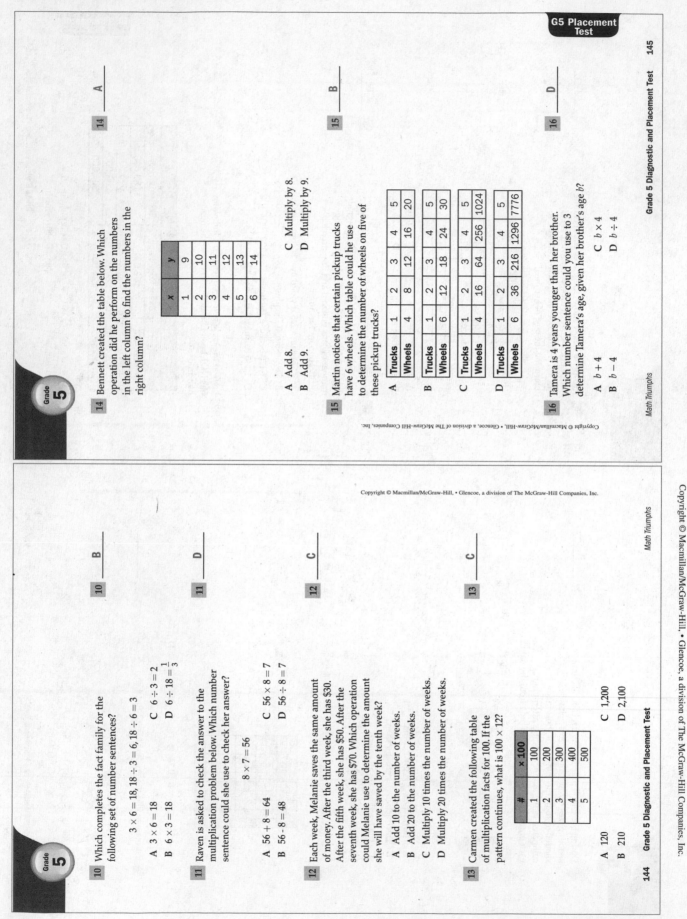

Grade 5

10 Which completes the fact family for the following set of number sentences?

$$3 \times 6 = 18, 18 \div 3 = 6, 18 \div 6 = 3$$

A $3 \times 6 = 18$ C $6 \div 3 = 2$
B $6 \times 3 = 18$ D $6 \div 18 = \frac{1}{3}$

10 ____ B

11 Raven is asked to check the answer to the multiplication problem below. Which number sentence could she use to check her answer?

$$8 \times 7 = 56$$

A $56 + 8 = 64$ C $56 \times 8 = 7$
B $56 - 8 = 48$ D $56 \div 8 = 7$

11 ____ D

12 Each week, Melanie saves the same amount of money. After the third week, she has $30. After the fifth week, she has $50. After the seventh week, she has $70. Which operation could Melanie use to determine the amount she will have saved by the tenth week?

A Add 10 to the number of weeks.
B Add 20 to the number of weeks.
C Multiply 10 times the number of weeks.
D Multiply 20 times the number of weeks.

12 ____ C

13 Carmen created the following table of multiplication facts for 100. If the pattern continues, what is 100×12?

#	× 100
1	100
2	200
3	300
4	400
5	500

A 120   C 1,200
B 210   D 2,100

13 ____ C

Math Triumphs

Grade 5

14 Bennett created the table below. Which operation did he perform on the numbers in the left column to find the numbers in the right column?

x	y
1	9
2	10
3	11
4	12
5	13
6	14

A Add 8.   C Multiply by 8.
B Add 9.   D Multiply by 9.

14 ____ A

15 Martin notices that certain pickup trucks have 6 wheels. Which table could he use to determine the number of wheels on five of these pickup trucks?

A

Trucks	1	2	3	4	5
Wheels	4	8	12	16	20

B

Trucks	1	2	3	4	5
Wheels	6	12	18	24	30

C

Trucks	1	2	3	4	5
Wheels	4	16	64	256	1024

D

Trucks	1	2	3	4	5
Wheels	6	36	216	1296	7776

15 ____ B

16 Tamera is 4 years younger than her brother. Which number sentence could you use to determine Tamera's age, given her brother's age *b*?

A $b + 4$ C $b \times 4$
B $b - 4$ D $b \div 4$

16 ____ D

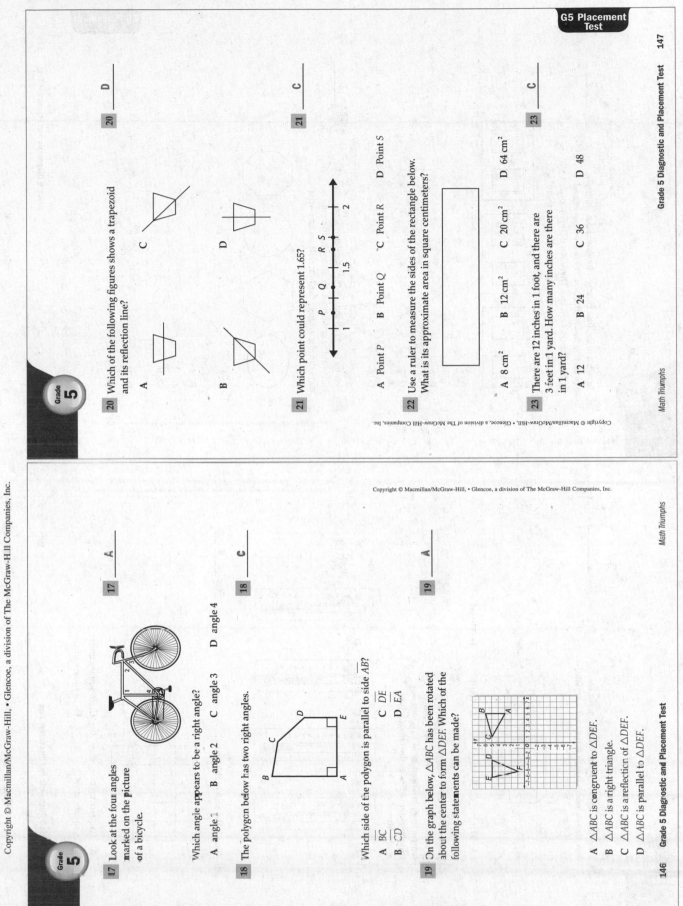

Grade 5

17 Look at the four angles marked on the picture of a bicycle.

Which angle appears to be a right angle?

A angle 1   B angle 2   C angle 3   D angle 4

17 ___A___

18 The polygon below has two right angles.

18 ___C___

19 Which side of the polygon is parallel to side $\overline{AB}$?

A $\overline{BC}$ C $\overline{DE}$
B $\overline{CD}$ D $\overline{EA}$

19 ___A___

19 On the graph below, △ABC has been rotated about the center to form △DEF. Which of the following statements can be made?

A △ABC is congruent to △DEF.
B △ABC is a right triangle.
C △ABC is a reflection of △DEF.
D △ABC is parallel to △DEF.

Grade 5

20 Which of the following figures shows a trapezoid and its reflection line?

A   C

B   D

20 ___D___

21 Which point could represent 1.65?

P   Q   R S
1   1.5   2

A Point P   B Point Q   C Point R   D Point S

21 ___C___

22 Use a ruler to measure the sides of the rectangle below. What is its approximate area in square centimeters?

A 8 cm²   B 12 cm²   C 20 cm²   D 64 cm²

23 There are 12 inches in 1 foot, and there are 3 feet in 1 yard. How many inches are there in 1 yard?

A 12   B 24   C 36   D 48

23 ___C___

Answers (Grade 5)

24 ___ **C**

Megan wants to estimate the volume of the box shown below. Which is the best estimate?
$(V = l \times w \times h)$

5.2 inches
1.76 inches
10.42 inches

A 50 in²   B 60 in²   C 100 in²   D 110 in²

25 ___ **D**

Jorgé notices the thermometer reads 38°F at breakfast. By lunchtime, he notices the temperature has risen by 14°F. Which thermometer indicates the temperature at lunchtime?

A   B   C   D

26 ___ **B**

What is the area of the figure?

A 10 square units   C 16 square units
B 14 square units   D 28 square units

27 ___ **D**

To win a prize, first choose a box and then choose a prize bag inside that box. There are 3 boxes and 2 prize bags in each box. There is a different prize in each bag. How many different prizes are there?

A 2
B 3
C 5
D 6

28 ___ **D**

Kendra wears all four of the bracelets shown below at the same time. How many different ways can she arrange the bracelets on one wrist?

A 4
B 8
C 16
D 24

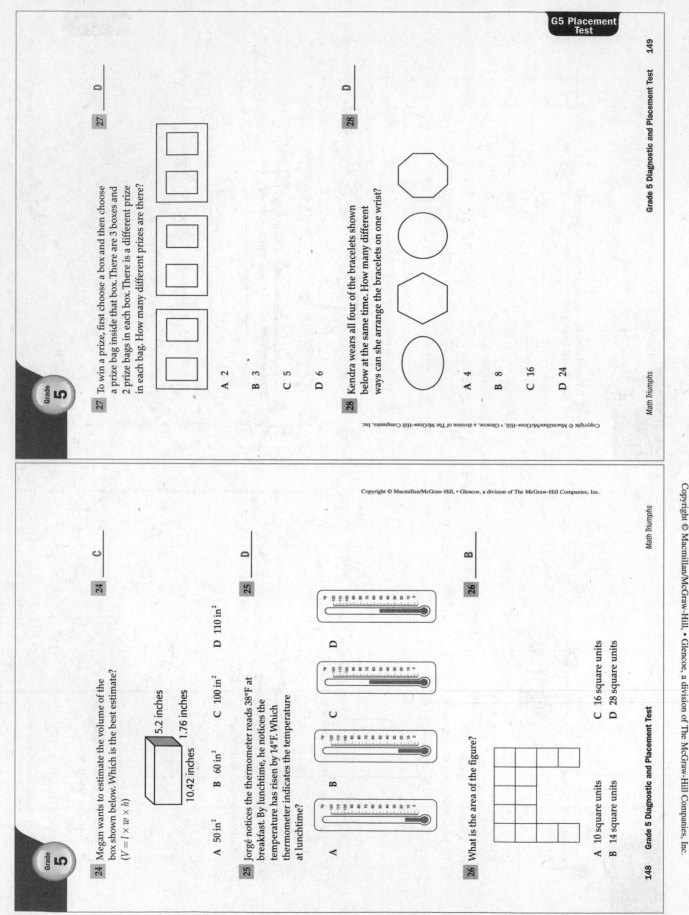

Answers (Grade 5)

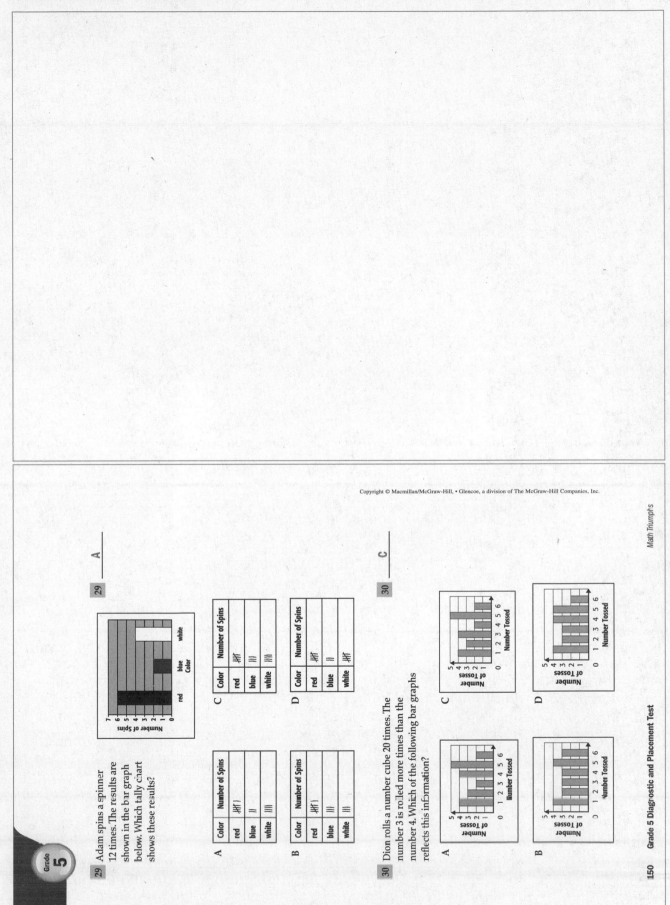

29   **A**

29 Adam spins a spinner 12 times. The results are shown in the bar graph below. Which tally chart shows these results?

A

Color	Number of Spins
red	JHT I
blue	II
white	IIII

B

Color	Number of Spins
red	JHT I
blue	III
white	III

C

Color	Number of Spins
red	JHT
blue	III
white	IIII

D

Color	Number of Spins
red	JHT
blue	II
white	JHT

30   **C**

30 Dion rolls a number cube 20 times. The number 3 is rolled more times than the number 4. Which of the following bar graphs reflects this information?

Math Triumphs

150   Grade 5 Diagnostic and Placement Test